REASONED POLITICS

MAGNUS VINDING

Ratio Ethica

Ratio Ethica, Copenhagen.
Copyright © 2022 Magnus Vinding
Paperback ISBN: 9798790853319
Hardcover ISBN: 9798790852930

Contents

PART V: SUMMARY

APPENDICES

Introduction

Politics is broken. To say that this is a cliché has itself become a cliché. But it is true nonetheless. Empty rhetoric, deceptive spin, and appeals to the lowest common denominator. These are standard premises in politics that we seem stuck with, and which many of us shake our heads at in disappointment.

Yet it is not only our politicians who fail to live up to their potential. The truth is that we all do. Our reasoning about politics tends to be biased by an unconscious commitment to tribalism and loyalty signaling — yay our team, boo their team (Hannon, 2021, p. 308). That is, our political behavior is often less about promoting good policies than it is about the desire to see our own team win, and to signal our loyalty to that team. As a result, our conversations about politics often go nowhere, and they frequently go worse than that.

The good news is that we have compelling reasons to think that we can do better. And it is critical that we do so, as our political decisions arguably represent the most consequential decisions of all, serving like a linchpin of human decision-making that constrains and influences just about every choice we make. This renders it uniquely important that we get our political decisions right, and that we advance our political discourse in general.

0.1 Problem: Unreasoned Politics

A dire problem with our political views and attitudes is that they not only fail to be carefully reasoned, but they are often positively *un*reasoned. As we shall see, our political behavior is commonly dictated by a mix of crude intuitions, motivated reasoning, and partisan loyalties — a mix that hampers our ability to think clearly about politics, and thus prevents good sense precisely at the level where it is most needed. We have a dysfunctional marriage between unusually biased reasoning and unusually important decisions.

Most of us can probably recognize this picture of biased reasoning without reviewing the relevant science, at least if we focus on the political behavior of the other side. *Their* primitive failings are all too transparent; *they* take unreasonable positions that are at odds with the evidence. But our own failings are much less visible to us, which is a large part of the problem. We are self-deceived about just how tendentious and unreasoned we ourselves are in the realm of politics (Tuschman, 2013, ch. 22; Simler & Hanson, 2018, ch. 5, ch. 16).

A related problem is that we rarely base our politics on clear values and well-grounded empirical views. As Richard Ryder puts it, contemporary politics often lacks two crucial ingredients: "a moral theory and a respect for the facts" (Ryder, 2006, p. 1). Indeed, we frequently fail to even distinguish moral and empirical views, let alone develop sophisticated views at these respective levels to help guide our policy decisions. Our tendency to settle for opinions announced by our most immediate intuitions precludes us from building our political views in a systematic way, and prevents us from engaging with arguments and evidence in a truly open-ended manner. We have yet to develop the kind of cultural operating system that can help us move beyond the politics of immediate intuitions and tribal loyalties, and toward a more systematic and reasoned approach.

In sum, while it must be acknowledged that modern political systems work well in a number of ways, especially compared to those systems that wholly suppress civil liberties, it is also true that our political culture and ways of thinking about politics remain starkly underdeveloped and suboptimal in many ways. At the level of our individual thinking, collective norms, and the overarching cultural frameworks with which we tackle politics, there is great potential to do better.

0.2 Remedy: Realistic Steps in a Better Direction

So what can we do to improve in these respects? And what reasons do we have for believing that we can do better? Answering these questions is among the key aims of this book, but the following hints at some of the main points.

An important step we can take, I argue, is to bring a more systematic and thoroughly reflected set of values into politics. More generally, we can seek to draw a clearer distinction between ethical views and empirical views in our political discourse, develop more advanced views at these respective levels, and let our policy decisions be guided by such views to a greater extent. An outline and defense of these ideals is found in Chapter 1.

In relation to our political biases and self-deception, we can seek to promote a greater awareness of these shared psychological pitfalls of ours. To clarify, the remedy here is not primarily a matter of increasing mere *individual* awareness, which is unlikely to be effective, but rather to increase our *collective* awareness of these devious tendencies, and in effect to foster norms that help limit rather than exacerbate the crude dynamics of our political psychology (Simler, 2016). One reason to be cautiously optimistic in this regard is that an advanced understanding of the mechanics of our biased political minds has only been acquired quite recently, and the most basic implications of this understanding have barely even begun to be explored. In other words, this newly gained understanding and its most basic implications have yet to percolate into our social norms. More on this in Chapter 4.

Taken together, the points above suggest a twin project of *limiting* the influence of biased intuitions, motivated reasoning, and dogmatic partisan loyalty, and then *replacing* this unholy trinity with something better — raising the standards of our discourse, and increasing the degree to which our politics is based on carefully reflected values and sound empirical evidence.

To be sure, this project is unlikely to be pursued on a large scale any time soon. It is not realistic to expect that most people will change their political behavior in significant ways upon simply being presented with certain findings and ideals. Any such expectation would be profoundly naive. But what *does* seem realistic is to improve things *on the margin*, by engendering a slow, gradual change that occurs disproportionally in certain communities open to such change — communities whose social incentives already to some degree reward open-minded reflection and efforts to reduce biases.

Having such communities develop and internalize better political norms (such as those outlined in Chapter 4) might already be a significant improvement with wide-ranging benefits. And if these communities have a certain level of repute, it is quite possible that such improved political norms would in turn spread further, and eventually come to have considerable force among a wider range of people. That is how norms can *realistically* change, and how they mostly seem to have changed so far (cf. Zaller, 1992; Taylor, 2015).

In short, I argue that we need (more) reasoned politics, pursued in gradual and realistic steps.

0.3 What Is Reasoned Politics?

I should clarify what I mean by the terms "politics", "reason", and "reasoned politics" in this context.

My definition of politics is rather broad and colloquial. I roughly use the term to refer to the realm of our large-scale collective decisions and decision-making, including the associated discussions, norms, and conventions. This definition goes beyond the practices of professional politicians, and indeed includes all activities, by everyone, that relate to large-scale collective decisions. The more directly certain views and activities relate to such collective decisions, the more political they are in this sense.

As for the term "reason", it is worth being clear that this term is commonly used in two rather different senses (Popper, 1945, ch. 24, I). The first is a narrow sense that contrasts "reason" with "empiricism". This conception of reason represents the rationalist side of the rationalist-empiricist dispute, the side that sees sensory experience as having less of a dominant role in the creation of knowledge. Second, there is "reason" in a broader sense that encompasses both systematic reasoning *and* experience, what Karl Popper defined as "an attitude of readiness to listen to critical arguments and to learn from experience" (Popper, 1945, ch. 24, I).

What I mean by "reason" in this book is decidedly the latter. Hence, when I advocate for reasoned politics, I am by no means advocating for reason divorced from experience, but in fact quite the opposite. I am advocating for an approach based thoroughly on experience in the widest sense, an approach that also acknowledges the limits of our faculties of reason themselves, such as the limits to our ability to predict future outcomes, as well as the social pitfalls and biases of these faculties (cf. Kahneman, 2011; Mercier & Sperber, 2017). After all, these limits and pitfalls are themselves facts that we can explore and come to (better) understand, and it would be most *un*reasonable to ignore these critical facts.

In a nutshell, one could say that I use the term "reasoned politics" to refer to reflection-based and evidence-based politics, in broad senses of the terms "reflection" and "evidence" — politics that embodies "an attitude of readiness to listen to critical arguments and to learn from experience" (Popper, 1945, ch. 24, I). The rest of the book will hopefully provide a fuller sense of what I mean by reasoned politics.

0.4 Outline

The book consists of four main parts followed by a fifth part that provides an overall summary.

Part I outlines a general framework for reasoned politics. This framework asks us to clarify our political views, to justify them with arguments, and to be willing to change our minds. These ideals are not at all original, and they probably sound agreeable to most people. Yet putting them into practice is nonetheless exceptionally rare, which underscores the need to spell out these ideals and explicitly commit to them.

Part II consists of descriptive groundwork, reviewing some key findings related to our political psychology and biases, as well as the influence of culture. These findings have universal relevance for how we think about and practice politics, and thus internalizing such empirical insights is a necessary step toward any reasonable approach to politics.

The rest of the book then seeks to apply the general framework and the descriptive groundwork laid out in the previous parts, and is thereby an attempt to apply the ideals of reasoned politics.

Part III presents an ethical view centered on the reduction of suffering that I and others have defended more elaborately elsewhere (see e.g.

Mayerfeld, 1999; Vinding, 2020a). I argue that the reduction of suffering ought to be a central aim of politics, and hence that political policies should be evaluated strongly on this basis. That is, how conducive are they to reducing suffering?

Part IV adopts this ethical view as its starting point, and explores which policies seem optimal in light of relevant empirical evidence and theoretical considerations. The goal of this examination is not to uncover definitive solutions, but rather to take a first step that provides some tentative answers, in turn hopefully motivating further discussions and investigations that will lead us to more mature answers.

Part V contextualizes and clarifies the aims of the foregoing policy analysis, and proceeds to summarize the book's main conclusions in the form of a party manifesto belonging to a hypothetical political party, the "Alliance of Reason and Compassion".

PART I

A GENERAL FRAMEWORK

1

The Two-Step Ideal of Reasoned Politics

"Political policy should be based, not upon mere opinion, nor upon a set of knee-jerk reflexes, but upon a scientific concern for the facts and an intelligent and open moral argument."

— Richard Ryder (Ryder, 2006, p. 1)

A problem with mainstream political discourse is that there is a striking lack of distinction between normative and empirical matters. That is, we fail to distinguish ethical values on the one hand, and factual questions about how we can best realize such values on the other, which in turn causes great confusion. And predictably so. After all, the distinction between normative and empirical issues is standard within moral and political philosophy, where it is considered indispensable for clear thinking. (Note that a meaningful *distinction* between facts and values does not imply a strict *dichotomy* between the two, Putnam, 2002.)

The framework I present below essentially amounts to applying this standard distinction to political practice, in turn yielding a simple yet, in my view, sorely needed ideal for how we should discuss and do politics. It is an open-ended ideal that entails a normative step followed by an empirical one.

1.1 The Normative Step

The first step is to clarify our values: what should be the moral aims of our policies? For example, should our policies generally aim to reduce suffering, or to maximize total happiness "minus suffering", or to protect certain fundamental rights?

The point here is not just to *state* our values, but also to argue for them, as well as to discuss and refine them through charitable and open-minded conversation. In other words, we should consider the strongest arguments for and against a variety of value systems so as to decide, provisionally, which values seem the most plausible basis for our policies. And this process is never fully finalized, as we should continue to be open to new arguments and further revisions of our views, even when we have considered them at length.

Unfortunately, our political discourse tends to proceed as though our values must be a given that cannot be evaluated or fruitfully discussed. But this is not the case. While it may be rare for people to *completely* change their minds about their values, it is nonetheless quite common for people's views and behavior to undergo at least *some* significant changes when they reflect on alternative moral views and novel arguments (Huang et al., 2019; Lindauer et al., 2020; Mercier, 2020, ch. 4).

1.2 The Empirical Step

Once we have identified a set of carefully reflected values or moral aims, it next becomes an open *empirical* question which policies are most likely to realize those values or aims. This holds true regardless of the nature of the values in question. For example, whether the values are centered purely on bringing about the best consequences (consequentialism), or on following ironclad rules (deontology), or some combination thereof, it is still a factual question which policies and institutions best accommodate these values.

For some values, ascertaining the optimal policy will be quite easy, such as in the case of deontological values that deem certain policies intrinsically right or wrong (e.g. some have argued that taxation is inherently wrong, cf. Rothbard, 1973). But for most values, the question of optimal policy is bound to be extremely complicated, dependent on myriad empirical factors. Yet these factors are nevertheless amenable to scientific investigation and discussion.

Thus, the aim of the second step is to assess which policies are most likely, given the available evidence, to realize the values identified in the first step. And it is crucial that we remain dispassionate and open-minded at this stage as well, continually being willing to look at new evidence and to have our minds changed.

Step 1: The Normative Step

Stating, arguing for, and refining our values

Step 2: The Empirical Step

Exploring empirical data, broadly construed, to clarify how to best realize our values

1.3 Openness as a Foundational Value

A key value that undergirds both the normative and the empirical step is intellectual openness. Karl Popper famously defended such openness at the level of our empirical convictions. Specifically, he argued that we can never be absolutely certain that our theories are correct, as they may always be overridden by further evidence, and hence we must remain open to such evidence (Popper, 1963, p. xi). What is less known is that Popper also defended openness at the normative level, essentially for the same reason: "though we should seek for absolutely right or valid [normative] proposals, we should never persuade ourselves that we have definitely found them" (Popper, 1945, "Addenda to Volume II, 13"; see also Popper, 1963, ch. 18).

I think Popper was right on this point. Intellectual openness is justified, indeed necessitated, by the fact that we are limited and fallible creatures. Nobody knows all the relevant empirical data and theories that bear on our decisions. Nor has anyone considered all the arguments that could be given for or against a given moral position. Therefore, we should be keen to have others inform us about the relevant facts, theories, and arguments about which we are currently ignorant, and which could potentially change our minds.

1.4 Who Should Engage in This Process?

The two steps outlined above do not provide much concrete detail as they stand, so it is fair to wonder how this two-step ideal is supposed to be realized. Specifically, who is supposed to engage in this practice of moral reflection and empirical investigation?

Ideally, everybody should reflect on their values, and then make empirically informed judgments about which policies seem optimal relative to these values. But it is, of course, not realistic for everyone to become an expert on moral philosophy or on the effects of various policies, let alone an expert on both. What *is* realistic, however, is that we have experts within these respective fields — moral philosophers specializing in normative issues and scientists specializing in empirical issues — who, beyond advancing the cutting edge of our understanding, can help inform the broader public.

Such experts will, of course, have their biases and blind spots like everyone else (cf. Tetlock, 2005). But that does not mean they cannot help advance the public understanding of complicated issues, especially if we listen to a variety of experts with opposing biases. So while the broader public may never realistically attain expert-level knowledge on these matters, they can at least still become considerably better informed, and thus come to adhere to the two-step ideal to a significantly greater extent.

It is especially important that politicians engage in this two-step process. That is, politicians should ideally state their underlying values in clear terms, along with explicit moral arguments supporting these values, and then justify their preferred policies with reference to relevant evidence that supports these policies as the best way to satisfy the values in question. To be clear, the point is not that politicians should elaborate on their values and provide detailed empirical arguments every time they engage in a political discussion, but rather that their values and arguments should be laid out *somewhere*, and serve as an underlying foundation for their policy decisions.

1.5 Is This Unrealistic?

One may object that the ideal I have outlined above is a complete pipe dream. Open and critical reflection, especially on values and policies, is just too far removed from human nature to have a chance of ever being realized. It is like saying that everyone should study advanced mathematics. (See Appendix B for some additional challenges to the two-step ideal.)

I agree that following this ideal is indeed quite far removed from our nature (see Section 6.6). But then it is also true that much, if not most of what we humans do cannot be said to "lie in our nature" in any straightforward sense (Henrich, 2015). For example, learning to read and write is not something humans just do naturally. On the contrary, acquiring these skills takes a vast repository of cultural knowledge and instructions, as well as persistent practice. The same can be said about democracy of any kind: creating and living within such a system is not something we just do by instinct, but is instead the product of (quite recent) cultural evolution through which we have domesticated our feral nature to a considerable extent (Henrich, 2020).

Note that it also used to seem unrealistic to have a society in which virtually everyone can read and write, or to create a democratic society. In fact, these aims probably seemed significantly *more* far-fetched hundreds of years ago than does a markedly greater adherence to the above-stated ideals today. But some people nonetheless dared to set out ambitious ideals for a literate and educated population, as well as for a democratic society.

By contrast, we appear to see little ambition for a better approach to political reasoning and discourse today. We mostly seem to have resigned ourselves to a fatalism of shallow and dumbed-down mainstream discourse. Yet the fact that a large number of people crave and consume deeper content, such as in the form of hour-long podcasts that do dive into fundamental issues, suggests that this resignation is unwarranted. Our mainstream political discourse *could* have significantly higher standards.

Regarding the comparison to advanced mathematics, it is worth noting that the mathematics we now teach teenagers and even young children was itself considered advanced mathematics at one point, and indeed beyond humanity's most advanced mathematics just a few thousand years ago. While it may have taken a Leibniz or a Newton to *discover* the fundamentals of calculus, it does not take a genius to teach it, let alone to learn it, especially given gradually improved techniques for formalizing and conveying these ideas. Such cultural progress means that a large fraction of the population *can* come to learn quite complicated ideas eventually. And the core ideas involved in the two-step ideal outlined above are arguably far simpler than the basics of calculus, or even the basics of fractions.

Moreover, one can argue that we in some sense already find ourselves more than halfway toward realizing this two-step ideal compared to hundreds of years ago, when there was no freedom of expression nor widespread literacy. After all, we now have at least *some* sensible discussions of ethical values that are accessible to many people, and we have at least *some* knowledge of the likely effects of various policies. We "simply" need to advance our discussions and knowledge further in these respects, and perhaps most importantly to *combine* these two levels — the normative and the empirical — in more sophisticated ways.

Of course, the tendency of university faculties and experts to specialize almost exclusively in just one of these two areas is not exactly helping us move toward more refined integrations of normative and empirical views. An obvious suggestion for remedying our shortage of such integrations would be to include ethics to a much greater extent in our schooling and education. After all, it is standard for education programs to include various empirical fields, such as history, biology, and physics, yet many such programs still do not include even a single school subject covering normative and evaluative fields, i.e. ethics and value theory. This absence of even the most basic of introductions renders it unsurprising that we see such a neglect of the normative side of things, and that we rarely see refined integrations of the normative and the empirical level.

Finally, it is important to stress that the two-step ideal can be worth striving for even if we can never fully adhere to it. Just as imperfect democracies are better than totalitarian dictatorships, an imperfect realization of the ideal of basing policies on carefully reflected values and empirical evidence still seems better than the alternative. For what, after all, *is* the alternative? That we base policies on poorly reflected values and mostly ignore empirical evidence? That we continue the current paradigm of failing to distinguish normative and empirical issues, with the consequent lack of reasonable discussion at either level? Those options seem worse.

Hence, even a slightly greater adherence to this two-step ideal would, I submit, still be a significant improvement, whether in the form of a relatively small number of people adhering strongly to it (e.g. certain political or altruistic movements), or a large number of people adhering to it just a bit more than they otherwise would. And nobody says that such improvements must be realizable overnight in order to be worth pursuing. Perhaps it would take decades to move us just marginally toward these ideals. But if this is what it takes to increase our adherence to these ideals, it seems worth taking the gradual steps required, starting with a clear statement of these ideals as a guidepost to aim for.

1.6 How the Two-Step Ideal Changes Things

To summarize, the framework outlined above divides our political reasoning and practice into two steps, one in which we clarify our values through moral argument and reflection, and one in which we identify which policies are most likely to realize those values in light of the empirical evidence. So how, in more specific terms, is this framework supposed to improve things?

For one, it brings greater clarity, both at the level of our individual thinking as well as in political disagreements. At the individual level, it gives us a method for assessing policies. Rather than trusting our immediate opinions on a given policy issue, we can instead split our appraisal into two steps that provide some structure, and in which we seek to adopt different mindsets — first the mindset of the ideal moral philosopher, then that of the ideal scientist. And while these ideal mindsets may be impossible to fully realize, the practice of actual moral philosophers and scientists shows that adherence to these ideals *is* possible at least to some extent, and certainly to a far greater extent than what we see in politics today.

Note too that if we have internalized this framework and identified a set of values that we find plausible, then we should have an interest in evaluating the empirical evidence regarding optimal policies in a fair and unbiased manner, since our biases will tend to be inimical to our values at this stage. We will, of course, still be biased in many ways, but the point is that we will have a self-directed incentive to be less biased, especially compared to a situation in which we simply follow our gut or the preferred policies of our ingroup. Questions of optimal policy are to be approached as open questions, which ought to close the door to political dogmatism. This would represent a significant improvement relative to the current condition in which our values and group loyalties all too often distort our empirical views, which in turn can fuel political polarization.

At the level of political disagreements, the two-step ideal brings greater clarity by enabling us to identify where exactly our disagreements lie. It is often unclear whether politically diverging parties disagree about aims or about the facts on the ground. If we presented transparent moral and empirical arguments in support of our preferred policies, it would be easier to pinpoint the cruxes of our disagreements, which could in turn enable more fruitful political conversations and compromises. It would bring greater precision and rigor into our political discourse, and experts would be better able to identify flaws in our reasoning, whether they be fallacies in our moral arguments or false empirical premises.

The two-step ideal also has the potential to highlight widely shared values that are neglected in our current political climate. The importance of reducing intense suffering is perhaps the most obvious example of such a value. Yet the way we think and do politics today tends to obscure the extent to which this value is shared, and often prevents us from acting on its most basic implications (cf. Hannon, 2021, pp. 307-308). If we adhered to a norm of explicitly spelling out our core values, our most widely shared values would likely become more visible and prominent, as would our common interest in realizing these values.

Lastly, by breaking our political thinking into these two steps, we may also become (at least somewhat) better able to change our minds and refine our views. Rather than being stuck in a condition where we each state our preferred policies and then, by assumption, reach an antagonistic impasse due to "a difference of opinion", this ideal would have us engage in reasoned conversation with moral and empirical arguments going back and forth, with the potential to advance everyone's views in the process.

1.7 From Here to There

How can we move toward realizing the two-step ideal of political practice, if only to a marginally greater degree? I see three basic things we can do. First, we can set out this ideal in clear terms and note its potential benefits. For example, we can point out how it could make politics more cooperative and more amenable to progress, both by enabling us to collectively refine our values and empirical views, as well as by facilitating a greater focus on widely shared values. This chapter has been an attempt to provide a basic such outline of the two-step ideal.

Second, we can raise awareness of the factors that prevent us from adhering to this ideal. Specifically, we can educate ourselves and others about the many political biases that influence our judgments, and then explore the implications of these biases — for example, that we should not trust our immediate intuitions but instead adopt a more self-scrutinizing and reflective mindset. The latter step of exploring the upshots of our biases is perhaps the most important and neglected one. For while quite a number of people have studied and written about political biases in descriptive terms, comparatively few have dared to say much about the normative implications of these biases, such as the necessity of disciplining ourselves and tempering our judgments. The next part of the book, Part II, will seek to explore both our political biases and their normative implications.

Third, we can attempt to show how politics can be done in accordance with the two-step ideal, and how this framework can help us reach well-founded policies. This may be in the form of elaborate moral arguments for the values we think should animate our policies (see e.g. Mayerfeld, 1999; Vinding, 2020a), or in the form of empirical examinations that shed light on which policies best satisfy our moral values. This is the kind of examination I will pursue in parts three and four, based on the value that suffering reduction deserves special priority.

PART II

DESCRIPTIVE GROUNDWORK AND ITS IMPLICATIONS

2

Political Psychology

It is commonly said that any political view must be based on a theory of human nature, at least implicitly. This seems difficult to deny, as our views of human nature influence just about every belief we have that concerns politics. Yet rather than adopting our view of human nature from philosophers who lived in a time in which we did not even understand our evolutionary origin — let alone modern genetics and anthropology — why not base our views on the best science of today? After all, we have learned a great deal about human nature in just the last few decades.

My aim in this second part of the book is to review some empirical data and theories that should inform our political thinking. This review can do little more than scratch the surface, partly because our knowledge of human nature is so vast, and partly because there is still much we do not know. Even so, I believe the following review suffices for the purpose of revealing some important ways in which we should update our approach to politics. I shall begin with a brief review of theories and findings in political psychology.

2.1 The Social Intuitionist Model of Moral Judgment

Psychologist Jonathan Haidt argues that our moral judgments are best explained by a social intuitionist model. According to this model, our moral judgments are usually the product of gut intuitions that we then rationalize after the fact. In other words, preverbal intuitions dictate our moral judgments, and our reasoning capacities are then given the task of making sense of our judgments to others (Haidt, 2001). On this model, our reasoning faculties mostly function like a press secretary tasked with the job of finding reasons that support the decisions made by the boss (our intuitions), with the purpose of making these decisions look defensible and prosocial to onlookers (Haidt, 2001; 2012, ch. 4).

One of the main pieces of evidence Haidt cites in favor of the intuitionist model is the phenomenon of "moral dumbfounding". For example, when people are presented with a thought experiment involving consensual incest between a brother and a sister that is stipulated to cause no harm and no risk of conception, people tend to grasp for reasons as to why the incest is wrong. They try to come up with ways in which the incest could cause harm, yet when it is pointed out that these harms were controlled for in the thought experiment, people eventually give up, often in laughter, with the admission that they cannot find a reason, but they still insist that it is wrong. They seem morally dumbfounded. This suggests, according to Haidt, that reasons are not the primary driver of our moral judgments, and that our judgments are instead driven by underlying intuitions, in this case intuitions about incest aversion that are easy to make sense of in biological terms (Haidt et al., 2000).

Beyond various studies that demonstrate the effects of emotions on our judgments (e.g. Lodge & Taber, 2005), the intuitionist model also meshes well with what we know about our evolutionary origins. The brains of our ancestors had to make judgments for hundreds of millions of years before they acquired the capacity to present reasoned arguments, and these judgments have increasingly been of a social and moral kind over the last tens of millions of years. By contrast, our ability to provide elaborate verbal reasons for our actions seems only to have emerged a few hundred thousand years ago (cf. Perreault & Mathew, 2012). So it makes sense that our reasoning capacity tends to function more as an appendix to our moral reasoning than as the primal source from which our judgments spring.

To be clear, Haidt's intuitionist model does not say that our reasoning cannot influence our judgments and underlying intuitions. Yet it does suggest that influence in this direction is the exception rather than the rule, and that our moral reasoning is in fact more likely to influence *other* people's intuitions and judgments than our own. Indeed, Haidt argues that this is largely the function of our ability to reason: to make us look good to others and to persuade others to agree with us (Haidt, 2001; see also Mercier & Sperber, 2017).

A number of critics have argued that Haidt understates the role that reasoning plays, or at least *can* play in our moral judgments. Specifically, critics have argued that it is quite common for our deliberate reasoning to shape both our moral intuitions and judgments, even if this is not how we make moral judgments most of the time (Pizarro & Bloom, 2003; Narvaez, 2008). Relatedly, one study reviewed evidence suggesting that "at least some kinds of moral reasoning play significant roles in moral judgment, including roles in abandoning moral intuitions in the absence of justifying reasons" (Paxton & Greene, 2010, abstract).

As most of the critics note, however, these points about the potential of deliberate reasoning to influence our moral judgments do not contradict the core claims of Haidt's model, which are generally accepted in at least a weak form. That is, researchers widely agree that our moral judgments *often are* just dictated by our intuitions, and that our accompanying reasons *often are* mere rationalizations made after the fact. But most researchers also agree that deliberate reasoning *can* influence our moral judgments in significant ways, especially when we are given the right tools and incentives (Greene, 2013, ch. 5; Mercier, 2020, ch. 4).

2.2 A Modular Mind

Evolutionary psychologists argue that our minds should be understood as consisting of distinct mental modules specialized to accomplish different tasks (Cosmides & Tooby, 1992; Kurzban, 2011a). One module recognizes edges in our visual field, another is responsible for blinking our eyes, and yet another detects unfairness. These modules should not be thought of in simple terms that have them occupy their own strictly delineated brain regions, but rather as different sets of mutually overlapping circuits that interact with other modules while also being part of many higher-level modules. Generally, mental modules are better thought of in functional rather than neuroanatomical terms, with their function being to solve adaptive problems that we faced in our ancestral environment (Cosmides & Tooby, 1997).

Especially relevant for our purposes is that this modular view applies to our moral cognition as well. That is, we also have distinct modules responsible for our many moral and political intuitions, and these "moral modules" develop and get expressed in different ways depending on our genes, childhood development, and adult life circumstances (Haidt, 2012, pp. 323-328).

Relevant, too, is that our mental modules often conspire to spin a self-serving story about our own beliefs and actions — especially when they pertain to politics — primarily for the purpose of making us look good to others. Yet the creation of this self-enhancing story is mostly unconscious to us, in part because being ignorant about it and deceiving ourselves with an unrealistically prosocial self-narrative makes us more convincing press secretaries on our own behalf (Trivers, 2011; Kurzban, 2011a, ch. 4; Tuschman, 2013, ch. 22; Simler & Hanson, 2018, ch. 5).

As Robert Trivers notes, "we deceive ourselves the better to deceive others" (Trivers, 2011, p. 3). Or more precisely: some of our mental modules hide unflattering information about us while other modules eagerly broadcast things that reflect well on us — to our own conscious selves and to others — all because it benefits us socially (Kurzban, 2011b).

As in the case of the social intuitionist model of moral judgment, there is some controversy around the edges of the modular view of mind, but a weak version that says that there is at least substantial modularity and specialization in the mind, and that there is considerable developmental plasticity in many of these modules, is widely accepted.

2.3 Moral Foundations Theory

Jonathan Haidt has proposed an extension to his social intuitionist model called "moral foundations theory". Where the social intuitionist model says that our intuitions come first and often directly dictate our moral judgments, the moral foundations theory seeks to say something about the nature of these intuitions. Specifically, it posits the existence of (at least) six different moral foundations, which can be thought of as distinct mental modules that each give rise to different moral intuitions (Haidt, 2012, Part II; Graham et al., 2013). The six moral foundations proposed so far are:

- **Care/harm:** Concern for suffering and the vulnerable.

- **Fairness/cheating:** Respecting shared rules and punishing cheaters.

- **Loyalty/betrayal:** Siding with one's family or group.

- **Authority/subversion:** Respect for tradition and for authorities perceived to be legitimate.

- **Purity/degradation:** Avoiding disgusting things, foods, and actions.

- **Liberty/oppression:** Resistance to being dominated and told what to do.

Haidt argues that these respective foundations, or moral modules, evolved to solve different problems in our ancestral environment. They enabled concern for our kin (care), successful cooperation (fairness), cohesive coalitions (loyalty), stable hierarchies (authority), the avoidance of pathogens (purity), and resistance against oppressive individuals and alliances (liberty) (Haidt, 2012, ch. 6-8).

A robust finding is that people vary greatly in terms of which foundations animate their moral judgments most strongly. For example, people who identify as liberal (here used in the modern American sense of the term) generally score higher on the care and fairness dimensions, while people who identify as conservative tend to score lower on these two dimensions, yet higher on loyalty, authority, and purity (Haidt, 2012, ch. 8). By comparison, Libertarians (in the modern American sense) tend to score uniquely low in the care dimension and, as one would expect, uniquely high in the liberty dimension — resistance to being told what to do (Iyer et al., 2012). Yet despite this relative variation, it is still true that people across the political spectrum all place considerable weight on both the care/harm and the fairness foundations in absolute terms (Haidt, 2012, ch. 8).

Another important difference, according to Haidt, is that liberals and conservatives tend to construe fairness differently, with liberals understanding it more in terms of equality while conservatives understand it more as proportionality, meaning that people should reap what they sow. Similar differences are found in the liberty/oppression foundation: liberals tend to be especially wary of oppression of the weak, as well as oppression from private corporations, whereas conservatives tend to be most wary of oppression from the government (Haidt, 2012, ch. 8).

A recent study tested the moral foundations theory across 30 diverse societies and found support for its core conceptualization, although there were some differences between Western and non-Western populations (Doğruyol et al., 2019). To be sure, moral foundations theory has its critics (Curry, 2019), yet the level of empirical support behind it suggests that it is, at the very least, a useful starting point for our thinking about political psychology.

2.4 Genes, Brains, and Personality

It is widely assumed that genes do not influence our political attitudes much, if at all. Yet this view is resoundingly false (Hatemi & McDermott, 2012; Hibbing et al., 2013). Studies consistently find that genetic factors account for 30 to 60 percent of the variation in our political attitudes (Tuschman, 2013, ch. 3; Hatemi et al., 2014). For example, the political orientations of identical twins reared apart have been found to be strongly correlated, whereas the same is not true for fraternal twins. Even more surprisingly, it does not seem to matter much whether identical twins are raised apart or together, as their views end up correlated to roughly the same extent regardless (Tuschman, 2013, ch. 3). As Bouchard and colleagues summarized their findings: "On multiple measures of personality [...] and social attitudes, monozygotic twins reared apart are about as similar as are monozygotic twins raised together" (Bouchard et al., 1990, p. 223; see also Klemmensen et al., 2012).

Genome-wide association studies have corroborated the significant heritability of political attitudes, and further identified a number of DNA regions that may account for a substantial fraction of the variation in political attitudes (Hatemi et al., 2011, p. 274; 2014; Benjamin et al., 2012). However, these studies also caution that political attitudes will tend to have a polygenic architecture, meaning that variation in these traits will usually be explained by many genes that each have only a modest effect (Benjamin et al., 2012; Hatemi et al., 2014). Another complication is that the heritability of various traits, including political attitudes, tends to differ across cultures, as different cultural environments create different "expression trajectories" for our genes (Uchiyama et al., 2021).

Researchers have also identified significant differences in the brains of liberals and conservatives. Liberals tend to have increased grey matter volume in the anterior cingulate cortex — associated with emotional awareness, among other things (Lane et al., 1998) — while conservatives tend to have a larger right amygdala, which is associated with negative emotions such as fear, among other things (Lanteaume et al., 2007; van der Plas et al., 2010; Kanai et al., 2011). Not only do these brain regions differ in size between liberals and conservatives, but they are also activated to different extents: liberals show greater activity in the anterior cingulate cortex in tasks where subjects have to override a habitual response, whereas conservatives show greater activity in their right amygdala in tasks involving risk-taking (Amodio et al., 2007; Schreiber et al., 2013).

Correlations have likewise been found between political attitudes and personality traits. Specifically, in a study exploring the relationship between left-right ideology and personality traits across 21 countries, openness to experience showed a significant correlation with left-wing attitudes, whereas conscientiousness showed a similar correlation with right-wing attitudes, though the pattern varied considerably across countries (Fatke, 2017). These correlations are consistent with a number of studies that have associated political conservatism with "preferences for stability, conformity, tradition, and order and structure", while associating political liberalism with "preferences for creativity, curiosity, novelty-seeking, and new experiences" (Mendez, 2017, p. 87). Relatedly, in terms of cognitive styles, highly politically conservative people tend to think less in terms of shades of grey and thus tend to be "hard categorizers", whereas liberals tend to be more tolerant of ambiguity and flexibility (Mendez, 2017, p. 87).

Note, however, that although research and books about political psychology often focus on the differences between staunch liberals and conservatives, the actual distribution of people's political views turns out to roughly fall along a bell curve in all societies, and only a minority of people fall into the categories of highly conservative or highly liberal. For instance, in a survey of more than 250,000 people in 97 different countries where people were asked to rate their political views on a left-right scale from 1 to 10, less than 15 percent placed themselves in one of the extreme categories of 1 and 10, and a large plurality, almost 30 percent, characterized themselves as a 5 (Tuschman, 2013, ch. 2).

2.5 The Importance of Environmental Factors

To say that genes exert a significant influence on our political attitudes is obviously not to say that the influence of culture is insignificant. It most certainly is not. A clear demonstration of this fact was provided by a twin study of more than 4,000 people that examined how attitudes on 28 different political issues were influenced by 1) biologically heritable factors, 2) the shared environment — e.g. shared family and shared peer groups — and 3) the non-shared environment, such as non-shared peer groups.

The study had two principal findings. First, the influence of these three factors varied from issue to issue, with each of them being the most significant factor for *some* issues. Second, for 23 of the 28 issues, the order of the influence of these factors was the same: the non-shared environment was most important, accounting for 53 percent of the variation on average (across all 28 issues), biologically heritable factors came second, accounting for 32 percent of the variation, and the shared environment came last, accounting for 16 percent on average (Alford et al., 2005).

So while our moral and political intuitions are strongly influenced by our genes, they are also strongly influenced by cultural factors, such as the prevailing attitudes in our peer groups and our culture at large (Haidt, 2001; 2012, ch. 3). A salient case in point is that most people in some cultures find it intuitively wrong to eat dogs, while in other cultures a majority of people deem it acceptable. There is, in this case, a profound difference in people's moral intuitions — a difference that is no doubt measurable in their hormones and brains (cf. Henrich, 2015, ch. 14) — yet this difference is chiefly due to cultural factors.

Our environment is also important in that it can determine what is in our self-interest, which likewise motivates our political behavior and attitudes to a considerable extent (Margalit, 2013; Page et al., 2013; Weeden & Kurzban, 2014). For example, a survey conducted in the US found that people whose family income is in the top 40 percent of the income distribution are almost 70 percent more likely to be opposed to wealth redistribution compared to people whose family income is in the bottom 40 percent (Weeden & Kurzban, 2014, pp. 154-156).

A similar survey found that people who are among the 25 percent most financially secure are 140 percent more likely to support a Republican candidate than are the 20 percent least financially secure (Pew Research Center, 2015). And while this result is partly explained by lower support for *any* candidate among the least financially secure, it is clear that this is not the full story, since the least financially secure are only five percent less likely to support a Democratic candidate than are the most financially secure (Pew Research Center, 2015). These variations in attitudes are probably to a significant extent *caused* by people's position along the income distribution. Indeed, another study found that sudden economic hardship, especially the loss of a job, has "a major effect on increasing support for welfare spending" — an effect that seems to disappear once people's employment situation improves (Margalit, 2013, abstract). (Of course, to say that narrow self-interest can influence our political views in significant ways is not to say our political views are always or even mostly determined by self-interest.)

2.6 Groups and Identity

The groups that we feel we belong to turn out to be an especially important determinant of our political views and voting behavior. In their book *Democracy for Realists*, political scientists Christopher Achen and Larry Bartels review a large literature that consistently shows that voters mostly vote based on their group membership and identity rather than their economic self-interest (Achen & Bartels, 2016). This contrasts with what Achen and Bartels call the "folk theory" of democracy, a more rationalistic view according to which voters primarily vote based on their individual policy preferences — a view that turns out to be mostly false (Achen & Bartels, 2016, ch. 8-9).

Achen and Bartels argue that people's social and psychological attachments to groups are "the most important factor" determining their political judgments (Achen & Bartels, 2016, p. 232). This is in line with the views of various authors who have argued that the main function of political beliefs and social identity has to do with social signaling and side-taking (Haidt, 2012, Part III; Park & Van Leeuwen, 2015; DeScioli, 2016; Simler & Hanson, 2018, ch. 16; Hannon, 2021).

On this view, the primary yet often hidden motive behind our political behavior is to signal our loyalty to our perceived ingroup, whether it be a given political party, ideology, or religion. So when people adopt a strong position on a contentious issue, such as climate change or immigration, the main motive, according to this view, will often be to signal loyalty to a particular group, even as the people sending the signal remain mostly unaware of this motive. In other words, political beliefs are, from this perspective, not too unlike a sports jersey or a religious symbol — an honest signal of one's allegiance (Haidt, 2012, Part III; Simler, 2016; Simler & Hanson, 2018, ch. 16).

The evolutionary logic behind such signaling, it has been argued, is that it increases cooperation and mating interest among the group one seeks to appeal to, even as it comes at the cost of reducing cooperation and mating opportunities with people on the other side (Miller, 1996; Park & Van Leeuwen, 2015, p. 119; Simler & Hanson, 2018, ch. 16, "Loyalty Demands Sacrifice").

2.7 Zooming Out

Some of the things I have said above may seem in tension — for instance, how can our political views both be strongly influenced by our genes *and* be mostly about group signaling? Let us therefore try to zoom out so as to get a clearer sense of how all these things fit together in a coherent picture.

If we look at a single politically active individual in a modern democratic society, call her Alice, the basic picture we get is roughly the following. First, genes and childhood socialization shape Alice's early moral and political intuitions, and these in turn influence which political positions and groups she finds appealing. When Alice becomes a young adult motivated to join a political movement, her many-dimensional moral profile (cf. Haidt's six moral foundations) is by no means a perfect match with the group she is most attracted to, yet it still fits okay on the dimensions she cares most about, and so she joins it. As Alice becomes increasingly socialized into her new political group, her ideological match slowly increases. This is partly due to signaling: though she is quite unaware of it, Alice is naturally drawn toward displaying her agreements with her group while she is less drawn, somehow, to express her points of disagreement. Over time, the points of agreement become even stronger while the disagreements generally become less significant, in part because Alice's social surroundings influence her political intuitions, gradually nudging them toward the group average (cf. Haidt, 2001; 2012, ch. 3; Achen & Bartels, 2016, p. 268).

This is, of course, a very generalized picture that fails to describe everyone. After all, some people, even among those who are highly politically involved, do flip their political stance in their adult lives (though this is the exception rather than the rule, as political views are generally quite stable in adults, Peterson et al., 2020). But Alice's story still helps to illustrate how genes, early socialization, and group signaling can all be highly significant, part of the explanation being that they are not independent. We tend to gravitate toward political groups that we were already disposed to agree with. Consequently, the political intuitions shaped by our genes and our formative environment will often end up pointing in much the same direction as the strong pull of loyalty signaling that we feel in our favored political groups as adults.

3

Political Biases

In this chapter, I will review a small selection of the many psychological biases that afflict our political thinking and decision-making. (Several books have explored such biases at length, see e.g. Achen & Bartels, 2016; Brennan, 2016; Shenkman, 2016.)

The previous chapter already hints at a general reason to expect our thinking about politics to be biased: we tend to base our moral and political judgments on gut intuitions, and given that our brains are mostly adapted to navigating small social environments, we should not expect these intuitions to yield sensible judgments on the complex issues of modern politics. As we shall see below, empirical research bears out such pessimistic expectations, and thereby highlights the need to go beyond mere gut intuitions in our political reasoning.

3.1 Irrelevant Factors Influencing Our Politics

Modern psychology has repeatedly shown that our judgments are subject to influences of which we are unaware. For example, one study found that people tend to make more calculating moral judgments when they have been exposed to cold temperatures compared to typical room temperature, seemingly because cold temperatures reduce empathic feelings (Nakamura et al., 2014). Another study had two groups watch different video clips — one positive and one neutral — and found a significant difference in the moral judgments made by the respective groups, with those watching the positive video being more willing to make a consequentialist choice (Valdesolo & DeSteno, 2006). Hunger, too, appears to influence people's moral judgments, with increased hunger leading to reduced disapproval of moral transgressions and greater support for social welfare (Aarøe & Petersen, 2013; Vicario et al., 2018).

In all these studies, people's judgments are influenced by factors that ought to be irrelevant. (Note that while the results of any one of these studies may seem uncertain in light of the replication crisis, the more general point they all support about how obscure factors often influence our moral and political judgments in significant ways does seem on solid ground, which is further supported by the studies cited below.)

Similar findings have been made in the context of real-life political judgments. A famous example is how a series of shark attacks that occurred in New Jersey in 1916 influenced voter behavior in the US presidential election of the same year. The shark attacks had an especially negative impact on the tourism of four counties in New Jersey — those located along the beach — and these counties all saw a significantly greater reduction in votes for the incumbent president than did other counties in New Jersey (Achen & Bartels, 2016, ch. 5).

This fits with a model of voter behavior proposed by Achen and Bartels called "blind retrospection", according to which swing voters tend to reward or punish incumbent politicians based on how the voters feel things are going, regardless of whether the incumbent politicians have anything to do with the causes of the voters' level of satisfaction (Achen & Bartels, 2012; 2016, ch. 5). After all, it makes little sense to punish the incumbent president for shark attacks and their effects on tourism — something the president had no control over. Yet similar patterns have been observed for droughts: voters seem to punish the incumbent politicians when there has been an increase in droughts, even though the politicians in question obviously did not cause these droughts, and even though voters have little information as to whether other politicians would have handled the droughts any better (Achen & Bartels, 2016, ch. 5). Likewise, sports fans whose teams have recently won a game will on average express significantly higher approval of the incumbent president (Healy et al., 2010; Shenkman, 2016, "Introduction").

The facial appearance of politicians is another factor with an undue influence. That is, people tend to judge the competences of politicians based merely on what their faces look like, and this tendency does not get modified much even when people get additional information about the politicians' party affiliation and campaign promises (Mannetti et al., 2016). Such assessments of competence based purely on facial appearances have even been found to predict election results (Sussman et al., 2013).

Other studies have found that we tend to trust people more when their faces resemble our own, which renders it natural to speculate whether facial similarity might influence our judgments of politicians as well (DeBruine, 2002). One study set out to test this hypothesis by surveying a representative sample of US voters in 2004, just a week before the presidential election between Republican George W. Bush and Democrat John Kerry. Participants were divided into three groups, one in which the voters watched unedited photographs of Bush and Kerry, one in which the voter's face had been merged with the face of Bush, and one in which the voter's face was merged with Kerry's face.

In the conditions with morphed faces, none of the participants noticed that their own face had been inserted in the picture, and yet the face merge had a surprisingly strong influence. In the condition where participants had been morphed with Kerry, the Democratic candidate won by six percentage points, while the group that had been morphed with Bush chose him with a 15-percent margin. In the unedited condition, Bush won by two percent, as in the actual election a week later. Unsurprisingly, people with a strong partisan identity were not swayed by the merged images (Bailenson et al., 2008; Tuschman, 2013, ch. 19).

Another striking example of a factor that should ideally not play a role in our political attitudes, yet which seemingly does, is physical strength. In particular, greater upper-body strength predicts support for financial inequality among men, but not among women (Petersen & Laustsen, 2019). More than that, one experiment suggested that strength training increases men's social dominance orientation — a personality construct that involves a preference for hierarchies and which correlates with conservatism (Pratto et al., 1994) — implying that increases in physical strength may increase men's opposition to egalitarian redistribution (Petersen & Laustsen, 2019).

These findings are not difficult to make sense of in evolutionary terms, since more formidable males would tend to have higher status and more resources in our ancestral environment. But in a modern society in which resources are largely decoupled from physical strength, it hardly makes sense to let one's physical strength determine one's political attitudes.

Relatedly, a study conducted in the US found that political views are also predicted by physical attractiveness. For instance, people rated as more attractive were more likely to identify as conservative and Republican compared to citizens who were rated as less attractive. And while physical attractiveness did not predict political beliefs quite as strongly as did income and education, the effect was still robust across different measures of attractiveness and when controlling for socioeconomic status and demographics (Peterson & Palmer, 2017, p. 4).

One can speculate that the explanation of this pattern is similar to the one outlined above in the case of physical strength: individuals who are considered more attractive may feel that they have higher status, which might increase their tendency to favor existing hierarchies and to oppose egalitarian sentiments and policies (cf. Pratto et al., 1994; Westfall et al., 2019).

3.2 Motivated Reasoning and Partisan Bias

It is well-documented that the human mind is subject to confirmation bias: a tendency to seek out and recall information that confirms our pre-existing beliefs while disregarding information that challenges these beliefs (Plous, 1993, pp. 233-234). Closely related is the phenomenon of motivated reasoning, which is when we seek to justify a desired conclusion rather than following the evidence where it leads (Kunda, 1990). It hardly needs stating that confirmation bias and motivated reasoning are rampant in politics (as indeed implied by Haidt's social intuitionist model).

For example, studies have found that people are more likely to agree with a given policy when it is proposed by a political party that they favor, while they are more likely to reject the same policy when it is proposed by a party they dislike — what has been called the "party sponsor effect" (Petersen et al., 2013). One could hope that this tendency reflects a rational heuristic through which voters try to defer to well-informed people who share their values, as opposed to just being a case of voters showing loyalty to their political team. Yet a study that set out to explore this question found significant evidence against the rational-heuristic hypothesis, and concluded that the source of the party sponsor effect does indeed appear to be motivated reasoning oriented toward team loyalty (Petersen et al., 2013; further support for this conclusion is found in Achen & Bartels, 2016, ch. 10; Hannon, 2021).

Studies have also demonstrated that our brains tend to process political leaders, groups, and issues in affectively charged ways. In particular, we instinctively process our own political tribe and leaders in a positive light and with positive affect while we process "the other side" in a negative light and with negative affect. Such charged cognition, commonly known as "hot cognition", is usually activated within milliseconds of exposure, well before we can form any conscious appraisal of the subject in question (Lodge & Taber, 2005). This is consistent with earlier work suggesting that motivated reasoning begins prior to conscious awareness, with underlying cognitive systems quietly pushing our thinking in the desired direction, in turn leaving us mostly unaware that we engage in motivated reasoning at all (Kunda, 1990; Trivers, 2011, ch. 7).

A later study showed motivated reasoning in action more directly. Subjects who read arguments for and against a set of contentious political positions did not moderate or even just maintain their original views, but instead buttressed their initial position by focusing on the arguments that agreed with their views while paying little attention to the arguments that spoke against them — all despite having been explicitly instructed to "rate the arguments fairly" and to be as "objective as possible" (Taber & Lodge, 2006).

Political partisans likewise tend to display a limited ability to faithfully represent the positions of the other side of a political debate, and tend to give straw-man accounts of opponents' views, even when given financial incentives to represent these opposing views accurately (Yeomans, 2021).

This suggests that straw-man representations of political opponents are often unconscious, and often require no deliberate distortions, as people just mostly fail to understand the opposing perspective. And while greater knowledge of political matters does increase people's ability to represent the position of their own side, it does not seem to improve their ability to represent the other side (Yeomans, 2021).

Even people's ability to solve a basic math problem can succumb to motivated reasoning when the problem is posed in a political context. One study presented the same mathematical problem to subjects, except that in one framing the problem was about the effects of a cream for skin rashes, whereas another framing made it about gun control. Not surprisingly, people with high numeracy scores could usually solve the problem when it was about skin cream. Yet when the problem was framed in a political context and the correct result went against the political ideology of the subjects — whether liberal or conservative — those with high numeracy scores suddenly did little better than those with the worst numeracy scores. Politics induced a near-total breakdown in reasoning abilities (Kahan et al., 2013).

Finally, although each side of the political spectrum considers the other side far more biased than their own, a recent meta-analysis of partisan biases among liberals and conservatives in the United States — titled "At Least Bias Is Bipartisan" — concluded that liberals and conservatives are generally biased to the same extent, although they tend to be biased about different issues (Ditto et al., 2019a; see also Haidt, 2013, 55:20). (The conclusion about *equal* bias has been criticized by Baron & Jost, 2019, who argue that the evidence suggests that liberals tend to display more epistemic virtues than conservatives, and that Ditto et al. included an unrepresentative sample of studies; this critique was in turn disputed by Ditto et al., 2019b. Yet the more general conclusion that partisan bias is significant and pervasive stands regardless.)

3.3 Political Ignorance and Overconfidence

Voters tend to be ignorant about politics. In fact, this has been characterized as one of the most robust findings in political science (Bartels, 1996; Brennan, 2016, ch. 2). And voters are not just wrong in small ways on insignificant matters, but in big ways on major issues. In the words of political scientist Jeffrey Friedman, "the public is far more ignorant than academic and journalistic observers of the public realize" (Friedman, 2006b, p. v).

For example, when US citizens were asked what percentage of the federal budget they thought goes to foreign aid, the median estimate was 25 percent, while people generally thought around 10 percent would be appropriate. Yet the actual amount that goes to foreign aid is less than one percent (WPO, 2010). A similar survey of registered US voters from 2014 found that 42 percent believe that US forces found weapons of mass destruction in Iraq (Cassino, 2015). And roughly three quarters of US adults cannot name all three branches of the US government (APPC, 2016). To be clear, this is not just a problem in the United States, as voters in other countries display similar levels of ignorance about political and social issues (Ipsos MORI, 2014).

A relevant phenomenon in this context is the "illusion of explanatory depth" — the widespread illusion of believing that we understand aspects of the world in much greater detail than we in fact do. For instance, a study asked people to rate their understanding of common objects such as a zipper and a flush toilet, after which they were asked to explain how these inventions worked. Not surprisingly, people's self-rated level of understanding dropped significantly when they were asked to explain the mechanic function of these things, as they came to realize how little they in fact knew (Rozenblit & Keil, 2002).

A later study demonstrated the same effect in the realm of political knowledge. When people were asked to explain how a set of policies work, there was a clear drop in their self-rated understanding of the policies, and people became significantly more moderate in their views. In contrast, when people were only asked to present reasons as to why they supported or opposed a given policy, there was little change in their self-rated level of understanding, and their positions did not become more moderate (Fernbach et al., 2013). We can thus extend Friedman's quote above: it is not just that most people are far more ignorant about politics than academics and journalists tend to assume, but we are also far more ignorant than we ourselves realize.

The illusion of explanatory depth is closely related to overconfidence bias: our tendency to overestimate how much certainty we can justify placing in our beliefs, a bias that is especially strong and influential in the realm of politics (Ortoleva & Snowberg, 2015). Yet the fact that overconfidence is prevalent in the political realm should not be surprising given that we often have an interest in persuading others about our political views, and studies show that we do become significantly more persuasive to others when we express our views with overconfidence (Schwardmann & van der Weele, 2019). Our brains unconsciously inflate our confidence to help us "win" with conviction, and the quality of our political discourse pays the price.

4

Implications of Our Political Psychology and Biases

The empirical findings presented in the last two chapters are clearly of great importance. Yet which specific implications we should derive from them may be less obvious. In this chapter, I will seek to highlight what I consider some of the key normative lessons that we should draw from this descriptive picture, lessons that should permeate our entire approach to politics if we are to realize the basic ideals outlined in the first chapter.

4.1 Don't Trust Immediate Intuitions

Perhaps the most important and general implication is, in short, that we cannot simply trust our intuitions. As we have seen, we often base our moral and political judgments on gut intuitions that we then seek to rationalize after the fact. Yet we have little reason to believe that our raw intuitions are a sufficient basis on which to rest our moral and political decisions, especially given that our intuitions can so easily be influenced by irrelevant factors such as how hungry we are or whether our favorite sports team has recently won a game.

The fact that genetic factors and personality traits can predict our political views is also a reason to be skeptical of our immediate intuitions.

Rather than just reflexively live out a stereotypical personality profile in the political realm, we can rise above the dictates of our immediate intuitions — to reflect more deeply on our ethical values (the normative step) and to explore the complicated empirical question of how these values can best be realized (the empirical step).

To be clear, the point here is not that our intuitions should be wholly disregarded. After all, our intuitions often do carry a lot of wisdom, sometimes even encapsulating centuries of hard-won cultural moral progress. For example, unlike a couple of centuries ago, most people now strongly intuit that human slavery is wrong. Moreover, our moral judgments must be based on *some* starting point, and it seems difficult to avoid having moral intuitions of some kind at the foundation of our ethics, such as the intuition that suffering is worth reducing.

But the point is that we do not have to go with the very first intuition that eagerly announces itself and tries to dictate our judgment. Instead, we can take a step back and behold multiple intuitions — to explore their mutual consistency and to hold them up against empirical data and arguments. By studying the mechanism of our political psychology, we can come to understand that our mind casts quick judgments that we are inclined to identify with and defend, which in turn can help us realize that we are not forced to identify with our most immediate inclination. We can view it as a data point to be evaluated rather than our final word.

In sum, when considering political issues, it generally seems advisable to suspend our judgment and take a closer look at the relevant moral arguments and empirical data before we draw any strong conclusions.

4.2 Beware Motivated Reasoning

A related proposal that seems helpful is to become aware of our tendency to engage in motivated reasoning. This is a greater challenge than one might naively suppose, not least due to the internal invisibility of our biased inclinations. As hinted earlier, the first steps toward motivated reasoning occur prior to conscious awareness, meaning that we often find ourselves on a moving train of motivated reasoning long before we can frame our first deliberate thought (Kunda, 1990; Lodge & Taber, 2005; Trivers, 2011, ch. 7).

The introspective invisibility of motivated reasoning is a problem, but what makes the problem even worse is that we are largely unaware of this invisibility. After all, if we have a folk model according to which motivated reasoning should be transparent to ourselves, it is no wonder that we fail to acknowledge that we engage in it — the absence of introspective evidence of motivated reasoning would seem to prove our innocence.

In contrast, if we at least had the meta-awareness that motivated reasoning is mostly invisible from the inside, then we could not pull this move of declaring ourselves innocent just because introspection yields no sign of misdeed. Instead, we would realize that our finding no trace of motivated reasoning in no way exonerates us, and we would realize that we should, at the very least, admit to the *possibility* of engaging in motivated reasoning. Such an admission alone would be a significant step toward better epistemic standards in our political discourse. But there will, of course, often be a very strong social pull not to admit to this possibility, which is another crucial pitfall to be aware of.

4.3 Resist the Pull of Loyalty Signaling

Recall that political scientists have deemed group attachments "the most important factor" in determining people's political judgments (Achen & Bartels, 2016, p. 232). This is at odds with the more common and more flattering view of ourselves that says that our political judgments are primarily determined by our individual reasoning — a picture that assigns little importance to our group affiliations, if any at all.

Unfortunately, most of us are probably self-deceived about the extent to which our political behavior is animated by the Do-Right motive of making the world a better place versus the goal of signaling loyalty to our group (Tuschman, 2013, ch. 22; Simler & Hanson, 2018, ch. 5, ch. 16). The fact that we vote in alignment with group interests, that we seem more concerned with position-taking than with influencing outcomes, and that we show little interest in being informed about actual policy issues makes little sense from a Do-Right perspective. Yet these and other observations fit well with the view that group loyalty is (at least often) the main motivation behind our political behavior (Achen & Bartels, 2016, ch. 8-9; Simler & Hanson, 2018, ch. 16; Hannon, 2021).

The main normative implication of the influence of our group attachments is that we should resist the pull of loyalty signaling. Specifically, we should be mindful of the urge to make our own political views conform to the views of our ingroup, and withstand the urge to say things chiefly because they signal our group affiliations. And as is true of motivated reasoning in general, our drive to signal group loyalty is rarely fully transparent to ourselves, in that it rarely comes with any indication that it serves the purpose of loyalty signaling. Both individually and collectively, we have little clue of the extent to which group loyalty motivates our political behavior (Achen & Bartels, 2016, ch. 10; Simler & Hanson, 2018, ch. 5, ch. 16).

Relatedly, to paraphrase Jonathan Haidt, we should realize that we tend to use our inner press secretaries to portray ourselves and our own side in the best possible light, while we portray the political outgroup in a bad light (Haidt, 2012, p. 319). We accentuate the strengths and downplay the flaws in our own views, whereas we do the opposite with the views of our opponents, emphasizing their flaws and downplaying their merits. Our minds thus naturally present us with a picture that is distorted along political lines, and it may take a lot of effort to control for this distortion — to really see the weaknesses in the views of one's own political group, and to see the merits in other groups' views. And even more effort is required to do these things publicly, where the pull of partisan bias and loyalty signaling is especially strong.

The point made here regarding group loyalty is not independent from those of the two previous sections, but rather an extension of them: our immediate intuitions are often strongly in favor of the ingroup position by default, and we routinely engage in motivated reasoning to reach the conclusions that are in line with the party position (Petersen et al., 2013; Achen & Bartels, 2016, ch. 10). Being aware of our proclivity for group loyalty is thus helpful in our efforts to reduce biased intuitions and motivated reasoning in politics, as it gives us a reasonable idea about which form we should expect them to take, namely the form of ingroup-favoring intuitions and reasoning.

4.4 Reduce Political Overconfidence

To say that overconfidence is pervasive in politics is an understatement. As we saw in the previous chapter, people vastly overestimate their understanding of political policies, so much so that they markedly downgrade their self-rated understanding of policies when merely asked to explain how they work (Fernbach et al., 2013). Another study that examined overconfidence in general found that people were correct less than 85 percent of the time when they claimed to be 100 percent certain about their answer to a given question (Fischhoff et al., 1977).

And yet the people in these studies did not even have a political audience to impress with posturing or grandstanding claims. Performing in front of such an audience — as we usually do when we behave politically — probably just further exacerbates our already damning tendency toward overconfidence, especially when it comes to the canonical empirical beliefs of our own political tribe (cf. Ortoleva & Snowberg, 2015; Simler, 2016; Schwardmann & van der Weele, 2019).

For example, just as no religious person wins many points among devout co-believers by expressing their credence in the existence of a God in terms of degrees of belief — even if it is a fairly high credence — no political loyalist will gain many points for expressing doubts, even minor doubts, about the core political gospels of their own side. Politics often incentivizes us to express our 80-percent credences as 100-percent credences, and thus to throw nuance and intellectual honesty under the bus (Vinding, 2018, "Thinking in Degrees of Certainty").

But the truth is that even our 80-percent credences tend to be overconfident (Fischhoff et al., 1977). We are generally far too sure about the consequences of different policies, and far too good at downplaying the inherent uncertainty of complex social systems (cf. Tomasik, 2013e; Vinding, 2020a, 9.1-9.2). Such uncertainty calls for nuanced views and balanced credences, neither of which make for clear loyalty displays in polarized disputes.

The term "political overconfidence" should be at the front of our awareness in political discussions, and the political overconfidence we should each be most aware of and most eager to expose is, of course, our own.

4.5 Be Charitable

Closely related to the points mentioned above is the need to be charitable and fair-minded toward our political opponents and their positions, engaging with the strongest and most generous interpretation of their views and arguments. As mentioned, our brains reflexively process and represent our political opponents in ways that are affectively charged and stacked against them, and hence an arduous effort is likely required to counteract our unconscious straw-man representations (Lodge & Taber, 2005). (This fact about human psychology may also be worth keeping in mind when others show a reflexively negative reaction toward us: they are not really reacting *to us*, but rather to their own negatively charged and unconsciously formed representation of us, which may indeed be an unpleasant cartoon figure to have to struggle with; a phantom struggle that merits both correction and compassion.)

Indeed, all of the tendencies outlined above plausibly conspire to make us uncharitable toward our political opponents. Our immediate intuitions and motivated reasoning provide knee-jerk justifications for less than generous representations of the other side's positions. And the pull of loyalty signaling then incentivizes us to express and perhaps further exaggerate our already uncharitable interpretations, and to be theatrically overconfident about them. In contrast, strong and charitable interpretations of the other side rarely feel intuitively good or effortless to come up with, and they are decidedly not a good way to signal one's political affiliations.

Thus, it seems that we should try to assume good faith on behalf of political opponents (unless we have clear evidence to the contrary), and try to gain a solid understanding of other people's views before rushing to attack them. A complementary heuristic that may be helpful in our age of screen communication is to strive to communicate with others exactly as we would in a face-to-face conversation, with the degree of interpersonal understanding and agreeableness that usually comes along with this mode of interaction (Vinding, 2020c, "Better norms for screen communication").

Other things that seem useful for promoting better political conversations include a willingness to criticize the excesses of one's ingroup, as well as a general nuance heuristic — e.g. avoiding black-or-white thinking, acknowledging grains of truth in different perspectives, and representing beliefs in terms of graded credences rather than rigid certainties (Vinding, 2018; Galef, 2021, ch. 6). And as usual, while it makes sense to encourage everyone to do better, it is probably most fruitful if all sides strive to be charitable and to observe high epistemic standards *themselves*, rather than mostly complain that the other side fails in these regards.

4.6 Not A Hopeless Endeavor

One may object that the recommendations outlined above are impractical, as our political biases are too deep-seated for us to ever transcend them. This is similar to the objection that says that the ideal presented in the first chapter is unrealistic (see Section 1.5), and my response is essentially the same: it is an understandable yet ultimately unwarranted sentiment.

First, we do not need to completely transcend our biases in order for debiasing to make sense. Bias comes in degrees, and so even if we will always be biased in significant ways, we can at least limit the extent and influence of our biases — to be *more* skeptical of our immediate intuitions, to have *more* awareness of our tendency to engage in motivated reasoning, to show *greater* resistance against the pull of loyalty signaling, etc.

Second, many empirical results directly contradict the notion that we are stuck with our pre-existing opinions and biases. For example, political scientist James Fishkin has arranged a number of "deliberative opinion polls", in which a representative sample of the public were invited to deliberate on policy issues through discussions with each other and with experts. The results are surprisingly encouraging: 70 percent of the participants changed their minds in the process, their views became more nuanced, and both liberals and conservatives generally allowed facts to sway their opinions (Fishkin et al., 2000; Klein, 2010; Shenkman, 2016, p. 17). These results suggest that most people *are* able to change their minds on political issues, if only the right cultural setting is provided.

Similarly, in one of the studies cited earlier, in which irrelevant factors such as recent sports victories influenced people's political judgments, it was found that the influence of these irrelevant factors could be significantly reduced by making people more aware of the reasons behind their momentary state of mind (Healy et al., 2010). Another study likewise found that people made fewer intuitionist moral judgments when they had been instructed to reappraise their emotional reactions (Feinberg et al., 2012).

Indeed, many studies have demonstrated that we *can* change our minds when exposed to rational arguments, and that our initial opinions and prejudices *can* be challenged to a considerable extent (see e.g. Huang et al., 2019; Lindauer et al., 2020; Mercier, 2020, ch. 4).

It is true, however, that better political reasoning does not come easily. As we saw in the previous chapter, when faced with arguments for and against their political views, people tend to be one-sided and to only strengthen their pre-existing convictions, even when they have been explicitly instructed to be as "objective as possible" (Taber & Lodge, 2006). Yet this finding is not surprising. First, it should be noted that the study in question included no control group that did not receive an instruction to be objective, so we do not know whether this minimal encouragement might in fact have had some positive effect. But more importantly, the debiasing effort in this study was indeed minimal, and we should not expect mere encouragements toward objectivity to reduce our political biases much, let alone to eliminate them entirely. Just as we cannot expect children to gain literacy by merely providing them with the instruction to "read as well as possible", we also cannot expect people to gain *political* literacy by providing them with similarly facile instructions. We should expect it to take *far* more.

A mere instruction to be fair-minded and objective does not teach us anything about our devious political psychology. It tells us nothing about the strong influence of immediate intuitions, or about the introspective invisibility of motivated reasoning. Nor does it tell us anything about the hidden yet powerful pull of loyalty signaling and political overconfidence. Without information about these particular pitfalls, we should hardly expect to be able to reduce their influence all that much. And we are unfortunately still largely unaware of these pitfalls.

This has been a major problem with the Enlightenment project so far: many Enlightenment thinkers failed to appreciate just how biased and tribal we are by nature, and how difficult it is for us to follow rational arguments (though some of these thinkers did acknowledge it to some extent,

Rasmussen, 2013). Indeed, we have pretty much *all* failed to appreciate how far from the ideals of reason and informed democracy the practices of actual people and societies in fact are (cf. Achen & Bartels, 2016). This is a sad fact, and yet acknowledging our massively biased and *un*reasoned (default) predicament may well be among the most promising steps we can take to remedy our situation, by giving us a more realistic sense of where we are and the serious effort that is required if we are to do better.

The truth is that a more reasoned approach to politics does *not* come easily, but nor is it impossible. Like literacy, it requires hard work and the right cultural circumstances. And there is reason not to despair completely: the scientific study of our political psychology and biases is still quite young, and its key findings are still to be widely disseminated. We have yet to turn this crucial self-knowledge into common knowledge, and to make it part of our culture. In particular, we have yet to see it change the perhaps most important aspect of our culture, namely our social incentives.

4.7 Change Social Incentives

We cannot meaningfully improve our political discourse by focusing on individuals in isolation. Indeed, this is another key point that was largely neglected in the original Enlightenment project: the *social* nature of human reason (cf. Mercier, 2020). Specifically, it has rarely been acknowledged just how strongly our thinking and our beliefs are subject to social incentives. When a given belief is unpopular in our ingroup, our minds may be inclined not just to *hide* such a belief, but to avoid believing it in the first place, since holding it could be too socially costly (Simler, 2016).

For example, a conservative person may be inclined to disbelieve in the existence of anthropogenic climate change, since believing in it might be seen as a sign of disloyalty (to the conservative team), while a liberal person may be inclined to disbelieve in the existence of innate sex differences for similar reasons (Haidt, 2013, 55:20; Simler, 2016; Simler & Hanson, 2018, ch. 16, "Loyalty Demands Sacrifice").

Yet loyalty signaling is not the only form of signaling that can introduce epistemically distorting incentives. We are also keen to be impressive: to hold beliefs that make us seem especially caring, smart, and creative, or whatever the trait may be that we wish to impress people with (Simler & Hanson, 2018, ch. 9). Rather than express the truth, we often opt to express the impressive, and the latter often diverges from the former (cf. Lewis, 2016).

One might think that the problem here is that we engage in these forms of signaling in the first place, and that the remedy is to simply stop this signaling behavior altogether. Yet while this may be true in some narrow and idealistic sense, it is hardly a realistic diagnosis. It is precisely the kind of individualistic approach that is unlikely to work (on its own) since our reasoning and behavior *do* respond to social incentives. Limiting the extent to which each of us individually seeks to signal loyalty and impressiveness is good and laudable, but the more effective remedy is to change the social incentives that surround us (cf. Lerner & Tetlock, 2003; Simler, 2016).

After all, the mere fact that we are trying to signal loyalty and impressiveness is not a problem per se. The problem, rather, is that we are trying to impress an ignorant audience — an audience that mostly fails to recognize and call out crude loyalty signaling and motivated reasoning when they encounter it (cf. Simler & Hanson, 2018, ch. 12, "Wrapping Up"). If we were instead trying to impress an audience that is deeply informed about the common shenanigans of human political psychology, and if we were trying to signal loyalty to a faction that values high epistemic standards and the curtailment of biases, then our social incentives and signaling efforts would be largely convergent with basic political ideals such as those outlined in the first chapter. We would thus be able to have our signaling cake and be (more) reasoned too (Simler, 2016).

Changing incentives in this way is not, of course, an easy task. Yet it is worth reiterating that even marginal improvements in our social incentives can still be highly significant. For instance, even if just a small number of sub-communities came to have a markedly greater awareness of common political biases, and in turn improved their collective epistemic incentives in the political realm, this might already represent valuable progress. And if such greater awareness and higher epistemic standards were to become prominent in some communities, there is a chance that they could eventually spread to other communities as well.

In general, if it were to become widely acknowledged just how strongly our default political behavior is animated by primitive biases and loyalty signaling, we might eventually come to see such behavior as a signal of poor self-awareness and embarrassingly low epistemic standards. As Kevin Simler notes, in such a condition, we would all be "cajoled into thinking more clearly — making better arguments, weighing evidence more evenhandedly, etc. — lest we be seen as stupid, careless, or biased" (Simler, 2016).

4.8 Reduce Zero-Sum Politics

Another important implication of our primitive psychology is that we should make an effort to focus more on win-win outcomes, as opposed to mostly engaging in zero-sum conflicts between "our group" and "their group". As federal policy expert Karl Smith observes, even businesses seeking to influence policy are often "not particularly interested in what is in their best interests [financially]. What they are very interested in is whether legislation is *pro* them or *anti* them [in terms of its perceived status]" (Smith, 2011). The fact that such a costly tribal dynamic is common even in a business context where financial incentives should militate against it says something about how deeply ingrained this way of thinking is — how natural it is for us to focus on coalitional position-taking and group status as opposed to beneficial *outcomes* (cf. Tooby & Cosmides, 2010; DeScioli, 2016; Tooby, 2017).

Indeed, this way of thinking is so strong in us that we sometimes even prefer policies that benefit "us" and hurt "them", even when we could choose mutually beneficial policies. As one study found, "high levels of perceived intergroup competition lead some Americans to prefer trade policies that benefit the ingroup and hurt the outgroup over policies that help both their own country and the trading partner country" (Mutz & Kim, 2017, abstract). A tribal zero-sum mindset runs deep in the human political psyche (Haidt, 2012, ch. 9; Sapolsky, 2017, ch. 11).

We have much to gain by transcending this mindset. Contrary to common intuition, politics often *can* be a matter of win-win for different factions, at least as long as we think about "winning" in terms of mutually beneficial policy outcomes rather than in terms of beating the other team. When we go beyond the paradigm of zero-sum tribalism, we can gain a clearer sense of the vast range of political issues that we in fact do agree on, such as reducing crime, security threats, air pollution, etc. This enables us to address these issues more effectively than if we waste most of our energy counteracting and undermining each other along party lines. Unfortunately, this is often exactly what we see today: our most important political problems become hostages in a tribal signaling game while concerns about policy outcomes, including those in which we have a strong shared interest, fade into the background.

Indeed, research suggests that disagreements in politics tend to be strongly overstated due to the "identity-expressive" nature of our political discourse. That is, people belonging to different factions often endorse opposing policy positions not because they strongly believe in or necessarily understand these positions, but rather because the endorsements serve as a clear signal of people's political loyalties. This frequently creates the appearance of major policy disagreements even when little disagreement actually exists (Hannon, 2021).

To be sure, some level of political competition is both inevitable and rational. But the point is that we likely focus too much on tribal antagonisms relative to what is ideal for creating mutually beneficial outcomes (cf. Mutz & Kim, 2017). For example, good policy outcomes often require compromises and cooperation across political divides, yet our crude "Us-Against-Them" psychology is arguably far too inclined to obstruct such cooperation relative to what is optimal in our modern world (cf. Tomasik, 2013a; Hanson, 2019b). Similarly, we may be able to find substantial policy wins if we look beyond the common hot-button issues that most political agents currently struggle over and signal their loyalties with, and if we instead focus on neglected yet important policy areas that people are less eager to explore or take opposing sides on — what has been referred to as "pulling the rope sideways" in the political tug of war (Hanson, 2007).

The most effective way to move to higher ground in these respects is probably, again, to change our social incentives. In particular, it seems beneficial to increase our collective awareness of our strong proclivity for zero-sum politics, and not least to increase our awareness of its common pitfalls and (frequent) suboptimality in today's world. This might in turn help us recognize the need to actively compensate for our tribal nature — by rewarding zero-sum tribal behavior *less* while rewarding a focus on mutually beneficial policies and outcomes *more*.

4.9 Candidate Tools: Mindfulness and Basic Probability Heuristics

Lastly, I should like to draw attention to a couple of specific tools that may be helpful for reducing our political biases and shortcomings. The first of these is mindfulness meditation. Yes, it is reasonable to be skeptical of this suggestion, especially given the current trend of overselling mindfulness meditation as the solution to just about all problems. But a connection between mindfulness and better political reasoning and behavior is not wholly unmotivated.

First, a number of studies suggest that meditation techniques such as mindfulness and loving-kindness can help reduce certain biases, such as the sunk-cost bias and implicit biases against outgroups (Hafenbrack et al., 2014; Kang et al., 2014; Lueke & Gibson, 2015; 2016).

Yet the connection also makes sense from a theoretical perspective. Mindfulness is basically a practice of becoming aware of what happens in one's mind, and such awareness is likely a key step to avoiding many of the pitfalls identified above: to notice our immediate intuitions *as* intuitions that we can behold and evaluate, rather than as something that we are compelled to identify with; and to notice that our political thinking is usually a case of "hot cognition", in which we process certain ideas and political figures with an affective charge that strongly colors our entire thought process (Lodge & Taber, 2005). Such noticing likely makes us better able to question and evaluate rather than follow the affective tainting of our thoughts (cf. Healy et al., 2010; Feinberg et al., 2012) — a claim that finds further support in studies suggesting that mindfulness training can reduce our reactivity to emotional stimuli (Hölzel et al., 2011; Farb et al., 2012).

Of course, a private meditation practice is not the only way to cultivate such a noticing ability. If people were open to it, this ability could likely also be practiced in live conversation, with people helping each other to become aware of their underlying intuitions and biases in real time, and not least rewarding each other for such awareness. Indeed, it could well be that a combination of both approaches is optimal: to practice paying attention to the flow of one's mind *and* to receive feedback from the outside about one's political biases.

Further empirical research will hopefully shed light on which specific practices and instructions tame our biases most effectively, but mindfulness meditation and rewarding each other for noticing our biases at least seem promising strategies that we could reasonably start trying out today.

Another powerful tool is formal thinking, such as basic probability theory. And this really can be basic, in that it need not involve any actual formulas. Merely thinking in terms of simple heuristics might already improve our thinking greatly. For example, there is the by now tiresome point that "correlation does not imply causation", which is important to keep in mind given that our motivated reasoning is inclined to selectively forget it. Or there is the heuristic that the credences we assign to mutually exclusive possibilities should not add up to more than 100 percent. So if we think there is at least, say, a 90 percent probability of A being the case (e.g. that a given politician is the single worst candidate on offer), we cannot simultaneously assign more than 10 percent probability to a belief that implies *not* A (e.g. that some *other* politician is the worst candidate).

This rule is trivial, of course, but its utility is not. It puts a hard constraint on our credences, and can thus mercilessly force consistency upon us and expose our biases when they are beyond the pale of mathematical possibility. (Worth noting in this regard is that we appear to think more accurately and consistently about probabilities when we visualize them as different sets, akin to Venn diagrams, cf. Mellers & McGraw, 1999; Yamagishi, 2003.)

A similar rule that may be useful is what is known as "Cromwell's rule", which says that we should never assign absolutely zero credence to any possible proposition (let alone to a plausible one). So while it might be tempting to completely dismiss one's political opposition, one should nonetheless admit that there is a non-zero probability — and indeed usually a non-negligible probability — that the political opposition will in fact end up realizing one's values better than one's own political party or team. (And the more the opposition shares one's underlying values, the greater this probability should generally be.) This point is *epistemically* trivial, yet it is anything but *socially* trivial, since just openly admitting it can be seen by the ingroup as a betrayal. But this is precisely why this heuristic, and formal thinking more generally, is so important: it breaks up our tribally motivated black-or-white thinking, and forces us to become more intellectually honest in our political reasoning.

To clarify, my point is not that we should *only*, or even *mostly* think about politics in formal terms, but simply that formal thinking of the kind outlined above may be a helpful tool for the purpose of limiting some of our most egregious biases and psychological shortcomings.

As we have seen, we tend to succumb to a host of psychological pitfalls and biases in the political realm. Knowledge of these biases has never been widespread, and so it is unsurprising that we have failed to develop a cultural apparatus to effectively counteract them. Indeed, the social infrastructure we have built around our politics often just serves to exacerbate our biased tendencies. We have come to a point where we have developed and disseminated highly advanced technology, yet where our modes of ethical and political thinking still remain profoundly primitive, often not going much beyond immediate emotional inclinations. This is a dangerous combination. If we are to improve our politics, we will have to develop and disseminate better social technologies as well — norms and institutions that help make our political judgments better informed and more reflective. I believe the norms and precepts outlined in this chapter are promising candidates to this end.

5

The Importance of Culture

Humans are a cultural species. We cannot understand human nature merely by studying individual brains and psychologies in isolation. Nor can we understand the space of possible institutions, and the cultural prerequisites for different institutions, without a basic understanding of human culture.

My aim in this chapter is to provide a brief descriptive review of the nature and significance of human culture. This is, of course, a vast research area spanning many different fields, and about which many books have been written (e.g. Henrich, 2015; 2020, on which I will draw heavily in this chapter). The following review will thus leave out many relevant aspects of human culture, yet it will nonetheless put plenty of things on the table that are much too neglected in our political discourse, and from which we can derive important lessons.

5.1 A Cultural Species

During the vast majority of humanity's evolutionary history, people lived in small groups with less than 200 members (Boehm, 1999, p. 76). Humans were able to survive in these forager groups, not by virtue of their individual smarts alone, but by virtue of accumulated cultural know-how, which has been essential for survival (Henrich, 2015, ch. 2). In fact, there are countless examples of people who were unable to survive in environments that were novel to them, including European explorers who possessed relatively advanced technology, yet in which local foragers survived quite easily because they had access to a vast repository of accumulated knowledge adapted to those environments (Henrich, 2015, ch. 3).

This relates to one of the defining features of our species, namely our ability to learn from others. For it turns out that chimpanzees can beat human toddlers on many tests of cognitive abilities — including tests of spatial, quantitative, and causal reasoning. Yet when it comes to cultural learning, i.e. learning from others, human toddlers are *far* superior (Tomasello, 1999, ch. 3-6; Henrich, 2015, ch. 2). This is where humans truly stand out: we have evolved unique learning abilities oriented toward the acquisition of cultural information. From a very young age, we pay disproportionate attention to those who seem most skilled and prestigious — those who may possess the most useful knowledge and habits (Henrich, 2015, pp. 42-43). Indeed, our tendency to copy the prestigious is so strong that even suicides are prestige-biased: when celebrities end their lives, suicide rates increase, especially among those who match the deceased celebrity in terms of age, sex, and ethnicity (Henrich, 2015, ch. 4).

Our distinctive ability to learn from other people is in large part what accounts for our species' flexibility and spread across the globe (Henrich, 2015, ch. 2). Rather than being hardwired for a few narrow tasks, we have specialized in social learning itself, which gives us the potential to learn a vast range of cultural knowledge and practices, including the knowledge and practices that happen to prevail and be fitness-enhancing in the cultural environment in which we are raised, whether it be a small band of foragers or a modern city.

5.2 Opaque Institutions

An important thing to realize about the culturally transmitted know-how we acquire is that we often do not understand its function. That is, there are many examples of practices, institutions, and beliefs that we simply learn and adhere to without knowing the underlying function they serve, or whether they serve any useful function at all. In fact, in some cases, it may even be adaptive *not* to know the functional purpose of a given practice, since being ignorant or having a mythic story about it might make people more motivated to follow the practice (Henrich, 2015, p. 99, pp. 105-106, p. 160).

The domain of food processing provides many examples of causally opaque practices (Henrich, 2015, ch. 7). Nardoo is a little seed-like spore that is indigestible and mildly toxic if not processed properly, yet aboriginal foragers have discovered an arduous multi-step process that renders it edible. This process includes grinding the spores in large amounts of water; exposing the resulting flour to ash, which makes it more acidic and likely reduces its toxicity; and finally consuming the resulting nardoo gruel using only mussel shells, which may have further detoxifying effects (Henrich, 2015, p. 30). Similarly, in the Americas, people relied on corn as their staple food, which required them to develop processing techniques to render the niacin (vitamin B3) in corn digestible. Such techniques could involve mixing the corn with burned seashells or with the ash from specific types of wood (Henrich, 2015, p. 103). And in certain Fijian tribes, women adhere to food taboos that selectively exclude the most toxic foods from their diets (Henrich, 2015, pp. 100-101).

A point of commonality in the examples above is that the people who adhere to these practices generally do not understand why they must be followed, only that they must. For instance, when the Fijian women were asked why they honored the food taboos, many of them admitted that they did not know, and found the question odd — it was simply custom (Henrich, 2015, pp. 100-101). It is not just that people in the examples above did not understand modern chemistry, but they often did not even understand that a failure to adhere to the established practices would have adverse effects on their health. After all, it takes a long time for unprocessed nardoo to cause adverse health effects, and the same is true of unprocessed corn, which eventually causes vitamin B3 deficiency (Henrich, 2015, pp. 29-30, pp. 102-103). Thus, individuals who decided to skimp on these practices would experience no immediate bad consequences, which makes it difficult for anyone to form even a rough causal model of the function of the practices in question (cf. Henrich, 2015, p. 99). And, of course, individuals who persisted in their defiance of these traditions would eventually meet their demise, with little clue as to why.

Now, why talk about opaque food processing techniques and food taboos in a book about politics? For one, because these are not heavily politicized matters, and thus the examples above help to illustrate a general point in what should be an uncontroversial sphere; the point being that many of our culturally transmitted practices serve crucial functions that we do not understand, and hence thinking we know better than tradition can *sometimes* be risky.

To be clear, this is *not* a point from which we should draw hasty political conclusions. Yet the causal opacity of (many of) our institutions *is* a key fact to understand about human culture, and one that *does* have significant implications that we must be thoughtful in teasing out (normative implications will be the focus of the following chapter). After all, food processing techniques are by no means the only opaque practices we have. We also have many social traditions that we fail to understand, such as rituals involving synchronous singing and dancing, which have been found to bind groups strongly together, and to increase trust and cooperation. Yet participants are usually not explicitly aware of these functions (Wiltermuth & Heath, 2009; Henrich, 2015, pp. 160-161).

Similar functions are served by religious traditions in general, which effectively bind groups of people together, sometimes actively pitting them against other groups (Rue, 2005; Haidt, 2012, ch. 11; Henrich, 2020, ch. 4). These social functions of religion also appear to remain hidden to most people, believers and non-believers alike (Henrich, 2015, p. 324; Simler & Hanson, 2018, ch. 15).

5.3 Cultural Differences in Human Psychology

A dichotomy between biology and culture is widely assumed, yet misguided (Henrich, 2015, ch. 14). As Joe Henrich writes, "recent evidence clearly shows how culture can shape biology by altering our brain architecture, molding our bodies, and shifting our hormones. Cultural evolution is a type of biological evolution; it's just not a type of genetic evolution" (Henrich, 2015, p. 263). In other words, different cultures give rise to significant cross-cultural differences in our biology, and our brains and psychologies are no exception (Muthukrishna et al., 2020).

An example is how people perceive individual objects relative to their surroundings. Collectivist cultures, such as those in East Asia, appear to foster a more holistic focus; for instance, people from such cultures seem better at judging the relative length of a line segment within a frame. Individualistic cultures, in contrast, foster greater attention to individual objects; Westerners appear better at judging the *absolute* length of a line, independent of its surrounding frame (Henrich, 2015, pp. 268-269). In general, Western cultures seem to foster analytic thinking over holistic thinking, which means that Western minds tend to think in terms of rule-based categories rather than in terms of relations between parts (Henrich, 2020, pp. 53-54).

Even something as apparently fundamental as whether we perceive certain visual illusions turns out to be culturally contingent, with some illusions being prevalent and virtually impossible to see through for people in some cultures, while being almost non-existent in others (Henrich et al., 2010, 3.1). Culturally induced differences of this kind are found in countless psychological domains, including our individual moral perceptions and intuitions (Henrich et al., 2010, 4.1). And it turns out that the individual psychologies found across different cultures strongly affect which formal institutions can be realized in these respective cultures (Henrich, 2015, ch. 17; 2020, pp. 51-52).

5.4 WEIRD Psychology

The acronym "WEIRD" refers to populations that are Western, Educated, Industrialized, Rich, and Democratic. The term was introduced in a 2010 paper that criticized modern psychology for mostly focusing on WEIRD populations, and for overgeneralizing from this highly non-representative sample (Henrich et al., 2010). This is particularly problematic given that Western minds turn out to be extreme outliers on many traits (Henrich et al., 2010; Henrich, 2020, ch. 1).

Joe Henrich sets out to document and explain some of the main ways in which Western populations are psychologically peculiar in his book *The WEIRDest People in the World* (Henrich, 2020). This book cannot be properly summarized in a short space, yet what follows are some of the main points (I encourage readers to consult the book for elaboration).

A defining feature of Western populations is that they are highly individualistic (Henrich, 2020, p. 29). For example, when asked to identify their own personal identity, Western people are prone to mention their occupation and personal achievements rather than their social relationships, as is common in other cultures (Henrich, 2020, pp. 24-25). People from more individualistic cultures tend to be uniquely overconfident, and to focus a lot on themselves and their own self-enhancement (Henrich, 2020, p. 56). They also tend to have weaker family ties and to be less loyal to their family and friends. As Henrich writes, "WEIRD people are bad friends" (Henrich, 2020, p. 30, pp. 44-46).

A consequence of this reduced loyalty is that WEIRD people tend to show less nepotism — e.g. managers and politicians are less inclined to promote relatives (Henrich, 2020, p. 30). Relatedly, WEIRD people are more likely to endorse moral universalism, including universal moral rights, and to adhere to impartial moral rules (Henrich, 2020, pp. 42-46, pp. 398-399). In particular, WEIRD populations are more likely to weigh impartial ethics and the law higher than helping a close friend who has acted immorally and broken the law (Henrich, 2020, pp. 44-45).

Note that our evaluative attitudes of these traits might themselves reflect a uniquely WEIRD mindset. For instance, seeing nepotism as wrong, rather than as rightfully putting family first, may itself be a fairly WEIRD way to view the world (cf. Henrich, 2020, pp. 21-22, p. 46). (Of course, the mere fact that there exists significant cross-cultural variation in moral attitudes toward certain behaviors, as a descriptive matter, has little to say about the normative validity of any of these attitudes; that would be a separate discussion.)

Another distinctive feature of WEIRD psychology is a greater trust in strangers (Henrich, 2020, pp. 46-48). For example, Chinese and South Korean individuals generally report less trust in both compatriot strangers and foreigners than do WEIRD individuals (Cheon et al., 2011; Henrich, 2020, p. 48). Western people also seem to place special weight on the intentions behind people's actions. In a hypothetical scenario in which a man either has his bag intentionally stolen or swapped by accident, WEIRD individuals see a uniquely significant difference in how the wrongdoer should be judged in the respective cases, whereas people in some cultures barely see a difference at all. Yasawans in Fiji, for instance, made no significant distinction in how severely they judged the culprit (Henrich, 2020, pp. 49-51, pp. 220-221).

Finally, WEIRD people are outliers in terms of how inclined they are to delay gratification, showing a greater willingness to wait so as to receive a larger financial reward later rather than receiving a smaller one immediately (Dohmen et al., 2015; Henrich, 2020, pp. 38-40). Such patience has been found to explain "a substantial fraction of development differences across countries" (Dohmen et al., 2015, abstract).

5.5 Explanations and Clarifications

What then explains these peculiar psychological traits? Henrich points to a number of factors, a crucial one being the low rates of cousin marriage found in WEIRD populations. The Catholic church made increasingly strict bans on cousin marriages in the Middle Ages, and this, Henrich and others argue, gradually paved the way for a more individualistic and less kin-partial psychology (Schulz et al., 2019; Henrich, 2020, ch. 5-6). Monogamous marriage has been another important factor, which likely reduced fertility, gender inequality, and violence, while increasing inclinations toward trust and long-term investments (Henrich et al., 2012; Henrich, 2020, p. 281). Also significant were increasing rates of urbanization and participation in commerce, which increased cooperation and adherence to impartial norms (Henrich, 2020, ch. 9-10).

It is important to note that there is no binary WEIRD versus non-WEIRD psychology. People across the globe occupy different parts of a high-dimensional space of psychological variation in which even neighboring countries are measurably distinct (Muthukrishna et al., 2020; Henrich, 2020, p. 31). Indeed, there is also great variation *within* countries. For example, there are significant psychological differences between urban and rural populations within the same society (Scala & Johnson, 2017; Henrich, 2020, ch. 9). And liberals likewise have a significantly more "WEIRD" thinking style compared to conservatives in the same geographical region, so much so that it has been suggested that the "WEIRD" acronym should be extended with an "L" for liberal, to highlight the close connection (Talhelm et al., 2015, p. 16).

That people in different cultures vary in the ways described above may not be to our liking, yet if we are to navigate well politically, we have to be honest about findings of this kind, and about the factors that might explain them. The temptation to deny such data, or to twist it so as to support one's political ideology, will undoubtedly be strong. But again, we should not rush to derive hasty conclusions. Rather, we should seek to gain greater clarity about the facts, and to reflect more deeply on the implications (the subject of the next chapter).

And to be clear, the findings reviewed above by no means support sentiments of Western triumphalism or anything of the sort — sentiments that have caused immense amounts of harm, and which Western ingroup biases will no doubt be all too eager to endorse. After all, in relation to moral universalism, there are many non-Western traditions, such as Jainism and strands of Buddhism, that far surpass the Western moral tradition in terms of how deep and extensive their compassion is, with an aspiration to practice Ahimsa (non-violence) toward *all* sentient beings (cf. Goodman, 2009; Pániker, 2010).

An overarching point emerging from Henrich's work is that various cultural innovations have paved the way for the unique formal institutions we see in WEIRD countries today, such as liberal democracy, and that this cultural and psychological groundwork has been long underway (Henrich, 2020, pp. 23-24). Thus, in order to really understand formal institutions — actual as well as potential ones — we must understand how they relate to broader cultural and psychological factors, both in terms of how these factors influence formal institutions and how formal institutions in turn change people's psychology. These influences are often opaque and highly counterintuitive, which underscores the importance of pursuing careful social science over brash intuitions.

In closing, it is worth clarifying that the significance of culture and cultural differences does not negate the significance of genes and universal features of human nature (cf. Brown, 1991). There is indeed a shared blueprint for mental modules and dispositions that are universal among humans (Cosmides & Tooby, 1992; Christakis, 2019, p. 16). We all share deep-seated instincts for things such as social learning (Henrich, 2015, pp. 13-15, p. 35), status-seeking (Anderson et al., 2015), and kin-favoritism (Brown, 1991, pp. 105-107; Akbari et al., 2020). Yet *how* these common drives get expressed varies greatly, as different cultures will evoke and develop different propensities based on what they teach their children and which feats they reward with status (cf. Henrich, 2015, p. 330). This is the cultural nature of human nature.

6

Implications of the Importance of Culture

Having reviewed some findings concerning human nature and culture, let us again turn to the normative side of things and explore the broader take-aways. The following, I will argue, are some of the main lessons to heed if we are to realize the ideals outlined in the first chapter.

6.1 Human Nature Is Tricky

It is no wonder that philosophers and political ideologies have by and large failed to get human nature right, seeing that the truth of the matter is a complicated middle position that, while perhaps obvious in hindsight, is difficult to get right a priori. At once profoundly universal *and* cultur-ally variable, the nuanced reality of human psychology defies any cartoon model. And it certainly does not conform well to any narrative tailored to signal one's party loyalties.

The upshot, yet again, is that we cannot rely on our immediate intu-itions. That is, we cannot reasonably base our politics on a merely intuitive understanding of human nature and culture, as neither is at all intuitive. Many things that are widely assumed to be culturally contingent turn out to be universal — e.g. trade and higher male aggression (Brown, 1991; Pinker, 2002, pp. 435-439) — while, as we have seen, many psychological traits assumed to be universal turn out to be highly variable, and to depend on obscure cultural factors such as the local rate of cousin marriage, urbanization, and the prevalence of commerce (Henrich, 2020, ch. 6, ch. 9).

Findings such as these have significant implications for the feasibility of different policies and institutions, which is why we must strive to base our policies on a science-based understanding of human nature *and* (local) culture. A trivial point perhaps, yet all too ignored nonetheless (cf. Henrich, 2015, pp. 328-331).

6.2 Optimal Policy Is Culture-Dependent

A related implication of the significance of culture is that good policy cannot be one-size-fits-all. For even if one thinks that there is ultimately a single set of policies that would be optimal for everyone everywhere, converging toward such a state would still require different policies in societies where highly distinctive cultures and psychologies currently prevail (cf. Henrich, 2020, pp. 487-488).

An example demonstrating this point is how people in different countries play a public goods game in which a group of people can increase their collective resources by contributing with individual donations. Not only is there great variation in how much people contribute across cultures, but it turns out that certain modifications to the game can have diametrically opposite effects in different societies. Specifically, a policy that allowed players to punish other players happened to *increase* cooperation in some cultures — especially the most WEIRD ones, in which it curbed free riders — while it strongly *decreased* cooperation in other cultures, where it fostered revenge cycles and punishments against those who made prosocial contributions (because low-contributors who had been punished chose to take revenge against the high-contributors) (Henrich, 2020, pp. 218-219).

The deeper point here applies beyond mere lab experiments. Real-world policies and formal institutions that work well in some parts of the world may be difficult, even harmful, to implement elsewhere — at least if done too hastily, as failed attempts to implement democracy in recently toppled dictatorships attest (cf. Henrich, 2015, p. 328). In Henrich's words, "the lesson is simple: policy prescriptions and formal institutions need to fit the cultural psychology of the population in question" — in addition to fitting the universal features of human psychology (Boyer & Petersen, 2012; Henrich, 2020, p. 219).

6.3 Consider the Long-Term Effects of Institutions

Beyond ensuring a sufficient fit with a society's pre-existing cultural psychology, we should also consider the effects that new policies and institutions will have on people's psychology down the line (cf. Henrich, 2020, p. 488). As illustrated by the example of marriage policies that increased individualism and impartial moral norms — perhaps eventually paving the way for the Industrial Revolution — even quite narrow institutional changes can end up having broad effects on people's psychology, and in turn influence the large-scale trajectory of entire societies (Schulz et al., 2019; Henrich, 2020, ch. 6).

In Henrich's words, "people's preferences and motivations are not fixed, and a well-designed program or policy can change what people find desirable, automatic, and intuitive" (Henrich, 2015, p. 330). This highlights the importance of understanding the likely effects that different policies and institutions will have on people's psychology, both in terms of immediate and long-term effects. Ideally, we should create an entire research program focused on such questions. In the meantime, we should approach policy and institution design with a degree of humility commensurate with our current state of knowledge of these complicated matters.

6.4 The Opacity of Institutions Implies Prudence

Cultural evolution is in many ways smarter than any individual, in that it can create institutions that reflect knowledge and adaptations accumulated over many generations, and which no single person could ever have discovered on their own — recall the elaborate food processing methods reviewed in the previous chapter (Henrich, 2015, pp. 99-103). In effect, the functions of our institutions are often difficult to understand, which implies that we should be somewhat cautious about changing them.

This is related to what is known as "Chesterton's fence", the principle that we should not remove a metaphorical fence, e.g. a law or an institution, unless we understand its function (cf. Chesterton, 1929, p. 35). Yet this principle can also be taken too far, since fully understanding the function of a given institution will often not be required for us to meet the more relevant bar of being reasonably confident that another institution would be better. After all, there will always be considerable uncertainty about the future effects of *any* given law or institution, including existing ones, meaning that there is no truly safe choice — especially not in a rapidly changing world. More than that, it is not guaranteed that all laws and institutions even have a meaningful function, or that such functions can be understood before a policy change is long overdue, in which case a rigid insistence on adherence to Chesterton's principle would also be dysfunctional.

Hence, the point is not that we should never alter our institutions, even radically, but simply that we have to go about such changes in thoughtful and sophisticated ways. Consider, by analogy, opaque food processing techniques: while deviation from such practices could be lethal, and hence worth limiting in a state of ignorance, it does not follow that better alternatives are impossible in principle. For example, a modern understanding of chemistry might enable far more efficient techniques for processing the foods in question. Or one may discover and adopt altogether different foods, a change one could surely make without fully understanding pre-existing food processing techniques.

A similar point might apply to religion. We know that religious institutions serve to bind groups together (among other things), and thus, speculatively, it *could* be the case that some elements of religion are critical for maintaining social cohesion in a large-scale society (cf. Haidt, 2012, Part III). These elements, if they exist, probably have little to do with deities or superstition. But they could well include a strong sense of shared identity and community (cf. Price & Launay, 2018), as well as singing and moving in synchrony — as mentioned, such synchronous activities have been shown to have a strongly cohesive effect on groups (Wiltermuth & Heath, 2009; Henrich, 2015, pp. 160-161).

Thus, like a modern chemist who is able to reverse-engineer the underlying mechanism of traditional food processing techniques, we may eventually, with a better understanding of social science, be able to understand the functional elements of our social institutions, including religion, and then update them such that we keep and enhance whatever beneficial elements they may have while abandoning the bad. (This is roughly what Karl Popper referred to as "piecemeal social engineering", Popper, 1945, pp. 148-149.)

6.5 Experiment-Based Politics

The fact that institutions often function in abstruse ways means that it can be challenging to design functional institutions from scratch, and suggests that we might benefit from a more experimental approach to institution design, sometimes called "policy experimentation". As Henrich writes:

> Humans are bad at intentionally designing effective institutions and organizations, though I'm hoping that as we get deeper insights into human nature and cultural evolution this can improve. Until then, we should take a page from cultural evolution's playbook and design "variation and selection systems" that will allow alternative institutions or organizational forms to compete. We can dump the losers, keep the winners, and hopefully gain some general insights during the process. (Henrich, 2015, p. 331)

What Henrich refers to by "cultural evolution's playbook" is the fact that a similar process has occurred throughout our species' cultural evolution. For tens of thousands of years, different groups of humans have been in competition over limited resources, with each group relying on slightly different cultural practices. Some of these practices proved more successful than others, and hence they persisted and spread, often by getting copied by other groups (Henrich, 2015, ch. 10).

The point is that we could copy this process, only in a more deliberate and systematic way. Instead of just testing random variations on policies and institutions, we could test institutional proposals derived from our best understanding of social science, and then pit many such proposals against each other in real-world trials. An example of an unusual proposal one could test would be to have international leaders sing and move in synchrony so as to increase the level of trust and cooperation between them — a suggestion that may sound silly, but which actually looks quite promising given our understanding of human nature (cf. Wiltermuth & Heath, 2009). More ambitiously, one could test proposals of altogether different governance structures (examples of such proposals are discussed in Section 14.4).

Such experiments would have to start on a small scale, of course, and then be scaled up to further test the proposals that seem most promising in the smaller trials. The hope would then be that we end up with policies that have strong evidence behind them, or at least enough evidence to convince us that the policies in question are better than the status quo. And while the process outlined above surely has its limitations — e.g. even fairly large experiments might fail to generalize to larger scales, and long-term effects might be difficult to assess — such experimentation may nevertheless be among the most promising tools we have for exploring and navigating the space of possible institutions. Yet it remains quite neglected (Bogenschneider & Corbett, 2010, ch. 1; Hanson, 2019a).

6.6 Reasoned Politics Is Unnatural

For most of human history, we had no deep theoretical understanding of the world around us on which we could base our decisions. Instead, we had to rely on traditional practices that were handed down to us from our ancestors, and which we generally just had to trust and stick to given that the alternative could be lethal, as exemplified by the many cases of opaque food processing techniques that had to be followed to the letter. Thus, in stark contrast with a view of ourselves as independently-minded thinkers geared toward "following the facts", we generally seem more geared toward following the status quo and the high-status individuals of our own tribe (cf. Henrich, 2015, pp. 328-329).

Capacities such as reflecting on our values and drawing inferences based on large amounts of data are recent and culturally dependent. They do *not* come naturally to us. This is obviously not to say that we do not have the potential to do these things. Yet it does underscore how much of an effort we should expect these endeavors to take. It also helps explain why we do not currently take a more reasoned approach to politics, the explanation being both that such an approach does not come naturally to us *and* that it has relatively little cultural precedent, the one thing that could compensate for the former. What instead does have ample cultural precedent, unfortunately, is a crude political dynamic that plays right into our primitive instincts, namely the familiar dynamic of tribal zero-sum politics (cf. Tooby & Cosmides, 2010; Tooby, 2017; Hannon, 2021).

This all further reinforces the point made earlier about changing social incentives: if we are to change our political culture toward a more reflective and reasoned state, we have to create more of a cultural precedent for it, and to promote norms that move us in this direction, however modestly. We will not get to a more reasoned political equilibrium otherwise.

6.7 More Research Needed

A final point worth highlighting here is that many of the key takeaways we should draw from the picture outlined in previous chapters more have the nature of questions rather than answers. That is, there are still many open questions concerning our political psychology and the mechanisms of culture, and further research on these questions should itself be a priority, along with further research on the normative implications of this emerging picture (the latter arguably being even more neglected and more urgently needed). What we have seen here barely scratches the surface of these important issues.

Even so, I believe we have seen enough to make it clear that a greater understanding of these subjects is greatly relevant to the manner in which we approach politics. Indeed, I would argue that such greater understanding is an absolute necessity. A sophisticated view of the facts on the ground and of their most fundamental normative implications must serve as a backdrop in any endeavor of reasoned politics.

PART III

REDUCING SUFFERING IN POLITICS

7

Suffering Reduction as a
Core Value in Politics

Having outlined a general ideal for political practice, and reviewed some relevant groundwork, my goal in the remainder of the book will be to put these elemental pieces to use. That is, I will seek to apply the framework described at the outset, by first briefly laying out a plausible normative foundation for our politics (the normative step), and then exploring which concrete policies and political strategies seem optimal from this normative perspective given the empirical evidence (the empirical step).

7.1 A Strong Moral Duty to Reduce Suffering

In technical terms, the ethical view or principle I propose as foundational for our politics is that we have a strong *prima facie* duty to relieve and prevent suffering (Wolf, 1997, VI; Mayerfeld, 1999, pp. 8-9). What this means, in simple terms, is that the reduction of suffering should be a foremost moral value guiding our politics, though not that it is necessarily the *only* moral value. (By suffering, I mean an overall negative experiential state, Mayerfeld, 1999, pp. 14-15; Vinding, 2020a, p. 13.)

A *prima facie* moral duty is a duty that we should adhere to *unless* we have other duties that override it. For example, one may hold that, in addition to a *prima facie* duty to reduce suffering, we also have a duty to observe various side-constraints that categorically prohibit certain actions — such as violating others' basic rights — even if such actions sometimes seem optimal relative to the aim of reducing suffering (Nozick, 1974, p. 29; Wolf, 1996, p. 278). Or one may hold that we have other *prima facie* moral duties, such as a duty to ensure that individuals are able to exercise certain liberties and capabilities (cf. Rawls, 1971, ch. 4; Nussbaum, 2011), and then further maintain that these other moral duties can sometimes override our duty to reduce suffering.

On the other hand, saying that we have a *prima facie* duty to reduce suffering is also compatible with views that hold that the reduction of certain forms of suffering, such as the most extreme forms of suffering, should *always* be of supreme importance, in effect overriding everything else (Mayerfeld, 1999, pp. 178-179; Vinding, 2020a, ch. 4-5). But the point is that a *prima facie* duty to reduce suffering does not strictly imply these latter, stronger views. (Some people dispute that the concept of "duty" is useful or even meaningful in the first place, and instead prefer to speak in terms of "what we have reason to do" and the like, see e.g. Leighton, forthcoming. Yet as I understand and use the term here, having a *"prima facie* moral duty" to do *x* is simply equivalent to having *"prima facie* moral reason" to do *x*.)

A strong duty to reduce suffering is in fact widely endorsed. It is, for example, entailed by the suffering-focused part of classical utilitarianism, the view that we should maximize the notional sum of happiness minus suffering. And many classical utilitarians hold that our resources usually go further when spent on reducing suffering rather than increasing happiness (see e.g. Mayerfeld, 1999, p. 149; Singer, 2018, 9:00-12:30).

And yet a *prima facie* duty to reduce suffering has much broader appeal and acceptance than does any utilitarian view. For instance, philosopher W. D. Ross, who coined the notion of a *prima facie* moral duty, and who explicitly rejected utilitarianism in favor of a pluralist view centered on various duties, still defended a strong *prima facie* duty not to cause harm — including suffering — as well as a *prima facie* duty to actively help others (Ross, 1930, pp. 21-22). Yet in contrast with classical utilitarianism, Ross endorsed a moral asymmetry between suffering and happiness, maintaining that we have a greater duty to reduce pain than to increase pleasure (Ross, 1939, p. 275; Mathison, 2018, 2.5.1).

Indeed, many philosophers and moral views endorse a moral asymmetry between suffering and happiness in some form (Vinding, 2020a, 8.17). And even more philosophers and moral views endorse a strong duty to reduce suffering. Beyond classical utilitarianism, these include consequentialist views united by a concern for the worst-off, such as egalitarianism, prioritarianism, and sufficientarianism, as well as various deontological views that entail duties to help those in distress and to prevent intense suffering (Mayerfeld, 1999, 5.2; Vinding, 2020a, ch. 6). The emphasis on abstaining from harm and preventing suffering is also strong in many Eastern philosophical traditions, such as in the traditions of Jain and Buddhist ethics (Keown, 1992, pp. 175-176; Goodman, 2009; Pániker, 2010, p. 200; Breyer, 2015; Jain, 2019, ch. 13).

The general population, too, is in wide agreement on the moral importance of reducing suffering. For instance, in a survey that asked more than 14,000 people what they thought a future civilization should ideally strive for, the most popular aim, favored by roughly a third, was "minimize suffering" (Future of Life Institute, 2017). Many more would presumably endorse the weaker claim that we have a duty to reduce suffering (cf. Caviola et al., 2022). Indeed, as far as positive moral duties go, a duty to reduce suffering is perhaps the most obvious and most widely endorsed duty of all, including in the realm of politics (cf. Friedman, 2019, 1.5; Enoch, 2021, p. 20). It is plausibly also the most bipartisan one, as concern for suffering is firmly endorsed across the entire political spectrum (Haidt, 2012, ch. 8).

7.2 Support for the Moral Importance of Suffering

I will not here provide an elaborate case for a strong *prima facie* duty to reduce suffering, as such a case has already been made elsewhere. For example, Jamie Mayerfeld defends precisely such a duty in his book *Suffering and Moral Responsibility*, and Clark Wolf has defended a similar view in various articles (Mayerfeld, 1996; 1999; Wolf, 1996; 1997; 2004). My own book *Suffering-Focused Ethics* likewise supports such a duty, and represents my own attempt to defend an ethical foundation for our politics, and for our conduct in general (Vinding, 2020a, Part I). (For additional arguments and support, see Tomasik, 2006; 2016; Leighton, 2011; forthcoming; Gloor, 2016; 2017; Pearce, 2017, Part II; DiGiovanni, 2021; Ajantaival, 2021a; 2021b; Animal Ethics, 2021; Vinding, forthcoming.)

I refer readers to these sources for a proper defense of a strong moral duty to reduce suffering, and for a fuller account as to why any reasoned approach to politics must entail a strong focus on reducing suffering. Below, I will just briefly sketch out some of the many views that support such a focus, while pointing to other sources that present more developed versions of these views and arguments in their favor. Note, however, that one need not endorse every single view outlined below, or even most of them, in order to grant a strong priority to the reduction of suffering. For instance, classical utilitarians will reject many of the views presented below, yet they still endorse a strong duty to reduce suffering, commonly on the basis of its directly felt badness (Mayerfeld, 1999, 6.5).

One class of suffering-focused views relates to future generations and the asymmetry in the moral importance of creating happy lives versus preventing miserable lives. For example, many people find it plausible that we have stronger moral reasons not to create a miserable life than to create a happy life (known as "the Asymmetry" in population ethics). Failing to create a happy life does not constitute a bad or a moral wrong on par with the creation of a miserable life, and so preventing miserable lives is plausibly more important than creating happy lives (Gloor, 2016, I; Vinding, 2020a, 1.1).

Another common view has to do with an asymmetry in quantity: the worst forms of suffering are much worse than the best states of happiness are good, and hence our primary focus should generally be on preventing the former rather than creating the latter (Singer, 2018, 9:00-12:30; Vinding, 2020a, 1.2). For example, in pain-pleasure tradeoffs, people's evaluations tend to skew heavily toward the negative, and many people further reject the notion that extreme suffering can be traded off with happiness at all — in one survey of about a hundred people, almost half said that no amount of happiness added to their lives could compensate for them having to experience just a single minute of very intense suffering (Tomasik, 2015b; Caviola et al., 2022).

Beyond the asymmetry in quantity, there is also an asymmetry in *quality*. That is, suffering carries a unique moral urgency and makes "a direct appeal for help" (Popper, 1945, ch. 9, note 2), whereas the mere absence of happiness, or the absence of other purported goods, carries no such urgency or appeal for betterment. The same applies to states of happiness that could be made more intense: increasing happiness to greater heights is not a moral emergency, whereas reducing suffering is (Mayerfeld, 1999, ch. 6; Vinding, 2020a, 1.4; 2020e).

This is closely related to Epicurean and Buddhist views of well-being, according to which the presence or absence of suffering is the most significant determinant of the value of our experiences. These views maintain that many, if not indeed all of our strivings for (apparently) positive experiential goods are in fact strivings to avoid bads, such as unsatisfied desires and discomfort, and that states that are absent of such bads are wholly optimal — e.g. a state of untroubled contentment is just as good as a state of intense happiness. Thus, according to these views, the greatest value in the context of our experiential well-being lies in the removal of bads rather than in the creation of (purported) positive goods (Breyer, 2015; Gloor, 2017; Vinding, 2020a, ch. 2; Ajantaival, 2021b).

As noted above, many people hold that no amount of happiness can outweigh extreme suffering, which is another view that lends support to a strong moral duty to reduce suffering, and to prioritizing the reduction of suffering over other possible priorities (Gloor, 2016, II). Specifically, it seems plausible that we should give foremost priority to the prevention of suffering that is so intense that the sufferers deem it unbearable and impossible to outweigh (Vinding, 2020a, ch. 4-5). (Various objections to the views presented above are discussed in Vinding, 2020a, ch. 8.)

7.3 Suffering as a Priority in Politics: Historical Precedent

Not only is the value of reducing suffering strongly endorsed by both moral philosophers and the general population, but there is also a strong tradition of defending the reduction of suffering as a core value within political philosophy in particular. My aim in this section is not to present a comprehensive review of this tradition (which would require a book in itself), but simply to give a sense of this tradition's breadth and depth, as well as to give a sense of the supreme unoriginality of my claim that the reduction of suffering should be a fundamental value in politics.

For instance, classical utilitarians such as Jeremy Bentham, John Stuart Mill, and Henry Sidgwick all placed the reduction of suffering at the center of political philosophy, along with the promotion of happiness (with this latter premise being more controversial, as we shall see below). Indeed, in line with their utilitarian views, these philosophers maintained that the reduction of suffering and the promotion of happiness should ultimately be the *only* ends of our political conduct (Bentham, 1789, ch. 1; Mill, 1859, ch. 1; 1863, ch. 5; Sidgwick, 1874, Book 1, ch. 2; 1891). And this strong focus on reducing suffering is, of course, likewise shared by modern political thinkers in the utilitarian tradition, such as Robert Goodin, James Wood Bailey, and Peter Singer (Goodin, 1995; Bailey, 1997; Singer, 1999; 2018; 2020b).

The emphasis on reducing suffering championed by Bentham, Mill, and Sidgwick was further defended by Karl Popper, though he strongly criticized their classical utilitarian view, especially their focus on promoting happiness. Popper endorsed a moral asymmetry between happiness and suffering, and argued that the reduction of suffering "must be considered a duty", and that it should further be adopted as a foremost principle of public policy (Popper, 1945, p. 442). In Popper's own words:

> All moral urgency has its basis in the urgency of suffering or pain. I suggest, for this reason, to replace the utilitarian formula 'Aim at the greatest amount of happiness for the greatest number', or briefly, 'Maximize happiness' by the formula 'The least amount of avoidable suffering for all', or briefly, 'Minimize suffering'. Such a simple formula can, I believe, be made one of the fundamental principles (admittedly not the only one) of public policy. (The principle 'Maximize happiness', in contrast, seems to be apt to produce a benevolent dictatorship.) (Popper, 1945, ch. 5, note 6; see also ch. 9, note 2)

As the last parenthetical remark hints, Popper believed it was "very dangerous" to seek to maximize happiness, at least at the level of public policy, as he considered it likely to result in utopian visions that could serve to justify totalitarianism and atrocities in general (Popper, 1945, ch. 11, note 62). Thus, Popper held that, unlike the reduction of suffering, "the increase of happiness should be left, in the main, to private initiative" (Popper, 1963, p. 465). (It is worth noting that Daniel Kahneman endorses a similar sentiment, based partly on his psychological research on happiness, which has led him to side with Popper's asymmetry over the classical utilitarians' symmetrical view: "what can confidently be advanced is a reduction of suffering. The question of whether society should intervene so that people will be happier is very controversial, but whether society should strive for people to suffer less — that's widely accepted" Mandel, 2018.)

Another philosopher who defended the reduction of suffering as the chief aim of politics is Judith Shklar (Shklar, 1982). Shklar defended liberal democracy, but with a unique emphasis on the avoidance of the worst forms of cruelty (such as torture), which she, in her own words, "put first" in the hierarchy of moral and political importance (Shklar, 1982, p. 17; 1989). Shklar further argued that our conception of injustice should include not only the act of causing harm and the immediate causes of disaster, but also failures to prevent harm and cruelty — what she called "passive injustice" (Shklar, 1992, pp. 40-41).

Shklar's view is related to the view that the primary purpose of moral rights is to protect individuals against extreme suffering, which has been defended by human rights theorists Roberto Andorno and Cristiana Baffone:

> Human rights norms are primarily focused on preventing the worst forms of human suffering, even if they only concern a small portion of the population. This task has moral priority over the promotion of the maximum well-being of the majority of people. [...] the entire human rights enterprise can be regarded as a social response to suffering [...] (Andorno & Baffone, 2014, abstract)

Similar views on rights have been defended by various political theorists (Felice, 1996; Talbott, 2005; 2010; Mayerfeld, 2016, ch. 1; Cochrane, 2018, pp. 28-29). Conversely, Clark Wolf has argued that some otherwise legitimate rights held by current generations, e.g. certain property rights, can legitimately be overridden if they cause significant suffering to future generations (Wolf, 1995).

Another important figure to mention is Richard Ryder, who defends a moral view called "painism". According to painism, our primary duty is the reduction of pain, especially the pain of the "maximum sufferer" (Ryder, 2001, p. 29). Ryder has proceeded to defend painism as the moral foundation for politics, arguing that our "political policies should extend to individuals of all nations, races, and species on an 'equal pain equal treatment' basis" (Ryder, 2006, p. 95).

More recently, political philosopher David Enoch has defended the "centrality of serious suffering" to politics (Enoch, 2021, p. 3). In contrast to Shklar's focus on cruelty in particular, Enoch argues that politics should be strongly concerned with *all* sources of "life-devastating suffering", and further argues that "in doing normative political philosophy we should by-and-large ignore all [other legitimate] values, and focus on serious suffering" (Enoch, 2021, pp. 3-6).

Other thinkers who have emphasized the political importance of suffering include Cynthia Halpern, who argues that suffering on a global scale is the "most urgent and least understood question of contemporary politics and political theory", and one that "demands a public response" (Halpern, 2002, first cover, p. 2), as well as Peter Berger, who argued that "the most pressing moral imperative in policy making is a calculus of pain" (Berger, 1974, p. xiii).

7.4 The Next Step

As is clear from the above, the reduction of suffering has been widely endorsed and elaborately defended at the level of the normative step. Yet the practical implications of this view nonetheless remain largely unexplored, especially at the political level. The baton has been dropped somewhere prior to the empirical step. My aim in the rest of the book is to help rectify this situation.

The main question going forward is thus essentially an empirical one: which political strategies and policies best satisfy a strong *prima facie* duty to reduce suffering? This, we should be clear, is an exceptionally complex question given the many facts and considerations that bear on the issue, and which often point in different directions. Partly for this reason, my aim in the coming chapters will not be to provide definitive answers (which is a misguided endeavor in any case, cf. Section 1.3), but rather to take a first step toward uncovering *plausible* answers.

What I seek to do in the coming chapters is just as much about exemplifying *how* one might approach answers to this question as it is about identifying the answers themselves. My primary goal will be to *explore* the question above — not to convince people of my tentative and no doubt incomplete answers, but rather to seek a more informed perspective and to encourage more refined discussions of our answers to this question going forward. The following exploration is thus a mere early step in what should ideally be a grand collective project.

7.5 Clarifying the Question

In order to answer a given question, we must first make sure that it is reasonably well-defined. Specifically, in the context of our question above, one can reasonably ask what a "strong *prima facie* duty" to reduce suffering entails in more specific terms. After all, as noted above, such a duty can be combined with a variety of other values that may each have distinct implications of their own, and the scope of the duty to reduce suffering can likewise vary depending on how we choose to interpret it. So how do I construe the scope of this duty here?

For one, I maintain that our duty to reduce suffering must reflect the ideal of impartiality. As Richard Ryder put it, we should seek to reduce suffering on an 'equal pain equal treatment' basis, meaning that suffering is no less important merely because it is experienced by an individual who has a different skin color, gender, or species — the suffering itself is sufficient to merit moral concern and priority (Singer, 1975, ch. 1; Mayerfeld, 1999, pp. 116-117; Ryder, 2006, p. 95; Cochrane, 2018).

Yet beyond clarifying this key feature of impartiality, I will mostly avoid specifying the nature of our duty to reduce suffering all that narrowly. My reason for this is that the practical implications will tend to be convergent for a variety of interpretations of our duty to reduce suffering, and hence I will mostly seek to explore a broad interpretation so as to keep my analysis compatible with a wide range of views that entail a strong duty to reduce suffering (which I maintain that any plausible moral and political view *must* entail, cf. Mayerfeld, 1999; Vinding, 2020a, Part I).

My analysis thus seeks to be compatible, for the most part, with both classical utilitarianism and purely suffering-focused views, as well as a wide variety of pluralist moral views that include commonly endorsed rights and other *prima facie* duties in addition to a strong duty to reduce suffering (cf. Wolf, 1996, p. 278; 1997, VIII). Indeed, as we shall see, a strong duty to reduce suffering will itself tend to recommend many such plausible rights and complementary duties in practice.

8

Notes on Consequentialist Politics

The moral view described in the previous chapter is a consequentialist one (i.e. it is focused on bringing about certain consequences). Or stated more precisely, a *prima facie* duty to reduce suffering represents a consequentialist *component* in a moral view; a component that entails that, other things being equal, we should bring about outcomes with less suffering (Mayerfeld, 1999, pp. 8-9, p. 117). Such a duty does not, as stressed in the previous chapter, commit us to a *purely* consequentialist view, since it is compatible with other values and side-constraints (Mayerfeld, 1999, pp. 93-94; Wolf, 1996).

Yet any view that includes such a duty will still grant significant prominence to consequences, which renders it worth clarifying what such a focus on consequences implies — as well as what it does *not* imply — before we dive into specific policy issues. (The discussion below will mostly be phrased in terms of the consequentialist aim of reducing suffering in particular, yet most of it applies to consequentialist views more generally.)

8.1 Marginal Realism vs. Broad Idealism

A key conceptual point is that we can approach consequentialist politics from two very different perspectives. The first is what may be called a "marginal realist perspective", where we consider what the relatively small group of people who are most dedicated to reducing suffering should do with their limited resources so as to reduce suffering most effectively on the margin. This stands in contrast with the "broad idealist perspective", concerned with what an entire society should ideally do to reduce suffering most effectively.

Note that I am not saying that the broad idealist perspective is necessarily *un*realistic — what I mean by broad idealism in this context is roughly "the best an entire society could realistically do *if* it were strongly motivated to reduce suffering". Yet the marginal realist perspective will nonetheless tend to be significantly *more* realistic, given that it pertains to existing groups of people as they are, and the immediately feasible actions they can take. (John Rawls drew a related distinction between ideal and non-ideal theory, yet his concepts do not clearly delineate broad versus narrow perspectives, and ideal theory in the Rawlsian sense is also more idealistic than what I mean by the term "broad idealism", cf. Rawls, 1971, pp. 241-247.)

These perspectives are clearly related, yet also importantly distinct. One way they are related is that the optimal thing to aim for from the marginal realist perspective will often be to actualize the broad ideal — i.e. to get all of society on board on a given policy issue. But in some cases, this might not be realistic, and then other strategies will be called for, such as aiming for compromises that benefit all parties.

Of course, these binary perspectives merely represent the endpoints of a continuous spectrum of marginal realism versus broad idealism, and we may fruitfully analyze consequentialist politics from various points of this spectrum. For example, there will likely be gradual variation in the amount of weight people grant to the political aim of reducing suffering, and so it makes sense to adopt an increasingly broad perspective when focusing on the more widely shared versions of this aim.

In the following chapters, I will seek to consider issues both from the marginal realist and the broad idealist ends of the spectrum, as both perspectives can provide action-guiding insights.

8.2 Empirical Uncertainty

Another important point is that there is bound to be substantial uncertainty as to which political strategies and policies will reduce suffering most effectively (within a given set of moral constraints). Our answers to the question of which policies best satisfy our duty to reduce suffering will always be fallible and probabilistic in nature.

This is not, however, to say that we cannot be reasonably confident about many things, especially as we move away from the most plausible proposals toward the least plausible ones. We can generally be very confident that proposals that seem exceptionally harmful are indeed just that. Yet when we consider the more sensible segments of the space of possible policies, uncertainty regarding which policy is best inevitably does get significant, and a closer look at the data and a deliberate suspension of our typical overconfidence will be necessary.

Such uncertainty obviously does not imply that the consequences of our policies somehow matter less, but instead implies that we need to carefully explore the likely effects of any proposed policy based on the best available evidence. To be sure, these questions are exceptionally complex and difficult to answer; for instance, recall how optimal policy is culture-dependent, and how institutions often function in opaque ways. Yet the alternative, i.e. making policy decisions in ways that are *not* informed by a careful examination of the likely consequences, still generally seems worse.

Underestimating uncertainty also appears to be a problem in much political philosophy and in politics more broadly: the step from values to policies is often too short and hasty, with little systematic exploration of the empirical matters. Even the very notion that we should look to the empirical evidence in order to clarify which policies are optimal seems surprisingly rare.

Worth noting, too, is that greater clarity about the consequences of different policies will tend to be useful to the political projects of many people, as it simultaneously helps clarify the empirical step for many different normative views. Gaining better estimates of the likely effects of policies is thus an aim that people should be able to support regardless of what their particular values may be.

A key implication of our inescapable uncertainty is that we should adopt an attitude of epistemic humility. In particular, we should be skeptical when it comes to untested claims about "clearly superior" institutions and policies. When we take all relevant considerations into account, these things are rarely intuitive, let alone obvious. We have to take a careful look at the evidence. (I say more on the implications of empirical uncertainty in Vinding, 2020a, ch. 9.)

8.3 The Long-Term Future

Earth-originating life may persist for millions, perhaps even billions of years, implying that the future might contain millions, if not billions of times more sentient beings than the present. Hence, the effects our policies will have on the long-term future are crucial to consider on any consequentialist approach to politics.

Increasing the priority we devote to the long-term future would change how we think about and practice politics in significant ways. Indeed, merely taking the next century fully into account in our policy decisions would already imply a great change in our political outlook relative to the prevailing one in which we rarely look beyond the next couple of decades.

To be clear, saying that the long-term effects of our policies matter greatly is not to say that the near-term effects are irrelevant, which they clearly are not. For one, the effects our policies have on the next couple of decades are clearly of great importance in themselves, and they can usually be estimated with much greater accuracy than can long-term effects. Moreover, if a policy is to have good effects in the long term, it will likely need to have good effects in the near term as well. After all, in a world very much focused on near-term outcomes, we should expect policies to possess a certain level of "near-term fitness" in order for them to have a chance of being instituted and maintained. Likewise, many long-term oriented policies will recommend the accumulation of certain resources — e.g. insights and technologies — and goals of this kind also require the near-term future to go well.

These considerations notwithstanding, a case can be made that the effects our policies have on the long-term future — i.e. beyond the next couple of decades — will generally be the most important thing about them given the vastly greater number of sentient beings that the future is likely to contain (cf. Animal Ethics, 2018). And this becomes increasingly true the more influential and less reversible our policy decisions get.

The moral and political importance of the long-term future raises many difficult questions, not least the question of how we can assess which policies best reduce suffering in the long-term future (within the bounds of whatever moral constraints we may endorse). I believe part of the answer lies in identifying various proxy aims that are robustly beneficial, and then striving to realize these aims (more on this in the next chapter).

Accepting even a weak version of the long-term thesis serves to further underscore the significance and inevitability of our empirical uncertainty, as well as the importance of making a serious effort to estimate the likely effects of our policy decisions. Again, the fact that these effects are difficult to assess is not a good reason to disregard them.

8.4 Taking Human Psychology Into Account

Politics is to a large extent an art of navigating human psychology, which renders it crucial that we understand human psychology and tailor our approach accordingly. This carries many important implications. For example, a policy might *appear* to bring about good consequences at first sight, but if it makes people react very negatively — either to the policy itself or to the people and the values that (seemingly) endorse it — then the policy may well be harmful all things considered. Policies recommended by a naive consequentialist analysis will thus often be strongly renounced by a more sophisticated analysis. And the difference between naive and sophisticated such analyses often comes down to how well human psychology is accounted for.

The example above highlights the importance of considering people's receptivity and overall reaction to any policy proposal we might have. Beyond that, it points to a heuristic that is usually wise to follow, namely that we should seek to be considerate of other people's preferences and values (Caviola, 2017; Schubert et al., 2017). Most people care about many other things besides suffering, and those of us who are most strongly committed to the reduction of suffering will generally increase our chances of striking gainful compromises and creating better outcomes if we take these other values into consideration (Tomasik, 2013a; 2014b; Vinding, 2020a, ch. 10). (Our tribal zero-sum intuitions will no doubt be inclined to oppose such compromises, even when they are positive-sum, which is all the more reason to consciously commit to placing outcomes above our primitive coalitional instincts, cf. Section 4.8; Tooby, 2017.)

8.5 The Necessity of Rule Following

Another point that becomes apparent when we take human psychology into account is the necessity of firm rules and principles. Again, from a naive consequentialist perspective, it may seem that we should just dispense with all such rules, and instead always seek to calculate optimal outcomes on a case-by-case basis. In other words, we might assume that a consequentialist *criterion of rightness* implies that we should always decide based on a consequentialist *decision procedure* (cf. Crisp, 1992; Ord, 2005). But a more sophisticated analysis will reveal that this is false, for many reasons.

First, in order for cooperation to be possible among a large number of agents, a certain level of predictability is required. Cooperation and trust can be facilitated far better among agents who stick to commonly acknowledged rules compared to if each agent were to make decisions purely on a case-by-case basis. As James Wood Bailey has argued, we cannot evaluate individual decisions independently of their effects on other decisions, and when we take a broader look at the overall equilibria that various kinds of decisions end up producing, it becomes clear that collectives that adhere to (at least some) firm rules are generally far superior at creating desirable outcomes (Bailey, 1997, ch. 4).

Second, since humans have evolved to be a cooperative species (Henrich & Henrich, 2007), the point above applies to us in a particularly strong and fixed sense. That is, we have deep-seated intuitions that in some sense mediate universal rules regarding fairness and cooperation — such as a strong intolerance of free riders (Price et al., 2002) — as well as various culture-specific rules that individuals must follow if they are to avoid failure and punishment (DeScioli, 2016).

Indeed, studies have found that people are significantly less willing to trust and cooperate with individuals who decide by calculating on a case-by-case basis, which suggests that this decision procedure is usually not the best way to create good outcomes, and hence that it is not what a sophisticated consequentialist analysis would generally recommend in the context of human cooperation (Everett et al., 2016; 2018).

Other studies have found that people tend to universalize the rules instantiated by a particular action, which underscores the point that we cannot evaluate actions in isolation (Levine et al., 2020). For even if a given decision produces good outcomes in a particular case, the generalized version of the decision may still be harmful, which is problematic if the decision sets precedent for future decisions, and if others judge the actor on the merits of the generalized version, as seems to often be the case. (Note that this tendency to universalize might be especially pronounced in WEIRD populations, cf. Henrich, 2020, ch. 12.)

The bottom line is that individuals cannot achieve their aims, including the aim of reducing suffering, by ignoring the many social constraints that surround them. One is bound to observe numerous established rules to succeed. And a similar point holds true at the collective level: it would be naive to think that we can avoid having myriad strict cultural rules, let alone that we can change the deeply rule-animated nature of people's moral intuitions.

Thus, on any consequentialist view, the question is not *whether* but rather *which* strict rules and norms should ideally be promoted, the answer to which will depend both on the cultural rules that currently prevail as well as the constraints of human nature (cf. Boyer & Petersen, 2012; Henrich, 2020, p. 219). (For additional reasons why adherence to firm rules is endorsed by consequentialist views, see Mayerfeld, 1999, pp. 120-125, pp. 196-205; Hooker, 2002, ch. 7; Vinding, 2020a, 9.7.)

8.6 Moral Software Amenable to the Human Mind

As hinted above, our psychology is in many ways geared to think in terms of set rules and precepts. We are not consequentialists by nature, trying to calculate how to create optimal outcomes in the world at large. Instead, our minds are adapted to handle more specific tasks in the moral domain, such as tracking and responding to norm violations (cf. Cosmides & Tooby, 1992; Price et al., 2002). Whether we realize it or not, we are all de facto moral pluralists of sorts, concerned about disparate moral dimensions whose importance has been drummed into us by evolution and culture (cf. Haidt, 2012, Part II; Henrich, 2020, ch. 4).

The fact that our minds are oriented strongly toward more specific moral tasks and precepts carries significant implications for the kinds of moral software that consequentialists should ideally promote. It suggests that, if we are to reduce suffering effectively, we will need other ideas — other "mental technologies" — than just the notion that we have a *prima facie* duty to reduce suffering. Such a consequentialist duty simply does not jibe well with our mental architecture. It is abstract and complicated, and intuitively unexciting (Vinding, 2020a, 7.13).

This is also evident in the history of political philosophy: as we saw in the previous chapter, many authors have defended the moral and political importance of reducing suffering, and hardly anyone has argued against it. Yet this view has nonetheless been largely ignored in the mainstream discourse within political philosophy, in large part, I think, because it lacks texture and has limited stickiness in our minds, unlike concepts such as justice and equality, which seem more intuitively appealing to most people (cf. Heath & Heath, 2007).

The lesson here is by no means that we should dismiss the aim of reducing suffering, but rather that it may sometimes be beneficial to translate this aim into more palatable and actionable terms. Thus, consequentialists might often do best by encouraging the cultivation of good character and common virtues, such as honesty and interpersonal respect, since these things fit well with our intuitive morality and because they tend to produce favorable consequences in the bigger picture (Crisp, 1992; Tomasik, 2013c; Bradley, 2018). Likewise, concepts such as justice and rights are powerful moral technologies that have proven exceptionally effective at creating good outcomes over the course of cultural evolution, which is a strong reason to endorse them even on purely consequentialist grounds (cf. Talbott, 2010; Henrich, 2020, ch. 12).

8.7 Being Realistic and Strategic

Modern politics is a popularity contest. That is a fact that anyone seeking to create good political outcomes has to contend with. Specifically, it means that one has to adopt a pragmatic approach and be realistic about what is feasible. This is not to say that one cannot be both honest and ambitious about one's political ideals. But it does mean that one should make an effort to choose strategies and framings that have the best impact all things considered (and things like honesty, ambition, and integrity will no doubt be critical in this respect, as they tend to have good consequences in the bigger picture, Tomasik, 2013c).

This is a case where the difference between the marginal realist and the broad idealist perspective becomes paramount. For the reality is that we do not live in a world in which most people are strongly dedicated to the aim of reducing suffering for all sentient beings — at least not in terms of their actual behavior. However, most people probably *are* willing to support policies that reduce suffering if only the cost is sufficiently low to them personally, which suggests that a promising strategy for those who are most dedicated to reducing suffering is to tap into this vast reservoir of potential support, making marginal pushes in just the right places such that our efforts inspire broad support rather than broad hostility.

Relatedly, if the moral importance of the long-term future and of reducing suffering are to become durable and widely accepted political memes, it is critical that they avoid getting tainted with naive ideas — for example, the idea that the near-term future is unimportant, or that unprovoked violence is a legitimate or effective way to reduce suffering (cf. Chenoweth & Stephan, 2011). The prevention of such failure modes of naivety should plausibly be a high priority, especially in a political context where people often present the ideas of their opponents in the worst possible light.

8.8 Not Just Formal Institutions

Another mistake worth avoiding is to think that the creation of good political outcomes is purely a matter of influencing formal institutions — effecting better legislation and better institutional structures. For while this is surely important, the truth is that our formal institutions do not exist in isolation. Our politics is also a product of our informal values and norms, which help set the stage for our political process at large, and to some extent even determine which formal institutions are possible in the first place (cf. Henrich, 2020, ch. 12). Consequently, improvements at this informal level are often just as crucial as improvements at the strictly formal level.

For example, reducing our tendency to engage in tribalism and zero-sum politics would constitute a great improvement in the way we do politics, not least since it could pave the way for progress on many other fronts, potentially improving the quality of our legislation and our political system altogether. (Of course, the causal arrow goes in the other direction as well, in that our formal institutions also influence our informal ones, cf. Sønderskov & Dinesen, 2014; Henrich, 2020, p. 30.)

More generally, consequentialists should be careful to avoid the trap of narrow optimization. For even if one has a singular aim at the normative level, it still holds true that political outcomes depend on myriad distinct variables. Sophisticated consequentialism will thus entail getting many things right — many laws, norms, insights, etc. — and success in each of these respects will usually be a matter of degree rather than all or nothing. (I say more on this point in Vinding, 2020a, 9.4-9.5.)

8.9 Awareness of People's Reaction to Suffering

It is challenging for the human mind to face up to the true horror of suffering, so much so that we seem to actively suppress its reality (Cohen, 2001; Metzinger, 2017). Most of us tend to give little thought to the fact that we live in a world that contains suffering of inconceivable awfulness (cf. Vinding, 2020a, 4.2-4.3, ch. 7). And when we are confronted with the fact that such suffering exists, and that it does so in horrifically large amounts, we easily feel overwhelmed and tempted to disengage. Indeed, even most scholarly writings on moral and political philosophy seem to treat these subjects as though extreme suffering does not *really* exist.

This "suffering denial" is a lamentable fact about our minds and our culture at large. But it is also a fact that those who seek to reduce suffering will have to acknowledge and adapt to, as it carries many strategic implications.

For example, given that people often react negatively to talk about reducing suffering (even when they acknowledge its moral importance), it is probably wise to avoid constantly framing issues in those terms. A political movement seeking to reduce suffering cannot be successful without an eye to people's limited capacity for hearing about the horrors of reality. One needs to find the sweet spot that inspires people to support efforts to reduce suffering without pushing them to the point of disengagement.

Relatedly, it is important that efforts to reduce suffering do not come to be seen as antithetical to people's individual pursuits of happiness and meaning. For not only need there not be a deep conflict between these respective aims, but a strong case can even be made that they are complementary, at least in that the aim of reducing suffering implies that we should place considerable importance on personal fulfillment and meaning in practice. This is partly because meaning and happiness help fend off suffering, partly because they keep us sustainably motivated and productive in our efforts to reduce suffering, and partly because movements and ideologies that allow for — and even encourage — the integration of happiness and meaning probably end up doing much better than those that do not (Leighton, 2017; Vinding, 2021; Ajantaival, 2021a).

8.10 Showing That We Care vs. Actually Reducing Suffering

An additional challenge we face is our tendency to be more concerned about *showing* that we care than about *actually* reducing suffering (cf. Simler & Hanson, 2018, ch. 12). This holds true even for those who are sincerely dedicated to reducing suffering — again, our minds are devious and up to more things than we consciously realize, such as signaling our loyalties and impressiveness (Trivers, 2011; Kurzban, 2011a; Simler & Hanson, 2018). (In light of this unconscious self-deception, one could argue that the attitude we should ideally adopt toward our own motives is roughly the same as the skeptical attitude that we tend to have toward the claims of a politician seeking to get elected.)

These unconscious drives risk distorting our assessments of which policies are most effective at reducing suffering. After all, we should expect there to be a substantial divergence between 1) those actions that best signal our impressiveness and loyalties, and 2) those actions that best reduce suffering (cf. Lewis, 2016). (Of course, honestly signaling certain traits can also be conducive to reducing suffering, yet this does not negate the point that our signaling drives often distort our views.)

Some of the signs that signaling motives are in charge include: an unwillingness to compromise with outgroups, dogmatic views, and a suspicious epistemic convergence with the views of our peers. In contrast, efforts strictly aimed at reducing suffering will tend to entail the opposite: a willingness to compromise, complex and nuanced views, and a healthy skepticism of groups and groupthink (cf. Simler, 2016).

This latter pattern does not come natural to us, whereas the former mostly does, which underscores the need to be keenly aware of these signaling-driven tendencies, and to make a serious effort to reduce their distorting influence. There is probably no greater source of bias in the realm of policy analysis than our hidden signaling motives (cf. Achen & Bartels, 2016, ch. 8-9; Simler & Hanson, 2018, ch. 16).

8.11 Objections to Consequentialist Politics

The following are five objections to consequentialist politics, along with my replies in brief.

8.11.1 *Consequentialist politics opens the door to dangerous actions. The risk of miscalculating is high, and it is too easy to justify atrocities in the name of creating good outcomes.*

First, it is worth reiterating that the consequentialist duty to reduce suffering that I outlined in the previous chapter is compatible with moral constraints of various kinds. Well-devised such constraints — e.g. fundamental rights and liberties — can plausibly address most of the worries one may have of this kind (cf. Wolf, 1996).

Second, we should be clear about the distinction between consequentialism as a *criterion of rightness* and as a *decision procedure*. As hinted above, a consequentialist criterion of rightness will often renounce consequentialist decision procedures. And this is especially likely if the decision procedure (or policy) in question is strongly objectionable by the lights of most people and most ethical views — in part because these other ethical views plausibly encapsulate a certain wisdom (also by consequentialist standards), and in part because of the importance of taking human psychology into account.

Third, it must be stressed that alternative moral views are also vulnerable to risks and pitfalls of this kind. There will *always* be a step from ideal to practical reality, and there will always be a risk of failing in this step, for any moral view. One may object that the risk of such failures, and of inadvertently causing bad outcomes in general, is smaller in the case of non-consequentialist views. Yet this is far from clear. Indeed, it is plausible that the dangers of *not* including a substantial consequentialist component in our political views are considerably greater, as we in that case seem more likely to overlook and fail to respond to future risks that we could otherwise have addressed (Vinding, 2020a, 8.15).

8.11.2 Consequentialist politics is dangerously radical, as it would make us too eager to implement sweeping changes on weak grounds.

A consequentialist and empirically-informed approach to politics would not imply that we should support radical changes on a weak basis. On the contrary, such an approach would require us to be no more confident and eager to change policies than what is warranted by the overall balance of reasons and evidence available to us.

A consequentialist approach to politics is thus entirely compatible with making only small and tentative policy changes, if any at all, when we do not have good empirical data or other good reasons that support significant change. After all, the point that institutions sometimes function in opaque ways that embody deep adaptations is itself a well-supported fact that a truly empirically-informed approach to politics should take into account; and this point does provide a *prima facie* reason to be cautious about policy change, especially as far as sweeping change is concerned (see Section 6.4).

8.11.3 *Consequentialist politics cannot support genuine moral rights.*

Again, a *prima facie* duty to reduce suffering is compatible with views that entail strong moral rights directly at the normative level. Beyond that, many consequentialists have argued that moral rights in fact *can* be defended on purely consequentialist grounds, which just serves to further support the adoption of moral rights in practice (see e.g. Brandt, 1984; Sumner, 1987; Pettit, 1988; Talbott, 2005; 2010).

As noted above, moral rights have proven an exceptionally powerful social technology in service of reducing suffering; indeed, individual moral rights are commonly defended on the grounds that they are critical for preventing extreme suffering (cf. Felice, 1996; Mayerfeld, 2008; Andorno & Baffone, 2014). Thus, just as consequentialist views can consistently support the use of other technologies that prevent suffering — such as anesthetics — so they can, when well-construed, support and uphold institutions of effective moral rights.

8.11.4 *A consequentialist approach to politics that is based on empirical evidence is at a serious political disadvantage given that it must, if honest and transparent, be phrased in the language of great empirical uncertainty. This is not a convincing language to most people.*

There probably is a real challenge in this respect, yet it is also important not to overstate this challenge. First, as noted in Section 8.2, it is by no means always the case that we have great empirical uncertainty about a given issue. When it comes to transparently harmful policy proposals, we really can be quite confident that the proposals in question are a bad idea.

Second, in cases where we do have great uncertainty about whether a given policy is good or bad relative to our values, it seems likely that honesty about this uncertainty is in fact ideal all things considered. After all, the alternative would be to lie about or hide our uncertainty, or to simply not base our policies on a set of underlying values combined with the best available evidence. These alternatives probably amount to a considerably worse political predicament overall (cf. Section 1.6).

Indeed, looking at our political discourse in general, it seems that we mostly express far too much confidence in our political views — not too much uncertainty. Thus, also when we consider the broader aims of reducing political overconfidence and improving our political epistemology, it would appear beneficial if we held and expressed much more uncertainty on just about all levels of our political discourse, even if such expressions of uncertainty involve certain costs as well (cf. Section 4.4).

Lastly, it is worth noting that uncertainty need not imply a lack of determination. For example, there is no contradiction between placing, say, a "mere" 70 percent credence in the claim that Policy A is significantly better than Policy B, and then working and advocating for the realization of Policy A with a strong resolve and determination (this point obviously applies more strongly when one's credence reflects a thorough examination of the issue rather than a mere hunch). After all, a 70 percent credence still means that Policy A appears to be the best policy, by a considerable margin even, which renders it rational to support it with dedication and commitment, despite the significant uncertainty. (The notion that we need to hide epistemic uncertainty in order to be convincing and achieve our aims is criticized more elaborately in Galef, 2021, ch. 9.)

8.11.5 Consequentialist politics of the kind advanced here could support killing innocent people, or even destroying the entire world in order to reduce suffering.

It must be emphasized, once more, that a *prima facie* duty to reduce suffering is wholly compatible with rights that protect individuals from violence. And such basic protective rights are no doubt among the most plausible and fundamental moral rights of all — also on purely consequentialist views, given how effective these rights are at ensuring safety and building trust (cf. Wolf, 1996, p. 278; Bailey, 1997, p. 148). Even on a consequentialist view focused *exclusively* on the reduction of suffering, there are many strong reasons to respect these basic rights, and indeed to actively protect them (cf. Vinding, 2020a, 8.1-8.2; 2020d).

The objection above is important to address, since this is often how a strong moral duty to reduce suffering is dismissed in moral and political philosophy: by associating it with violence and destruction (cf. Knutsson, 2021). So it is worth driving home, repetitiously if necessary, that this *is* a non sequitur. The most prominent philosophers who have defended a strong *prima facie* duty to reduce suffering have all rejected such violent implications, often with reference to non-hedonistic values (see e.g. Popper, 1945, p. 501; Wolf, 1996; 1997; Mayerfeld, 1999, pp. 98-101, pp. 159-160).

In truth, nothing prevents us from reconciling a strong duty to reduce suffering with a peaceful approach that also respects other sensible values, such as respect for autonomy and individual rights.

9

Identifying Plausible Proxies

It is difficult to assess how a given policy will affect future suffering. Evaluating policies by trying to measure their direct effects on suffering is unlikely to be the best approach, one reason being that suffering itself can be difficult to measure directly, especially on a large scale. This suggests that we should instead look at factors that are easier to measure or estimate — factors that can serve as *proxies* for future suffering. Ideally, we should build a framework that incorporates many such proxies; a framework with more structure than just the bare question "How does this policy influence suffering?", and which can help us analyze policies in a more robust and systematic way.

My aim in this chapter is to build a preliminary such framework. The proxies included in this framework are, of course, bound to be imperfect. Indeed, beyond the inevitable imperfection of any given proxy, the particular proxies that I will present and argue for below are likely not the best proxies possible. Future work and criticism will hopefully refine them and identify better ones. But we have to start *somewhere*, and the proxies I will present are, I believe, still quite useful.

9.1 The Importance of Avoiding Worst-Case Outcomes

A key point to appreciate in our endeavor to reduce future suffering is the importance of avoiding worst-case scenarios (Tomasik, 2011; Althaus &

Gloor, 2016; Baumann, 2017a). This is supported on both theoretical and empirical grounds. In theoretical terms, expected value calculations suggest that it can be particularly important to prevent future outcomes with especially large amounts of suffering (Gloor, 2018; Vinding, 2020a, 9.8.2, 14.1-14.3). Hence, even if there is only a, say, five percent probability that humanity will increase suffering by many orders of magnitude, the large amount of suffering that such a scenario may entail means that we should nonetheless take it seriously.

In empirical terms, we find reasons to expect that most future suffering could result from a relatively narrow range of worst-case scenarios — e.g. among the worst 10 percent of expected outcomes. One reason is that the severity of many kinds of catastrophes, including natural disasters and wars, fall along a power-law distribution, meaning that the majority of the casualties have been due to a relatively small number of particularly bad events (Newman, 2004). Another reason is that the universe could contain a *vastly* greater amount of suffering than it does today, such as if we colonized space in a way that steeply increases the number of beings experiencing extreme suffering (Vinding, 2020a, 14.1-14.3).

A few clarifications may be in order. First, to say that it is important to avoid worst-case outcomes is not to say that we should only focus on a narrow sliver of future scenarios, such as a very specific kind of future risk that might be salient to us. For not only might the range of worst-case outcomes we should focus on be fairly broad — e.g. the worst 15 percent rather than the worst 0.1 percent of expected outcomes — but we also have little knowledge about which particular risks are the most worrisome, implying that a near-exclusive focus on any one such risk would be dangerously narrow. We should seek to avoid worst-case outcomes with a broad range of risks in mind (Baumann, 2020a; Vinding, 2020g).

Nor does the importance of avoiding worst-case outcomes imply that we should focus exclusively on avoiding such outcomes. The unspeakable suffering in the world of today is obviously urgent, and much of it can be prevented an exceedingly low and obviously worthwhile cost. What does follow, however, is that the avoidance of worst-case outcomes should at least be a significant consideration, and perhaps even the *main* consideration, when we evaluate policies with an eye to reducing future suffering. Hence, the proxies we should be looking for are probably to a large extent proxies for worst-case outcomes.

9.2 The Bounding Approach to Avoiding Worst-Case Outcomes

Before exploring particular proxies, I first wish to outline a useful way to think about these proxies, and about how to avoid worst-case outcomes in general. I propose that we should think about this challenge in terms of a bounding approach of sorts, in which we view ourselves as situated in a high-dimensional landscape of worst-case risks, with different dimensions representing different kinds of risks (cf. Baumann, 2018). And our aim should then be to bound ourselves off from these risks, building a protective wall, as it were, that keeps us at a safe distance from worst-case scenarios in which things spiral out of control toward a runaway moral catastrophe — potentially on a cosmic scale (cf. Gloor, 2018; Vinding, 2020a, ch. 14). This notional safety wall cannot, of course, be the product of any single policy, or indeed any single human generation, but must instead be built and strengthened in gradual steps, with each generation thoughtfully updating and refining it.

The fact that we face many different risks simultaneously, about which we have limited knowledge, lends support to such a strategy aimed at broad worst-case safety. For even if we do not know which particular risks are most worrisome, we can likely still pursue actions that are robustly positive in that they help "bound us off" from many different risks at the same time. In this way, we can pursue policies that are in a sense wiser than our state of knowledge, since policies need not be contingent on the exact details about what the "danger zone" looks like in order to protect us from getting there.

It seems that we should generally search for and pursue policies that contribute to such robust safety — i.e. policies that help steer us toward and within the low-risk zone in the space of worst-case risks. At the very least, the promotion of such robust safety should be considered a key policy desideratum.

9.3 Plausible Proxies

Two kinds of proxies are worth distinguishing. First, there are those proxies that track suffering; in this context, these will be suffering-conducive factors, or risk factors for increasing future suffering (cf. Baumann, 2019). We may label these "negative proxies", since we will generally want to minimize them.

Second, there are proxies that track the opposite, namely the reduction of suffering. These will be suffering-reducing factors, or protective factors against increasing future suffering. We may label these "positive proxies", since we will generally want to advance them. Each negative proxy will tend to have a roughly corresponding positive proxy, yet it will nonetheless be convenient to be able to refer to both kinds of proxies separately.

9.3.1 Greater Levels of Cooperation

There are many reasons to think that a greater overall level of hostility and conflict will lead to more future suffering. Conversely, greater levels of cooperation will probably tend to reduce future suffering (Tomasik, 2011; 2013a; 2014b; Vinding, 2020a, ch. 10; 2020d).

In more specific terms, we should likely seek to reduce things such as (excessive) political polarization, international conflicts, and arms races, and instead seek to promote institutions that enable conflict resolution, compromise, and mutual understanding.

The avoidance of large-scale conflicts seems good for reducing suffering for two principal reasons. First, conflicts on a large scale could directly cause vast amounts of suffering; indeed, such conflicts likely represent one of the most serious worst-case risks (cf. Baumann, 2017a). Second, conflicts are bad because they tend to impede moral progress. Resources spent on needless conflicts are resources not spent on reducing suffering. So even if a conflict does not directly increase suffering, it may still cause a lot of suffering indirectly, by getting in the way of betterment.

Cooperation, on the other hand, can actively promote moral progress, such as by enabling us to update our views and to strike win-win compromises that help reduce suffering (cf. Tomasik, 2013a). Consequently, we have reason to think that the dual aim of avoiding conflicts and promoting cooperation is robustly good relative to a broad class of worst-case risks, and hence that it is a highly plausible aim to adopt when trying to reduce future suffering. And the fact that this aim is recommended by a wide range of value systems, including common-sense morality, only lends it additional support.

9.3.2 Better Values

Our decisions are in a sense downstream from our fundamental values, which renders our values a significant determinant of future outcomes. In particular, we should expect the level of concern for suffering held by future moral agents to correlate reasonably well with future suffering reduction, and hence it is critical to ensure that future agents will have a sufficient level of concern for suffering (Vinding, 2020a, 12.1). However, concern for suffering is not sufficient, at least not if that concern is confined to human suffering only. Better values must mean greater concern for the suffering of *all* sentient beings (Vinding, 2015).

In line with the previous point concerning cooperation, it is crucial that concern for suffering is mostly advanced in a non-partisan way, such that suffering reduction becomes a common goal rather than a needless hostage of political strife. After all, as noted earlier, concern for suffering is already a bipartisan value to a considerable extent; it is just not a value that we have fully extrapolated and acted on in a manner consistent with our stated level of concern (Vinding, 2020a, 12.3).

To advance our collective moral values, we will likely also need to promote norms that enable such value advancement in the first place — for example, norms of open-mindedness, reflection, and charitable interpretation. Beyond helping us advance our moral values, such norms also seem conducive to cooperation in general, which is an additional reason to think that better norms and values at this more epistemic level are a positive proxy as well (cf. Tomasik, 2013d).

Perhaps even more important than the attainment of better values is the avoidance of worse values — i.e. a deterioration of values that leads agents to have outright malevolent attitudes and goals, such as vindictiveness and sadism, or a regression of the political process that leads people with such traits to rise to (even more) power (cf. Althaus & Baumann, 2020). The reason this might be more important is, in short, that there is more room for our values to get worse than there is for them to get better. For example, the vast majority of people lean at least slightly toward reducing the suffering of others, while few people endorse values that entail the deliberate increase of suffering — though some sadly do. Keeping such individuals and their values from gaining influence is of utmost importance (more on this in Section 14.6).

The fact that the potential for value deterioration is in some sense much greater than the potential for value improvement is a reason to be prudent and amiable in our endeavor to improve values, lest we inadvertently push people toward worse values (e.g. by provoking resentment and hostility). After all, the act of pushing a relatively small number of people toward harmful values may undo the good done by improving the values of a much larger number of people (Vinding, 2020a, 9.3, 9.6).

9.3.3 Greater Capacity to Reduce Suffering

Another important factor, quite distinct from our willingness to reduce suffering, is our level of competence in this endeavor. Specifically, to reduce suffering, we also need the requisite insights, tools, and resources, which represent yet another set of positive proxies. Note, however, that these proxies are not just about increasing our capabilities and resources indiscriminately, since some insights and technologies likely will tend to increase rather than reduce future suffering, especially in the hands of the wrong agents.

We should thus ideally advance insights and technologies that make us wiser and better able to avoid catastrophic outcomes — e.g. insights into social science and practical ethics — while limiting the advancement of insights and technologies that are likely to cause enormous harm (cf. Bostrom, 2011). This has been referred to as "differential intellectual progress" (Muehlhauser & Salamon, 2012; Tomasik, 2013d). It is such differential capacity-building in particular that we should seek to promote and regard as a positive proxy. The development of disproportionally harmful capacities, in contrast, should be regarded as a negative proxy and something to actively prevent.

9.4 A Robust Framework

We may view the proxies above as criteria that policies should ideally satisfy, and the more of these criteria that a given policy satisfies, the more confident we should generally be that the policy is good and worth pursuing. In more exact terms, we should plausibly judge policies based on their combined score on these dimensions, at least as a first approximation. This represents (the beginning of) the kind of framework we set out to construct: it gives us a set of measuring rods that are at least somewhat tangible, and from which we can seek to triangulate how good or bad a policy is relative to future suffering — supplemented, of course, by whatever considerations and additional criteria that seem relevant in the particular case at hand.

Objectives such as "accumulating insights" and "avoiding value deterioration" are hardly among the first criteria that come to mind when thinking about policies that best reduce suffering. The most intuitive criterion in this regard is perhaps something like "immediate impact on suffering" — which is no doubt a significant factor to consider. Yet the importance of the long-term future means that immediate impact should not be the only, and in many cases not even the main criterion for evaluating policies. When we take the long-term future into consideration, we see that the effects on our future *capacity* to reduce suffering will often be more significant than the direct effects on suffering in the near term.

Hence, it might generally be ideal to aim for policies that place us in a position to be more rationally compassionate going forward. This point bears emphasis, not least because policies that are promising from a near-term perspective may at the same time be harmful from a long-term perspective. In particular, controversial actions aimed to reduce current suffering might in effect provoke backlash and value deterioration, and thereby greatly increase suffering in the long term.

9.5 Turning to Policy

The next part of the book will examine a number of policy issues, with the aim of exploring which specific policies, principles, and institutions best serve the aim of reducing suffering. A few preliminary notes about this project are in order. First of these is that my analysis will not — indeed *could* not — be a matter of simply presenting empirical data and then directly "reading off" which policies seem optimal. For although it is in principle an empirical question which policies best reduce suffering, the reality is that we often lack data that can settle this question directly; in part because we do not have perfect data on the outcomes of existing policies, and in part because relatively few things have been tried so far in the vast space of possible institutions and policies. Consequently, it will be necessary to rely on both empirical data and theoretical considerations when trying to identify good policies, and theoretical considerations will often have to do much of the work when the empirical evidence is scarce.

Second, there is the limited scope of my analysis: given the large number of relevant policy issues one could explore, I have been forced to pick out a relatively small set of issues to focus on, in turn neglecting many other relevant ones. Yet not only is my analysis limited in terms of the set of policy issues and institutions it explores, but it is also far from exhaustive in its treatment of the few issues that it *does* explore. Both in terms of breadth and depth, one could go much further than does the following analysis. And my hope is that we will.

In general terms, the goal of the following analysis is to illustrate how the two-step ideal of reasoned politics can be used to infer evidence-based policies. In more specific terms, the goal is to provide tentative recommendations that can inform the actions of people seeking to reduce suffering, as well as to encourage further exploration into these issues so that we can approach better answers still to the question of how we can best prevent unspeakable suffering.

PART IV

POLICY ISSUES

10

Non-Human Beings and Politics

We think with our culture. That is, we rarely think from first principles, even first principles we ourselves sincerely endorse, but rather from sentiments instilled in us by our culture. Nowhere is this more obvious than in the case of humanity's moral attitudes toward non-human animals. Even most utilitarians, who by their own ideals ought to consider the suffering of all beings important, are still in fact exceptionally anthropocentric in their attitudes. The insights of Darwin have not yet trickled fully into our moral consciousness, not even among those whose moral views demand it. Such is the heavy momentum of culture, which is reflected in every facet of modern politics and political thought. The anthropocentrism of most political philosophy is, to put it mildly, a massive failure.

10.1 The Case Against Speciesism

Speciesism is discrimination against sentient individuals based on their species membership (Horta, 2010b). Such discrimination, and the cruelty against non-human animals that it supports, is evidently widely practiced in today's world. Yet what could justify such discrimination? A common defense is to invoke some particular trait or ability that humans possess and which non-human animals are said to lack, such as intelligence, moral responsibility, or a capacity for language.

The problem, however, is that this supposed defense runs into the argument from species overlap: for any trait we may point to that non-human animals are said to lack, we can also identify humans who do not possess this trait. And yet in the case of human individuals, virtually everyone agrees that the absence of these traits — such as the capacity for linguistic communication, or to plan for the future — does *not* justify discrimination, let alone a complete moral disregard of these individuals. Hence, the claim that the absence of the trait in question can justify discrimination does not seem tenable, by our own standards (Horta, 2014).

In the case of humans, we recognize that sentience alone — the capacity to have experiences — is enough to warrant moral consideration. For example, we do not accept discrimination against people whose cerebral hemispheres are largely absent, such as due to hydranencephaly, since these individuals show every sign of being conscious, and indeed to experience strong emotions (Beshkar, 2008). But we have yet to realize that this underlying premise regarding the moral relevance of sentience per se also implies that we should grant moral consideration to non-human animals, since the evidence for sentience among non-human animals is just as overwhelming at this point. As the Cambridge Declaration on Consciousness states:

> Convergent evidence indicates that non-human animals have the neuroanatomical, neurochemical, and neurophysiological substrates of conscious states along with the capacity to exhibit intentional behaviors. Consequently, the weight of evidence indicates that humans are not unique in possessing the neurological substrates that generate consciousness. Non-human animals, including all mammals and birds, and many other creatures, including octopuses, also possess these neurological substrates. (Low et al., 2012)

This statement does not explicitly mention fish, yet the evidence for sentience in fish, including pain in particular, has since been declared similarly strong by various scholars (Brown, 2015; Balcombe, 2016; Jabr, 2018).

These findings leave our discriminatory attitudes in a rather awkward position, as they reveal them to be animated by a strange bodyism of sorts

(Vinding, 2015, ch. 1). They imply that if only we could transplant the nervous system of a non-human animal into a human body, then this would apparently be enough to protect this being from our speciesist attitudes. Yet this clearly conflicts with the widely accepted moral principle that the encapsulating shell that a being happens to reside in should not be relevant to the moral consideration we grant them. Our speciesism essentially amounts to discrimination based on external appearances. (More elaborate arguments against speciesism can be found in Horta, 2010b; Vinding, 2015; the psychology of speciesism is explored in Caviola et al., 2019.)

The moral and political relevance of non-human animals is only further underscored by their numbers. For not only are non-human animals subjected to uniquely severe harms, and generally worse off than humans (Faria, 2014; Horta, 2016), but they are also far more numerous, representing more than 99.999 percent of sentient beings on the planet (Tomasik, 2009; Bar-On et al., 2018).

A political project that takes seriously our moral duty to reduce suffering cannot ignore more than 99.999 percent of the suffering beings on our planet. It must bring this majority and their suffering to the very top of our moral and political agenda.

10.2 Wild-Animal Suffering and the Idyllic View of Nature

The point made above also applies to wild animals in particular, as the vast majority of sentient beings on Earth, more than 99.9 percent of them, happen to live in the wild, where many experience great suffering (Tomasik, 2009; Bar-On et al., 2018). And as just noted, we cannot defend ignoring the vast majority of sentient beings in our political endeavors. Politics for all sentient beings will to a large extent mean politics for non-human beings in nature (cf. Johannsen, 2020, ch. 3).

This will seem starkly counterintuitive to many, including many animal advocates. One reason for this is speciesism: we discriminate against wild animals, and wholly disregard their interests in ways we would never deem acceptable in relation to (beings with the bodies of) humans. Another reason we tend to disregard the interests of wild animals is an idyllic view of nature, according to which wild animals live comfortable and happy lives, implying that there is little need to take wild animals into consideration, except perhaps to ensure that we leave them alone to flourish in their natural state. Unfortunately, this idyllic view is wrong, for many reasons (Horta, 2010a).

For one, there is the fact that wild animals tend to have vast numbers of offspring, of whom only few can survive to adulthood. In a condition where reproducing pairs have thousands of offspring, and where populations remain roughly stable, all of these thousands — minus a few — must die before they reach the age where they themselves can reproduce. In effect, most beings born in nature live short lives where their basic needs mostly fail to be met, and where they die what is likely a painful death (Horta, 2010a; 2015; Villamor Iglesias, 2018; Johannsen, 2020, ch. 2).

Yet wild animals suffer from a wide range of harms regardless of their reproductive strategies, including hunger, disease, parasitism, and natural disasters. These harms often cause intense suffering, and we should not disregard this suffering merely because the sufferers happen to live in the wild, or because they happen to have non-human bodies. We rightly acknowledge a moral duty to relieve intense suffering experienced by humans, including when it is due to natural causes, and there is no justification for restricting this moral duty to humans only (Vinding, 2015; Horta, 2017a; 2017b).

A common objection against trying to help wild animals is that we would only make things worse, and that the track record of human interventions in nature supports this pessimistic view. Yet this objection is problematic for at least three reasons. First, large-scale human interventions in nature have so far not been done with the aim of helping wild animals, and hence the track record so far is not representative of what human interventions might accomplish if they were done for this purpose (Tomasik, 2015a; what such beneficent interventions might consist in is explored in Section 10.7.1).

Second, we do not accept a similar defeatism in the case of human suffering. Again, when it comes to catastrophes involving humans, such as genocides and famines, we realize that we have strong reasons to help, and we often try to do so *despite* the fact that helping may be difficult, and despite there being no perfect guarantee that we can make things better.

Failing to display a similar level of moral ambition when the victims are non-human beings amounts to unjustified discrimination (Horta, 2010b).

Third, this objection seems to overlook just how catastrophic the situation of wild animals actually is: a condition of famine, disease, and destitution in which the vast majority of beings are unable to find food, and in effect die very young (Horta, 2010a; 2013a; 2015; Mannino, 2015). When the condition we are trying to ameliorate is extremely severe, our conception of what it would mean to make things worse must be adjusted accordingly, as must the level of risk that is acceptable when pursuing compassionate interventions.

There is, to be sure, a risk that interventions to help wild animals will end up making things worse, which highlights the importance of a well-informed and cautious approach to compassionate intervention. Yet this is very different from a stance of moral defeatism that simply dismisses the issue out of hand. (A collective duty to help wild animals is defended at greater length in Johannsen, 2020, ch. 3. Various biases that prevent us from caring about wild-animal suffering are reviewed in Davidow, 2013; Vinding, 2020b.)

10.3 Animal Exploitation: A Moral Catastrophe

Humanity's industrial exploitation of non-human animals arguably represents the greatest source of readily preventable suffering in the world today (Pearce, 2015, p. 161). Each year, we exploit non-human animals in unspeakable ways on an enormous scale. We raise pigs and chickens in horrific conditions, crammed in small spaces where they are confined for life and subjected to cruel mutilation — for example, it is common practice to "debeak" chickens and to castrate and cut off the tails of pigs, all without any pain relief (Capps, 2013a; 2013b; American Veterinary Medical Association, 2013).

We raise more than 70 billion land vertebrates in such horrific conditions each year, and even more beings are raised on aquatic "farms", where large numbers of fish are crammed into small, dirty basins in which they develop myriad health complications due to poor water quality, and they are usually killed by asphyxiation, again without any pain relief (Mood

& Brooke, 2012; King-Nobles, 2019). In addition, we kill an even larger number of "wild-caught" fish — more than a trillion each year — also in extremely painful ways, such as asphyxiation or by freezing them to death in an ice bath; both these methods commonly cause the fish to suffer for more than an hour before they die, and in many cases it takes several hours (Mood & Brooke, 2010; Fishcount, 2014; 2019).

The sad reality is that the number of sentient beings raised on factory farms has been growing exponentially for decades (Ritchie & Roser, 2017; Bollard, 2018). And something that risks making the problem much worse still is the burgeoning trend of farming insects for human consumption, which not only involves far more animals killed per calorie, but also routinely involves boiling, frying, and roasting the insects to death as a method of slaughter (Tomasik, 2014c; Rowe, 2020; Molloy, 2021). Even if we may be uncertain about the degree of sentience among insects, we should still avoid the risk of creating what *could* be intense suffering for them on a vast scale (Birch, 2017; Knutsson & Munthe, 2017; Balcombe, 2021, ch. 3) — not least given that there are alternatives that are much less harmful, such as plant-based, cultivated, and even air-based meats (cf. Tetrick, 2013; Dyson, 2016).

Non-human animals are, as Judith Shklar put it, the "ultimate victims of human cruelty" (Shklar, 1982, p. 20). Preventing this cruelty and the suffering it causes must be a key priority, not just according to moral views concerned strongly with the reduction of suffering, but according to all moral views that entail but a modest degree of impartiality (Korsgaard, 2018; Animal Ethics, 2020e).

10.4 Future Risks: Increasing Animal Suffering and Novel Forms of Suffering

Working to avoid worst-case outcomes with vast amounts of suffering may, as argued in the previous chapter, be the most effective way to prevent future suffering in expectation (Baumann, 2017a; 2020e). And risks of increasing non-human suffering likely represent by far the greatest and most worrisome class of such worst-case risks, partly because the set of plausible worst-case outcomes whose main victims are non-human beings is considerably larger than the set of plausible worst-case outcomes whose main victims are humans, and partly because non-human suffering is uniquely neglected (cf. Tomasik, 2011).

One way we might increase non-human suffering in the future is by simply continuing the ongoing exponential increase in the number of animals suffering on factory farms. Additionally, there is the risk of vastly increasing wild-animal suffering, such as by spreading wild animals to other planets — something that certain groups are currently advocating (Tomasik, 2014d). In fact, we have *already* sent animals to space. In 2019, a private spacecraft flew to the moon with thousands of tardigrades, also known as water bears, which are small invertebrates with around 200 neurons (Martin et al., 2017; Oberhaus, 2019). (The spacecraft crashed in its attempt to land, but it is speculated that the tardigrades may have survived, at least for a while, as they are known to be able to survive harsh conditions, including prolonged exposure to space, Jönsson et al., 2008; Oberhaus, 2019.)

Even if these risks of increasing suffering on a large scale do not seem particularly likely, they are still very much worth reducing given the stakes. The same can be said about another class of risks, namely the risk of creating suffering in new kinds of beings. This could, for example, be in the form of future sentient machines (Ziesche & Yampolskiy, 2019), highly developed in vitro "mini brains" (Trujillo et al., 2019), or brains in vats (Vrselja et al., 2019). Such risks may seem remote and unduly speculative, yet given that the further development of such technologies might vastly increase the potential size of future moral catastrophes, these risks deserve to be taken seriously, including at the level of public policy (cf. Tomasik, 2011; Baumann, 2017a).

As philosopher Thomas Metzinger writes, a potential risk of the development of new kinds of conscious beings is that we might "dramatically increase the overall amount of suffering in the universe, for example via [...] the rapid duplication of conscious systems on a vast scale" (Metzinger, 2018, p. 3). In light of such dangers, Metzinger recommends a policy of banning all research that "risks or directly aims at the creation of synthetic phenomenology", as well as greater funding of research into the ethics and risks of creating novel systems capable of conscious experience (Metzinger, 2018, p. 3; 2021).

A ban on attempts to create new kinds of suffering beings would also be well in line with the bounding approach to worst-case risks outlined in the previous chapter, as such a ban could help serve as a protective wall preventing us from getting into the "danger zone" where novel technologies can vastly increase suffering (cf. Baumann, 2019).

10.5 What to Do?

The last few sections have outlined three classes of problems: two pertaining to existing sources of non-human suffering, and one pertaining to future risks. The pressing question that arises is how we can best address these problems. One level at which we can approach this question is the broad level of what society at large should ideally do, which is perhaps the easiest question to answer given its idealized nature, at least with respect to some of the main issues:

- Outlaw all industrial practices of imposing intense suffering and death on non-human beings for trivial purposes, such as taste and fashion preferences (cf. Cochrane, 2012, ch. 4; Vinding, 2014; Huemer, 2019; Singer, 2020b).

- Fund research on and eventually implement large-scale interventions that help non-human beings in nature (cf. Horta, 2017b; 2019; Johannsen, 2020, ch. 3).

- Outlaw the creation of novel forms of suffering (cf. Metzinger, 2018; 2021; Ziesche & Yampolskiy, 2019).

This is essentially just to say that we, as a society, should seek to prevent the sources of suffering outlined in the previous sections (though I do not claim these proposals are by any means sufficient, as there is surely far more to be said at the broad idealist level; see e.g. Horta, 2013b; Animal Ethics, 2017; Cochrane, 2018; 2020; Sebo, 2022).

Yet since the large-scale adoption of these laws and ideals is quite remote from where we are today, the main question I shall focus on here is how we can best prevent these sources of suffering at the marginal realist level. What can individuals and organizations do today in the political realm to reduce non-human suffering most effectively?

10.6 Individual Actions

A first step that everyone seeking to help non-human beings can take is to learn more about the issues reviewed above. Specifically, this means learning more about:

- The main arguments concerning speciesism and the implications of rejecting it (Horta, 2010b; Animal Ethics, 2012; Vinding, 2015).

- The problem of wild-animal suffering (Tomasik, 2015a; Animal Ethics, 2016a; 2020a; Johannsen, 2020).

- The best strategies for reducing wild-animal suffering (Animal Ethics, 2013; 2022; Johannsen, 2020).

- The difference between animal ethics and environmental ethics (Animal Ethics, 2014; Horta, 2018; Faria & Paez, 2019).

- The arguments surrounding the exploitation of non-human animals (Vinding, 2014; 2020f; Huemer, 2019; Singer, 2020b).

- The importance of the long-term future (Animal Ethics, 2018; Vinding, 2020a, 9.8.3; Baumann, 2020f).

- The risks of increasing non-human suffering in the future (Tomasik, 2011; Althaus & Gloor, 2016; Baumann, 2017a; Vinding, 2020a, ch. 14).

This recommendation of educating oneself may sound trivial, and perhaps not particularly political. But the truth is that knowledge about these issues is crucial to identifying the right political strategies and policies. Optimal political advocacy requires the advocates themselves to be well-informed, and to take the suffering of *all* beings into account.

Unfortunately, there might be a kind of "bias blind spot" at work among animal advocates in this respect (cf. Pronin et al., 2002). That is, animal advocates may tend to see *others* as being ignorant and urgently in need of information, but not so much themselves, which is unfortunate given that we are *all* urgently in need of additional insights regarding the various problems of non-human suffering and their potential solutions. And the concrete step of educating oneself also happens to be an eminently feasible one, especially compared to the task of educating the morally apathetic.

Further educating oneself about the issues mentioned above is plausibly the most important first step one can take toward creating political improvements for non-human animals. The next, and closely related step is then to inform others about these issues. This includes the broader public in general, but also animal-focused organizations and political parties in particular. For most such organizations and parties do not, unfortunately, exhibit a thoroughly informed stance on most of the issues mentioned above. Such groups might be well-versed in the issue of animal exploitation specifically, but they usually seem much less informed about issues such as speciesism, wild-animal suffering, and the differences between environmental and animal ethics. Consequently, they tend to neglect these crucial issues.

Informing animal-focused organizations and political parties about these issues may well be more effective than trying to educate the general public. After all, such dedicated groups will tend to be the main source of information about animal issues for the general public (suggesting a strategy of "influencing the influencers"), as well as being the main instrument through which the public can push for improvements for non-human beings. And such pushes for betterment might only be as good as the organizations that serve as their formal mediators.

Another concrete thing one can do is to donate to organizations that do research and advocacy on the issues described above. One such organization is Animal Ethics, which works to inform people about speciesism, wild-animal suffering, and future risks of non-human suffering (see animal-ethics.org).

Political parties that seek to protect non-human animals are another potential donation target. Yet given their de facto neglect of most suffering beings, a donation to organizations with a more comprehensive focus seems considerably safer at this point. After all, many such political parties currently champion environmental ethics and policies that reflect little to no consideration of individual non-human beings (cf. Animal Ethics, 2014; Faria & Paez, 2019).

Finally, there is the option of devoting one's career to the cause of reducing non-human suffering. This could mean becoming a philosopher who explores the moral and political importance of non-human beings, or a social scientist who studies empirical questions concerning how we can best reduce non-human suffering, in the political realm or otherwise. Alternatively, one could become a full-time advocate for non-human beings, or a politician who works to reduce their suffering. More information about career choice for reducing non-human suffering can be found at animaladvocacycareers.org (see also Baumann, 2022).

10.7 Policies and Initiatives to Support

Which policies and initiatives should individuals and groups promote to best reduce non-human suffering? This is an open question that we should investigate in depth. Below are some proposals that we can explore further and potentially pursue in the near term.

10.7.1 Wild-Animal Suffering

There are many initiatives and policies that could already be realized today to help wild animals, such as interventions to help individual wild animals afflicted by disease or injury (Animal Ethics, 2016b; 2020b; 2020c). For example, a number of countries, including Sweden and Denmark, already have emergency call centers for non-human animals, as well as associated ambulances that are dispatched to help injured wild animals. Such ambulances are currently run by non-profit organizations that are mostly privately funded (e.g. Svenska Djurambulansen and Dyrenes Beskyttelse). But these initiatives should also be regarded as a public responsibility, and should receive greater public support, which would help expand these much needed and already widely used services — for instance, in Denmark, the animal ambulance service receives over 70,000 calls a year and dispatches more than 8,000 times (Toft, 2013).

Beyond such initiatives focused on helping individual animals, there are also many ways we already can and do help wild animals at the level of large-scale interventions (Horta, 2019). For example, we have developed vaccines that protect wild boars against swine fever and tuberculosis, as well as vaccines that protect various wild animals against rabies, and which have eradicated the disease in large geographical areas (Koenig et al., 2007; Garrido et al., 2011; Maki et al., 2017; Animal Ethics, 2020d).

As Oscar Horta has noted, these interventions have so far mostly been done because we were trying to benefit humans in particular, which hints at the potential for helping wild animals on a large scale if we intervened for their sake (Horta, 2019, 9:30-10:00). Supporting further research on and implementations of such vaccination programs could serve not only to help a lot of wild animals in the near term, but also to expand already existing concerns for wild animals, and to further reinforce the view that we can and should help wild animals who are suffering.

More ambitious interventions have also been proposed, such as using already available technologies to create a "welfare state for elephants" (Pearce, 2015), which could then pave the way for still more ambitious interventions in the future, when we are better informed about how to intervene safely. Such ambitious interventions may include using CRISPR-based gene drives to reduce wild-animal suffering (Pearce, 2016; Johannsen, 2017; 2020, ch. 5).

It is worth noting that many *concrete* ways of helping wild animals seem widely supported — e.g. nursing individual animals back to health and distributing vaccinations — whereas people tend to be more resistant to the idea of helping when the issue is presented in more abstract terms, which is a reason to focus on concrete interventions when introducing the issue (Pearce, 2015, p. 162; Horta, 2020, 59:00-60:30).

Another important task that people working in this field have emphasized is the establishment of welfare biology — the study of the welfare of all sentient animals — as a proper field of study (Ng, 1995; Faria & Horta, 2019; Soryl et al., 2021). This is first of all important for helping us better understand the ways in which wild animals suffer and how we might help them, but also for establishing a more formal and well-regarded basis on which policies for helping wild animals can eventually be based in the future (Animal Ethics, 2020f).

10.7.2 Ending Animal Farming

Many promising strategies have likewise been proposed to address humanity's industrial exploitation and cruel treatment of non-human animals. One such strategy is to push for greater enforcement of existing laws against animal cruelty and the pollution caused by animal farming, which some have argued is a strategy that, if pursued with ambition, could serve as an important step toward undermining factory farming (Merkel, 2015; Shooster, 2018). That is, several countries already have laws that forbid many common practices employed by factory farms and slaughterhouses, but a problem is that serious attempts at prosecuting the companies and the farms that perform these practices have rarely been made (Sunstein, 2009, II.A-B; Shooster, 2018).

A consideration favoring this approach is that greater enforcement of existing laws against the most egregious (yet sadly common) forms of cruelty likely would find broad public support, even as there are still only relatively few people who identify strongly as animal rights supporters. Moreover, animal advocates in the United Kingdom have already used this strategy of documenting breaches of law and failures of law enforcement, and have successfully pushed for the enforcement of laws that nobody else worked to enforce, in some cases leading to the abolition of exploitative practices and institutions (Tyson, 2013; see also legalimpactforchickens. org).

Along with pushing for the enforcement of existing laws, we can also push for increasingly extensive bans on cruel and exploitative practices, with the end goal of abolishing all such practices (Sunstein, 2009, II.C-D). Several well-known politicians have already taken ambitious steps in this direction, and said that factory farming should be abolished. In the United

States, these politicians include recent presidential candidates Tulsi Gabbard and Cory Booker (Matthews, 2019; Singer, 2020a). In other countries, there are entire political parties that call for the end of factory farming, including the Dutch Party for the Animals ("Partij voor de Dieren"), which gained 3.2 percent of the vote in the Dutch general election of 2017, and which at the time of writing has a total of 80 elected representatives, including one in the European Parliament (Party for the Animals, 2020).

Such animal-focused parties and politicians can create positive change not only through their direct influence on legislation and policies, but also by putting the issue of animal suffering on the political agenda, by forcing other political parties to take the issue more seriously, and by changing society's attitudes toward non-human animals. These more indirect effects may well end up being more significant than the direct effects.

We can all join and support the growing international movement that seeks to protect non-human animals from suffering through political and legal change — whether by engaging in local political groups, reaching out to representatives, or by supporting international efforts to secure legal protections for non-human animals (cf. Horta, 2013b; Peters, 2016; Brels, 2017). (Though as hinted above, a worry with respect to this broader movement in its current form, including the most successful animal parties, is the lack of awareness of the problem of wild-animal suffering, which is a critical omission that must be rectified, cf. Johannsen, 2020.)

Beyond pushing for policies that ban an increasing range of cruel and exploitative practices, it also seems worth pushing for an end to subsidies to animal agriculture, which keep the price of animal products artificially low (Horta, 2013b). For example, around 20 percent of the total budget of the European Union — roughly 30 billion euros annually — is devoted to livestock subsidies, and globally, an estimated 35 billion US dollars are spent subsidizing the fishing industry each year, in effect significantly increasing the number of beings who are killed in the horrific ways mentioned above (Teffer, 2019; Sumaila et al., 2019). If we are to subsidize food products, it would make more sense to subsidize plant-based foods — or to invest in the development of new foods — that are less harmful to both non-humans and humans alike.

Indeed, human health concerns alone provide a strong case for ending subsidies to all forms of animal agriculture, and for phasing out this harmful institution altogether. One reason is the increased risk of zoonotic diseases: many of the greatest pandemics of the previous century have spread to humans due to animal agriculture or animal consumption, including the 1918 flu (50-100 million deaths) and AIDS (30-40 million deaths) (Greger, 2020a; 2020b, ch. 1-2). And the same is true of many of the largest epidemics so far in this century (Greger, 2020b, "Prologue").

Another compelling reason not to subsidize animal agriculture is that greater consumption of animal products significantly increases the risk of many of the leading causes of human misery and death — including cardiovascular disease and cancer, which together are responsible for around half of all human deaths globally (Ritchie & Roser, 2018) — while a greater consumption of fruits and vegetables actively reduces many of these risks, including the risk of depression (Wang et al., 2014; Greger, 2015, Part I; Conner et al., 2017; Madigan & Karhu, 2018; Saghafian et al., 2018).

Making people aware of this information may be helpful for ending the extensive subsidies currently provided to the animal industry, and for ultimately phasing out this industry that harms both humans and non-humans with impunity.

10.7.3 Risks of Novel Forms of Suffering

Of the three idealist policy proposals listed earlier, the proposal pertaining to future risks — "outlaw the creation of novel forms of suffering" — might be the most feasible one in the foreseeable future. For unlike in the case of animal farming and wild-animal suffering, there is not yet an extensive problem to ameliorate in this case. There is "merely" a potential for things to go very badly (Metzinger, 2018; 2021).

This does not, of course, mean that it would be easy to create legal safeguards against the creation of novel forms of suffering. It may, after all, be difficult to specify what kinds of novel brains we should protect, not to mention the difficulty of convincing politicians that any protection is necessary. These complications suggest that the ideal strategy might be to first engage with scientists and ethicists whose work relates to these risks — a group of experts who can contribute important insights, and who are likely to be taken seriously by legislators (cf. Harris, 2021).

An encouraging sign is that many such experts already show considerable concern for the issue (Harris & Reese, 2021). Even so, one would probably need to go about these efforts in a thoughtful manner, as one could easily frame the issue in a way that makes it seem alarmist or uninformed. Outright advocacy is likely ill-advised, as opposed to making reasoned arguments about the ethics of risk and the moral significance of suffering, including uncertain suffering (cf. Birch, 2017; Knutsson & Munthe, 2017; Ziesche & Yampolskiy, 2019; Metzinger, 2021).

10.8 One Movement for All Sentient Beings?

The three broad issues outlined above — wild-animal suffering, animal farming, and the risk of creating novel forms of suffering — may well end up being addressed by the same movement eventually: the movement to protect non-human beings from suffering. In fact, significant steps toward such a single movement have already been taken.

For example, as an expansion of our current human rights framework, Alasdair Cochrane has defended "sentient rights" — rights pertaining to *all* sentient beings purely on the basis of their sentience (Cochrane, 2013; see also Kymlicka, 2018). Moreover, a number of recent academic books have explored issues of non-human rights from a broad perspective that includes both non-human animals and (potential) future sentient robots (see e.g. Schulz & Raman, 2020; Gellers, 2020). And various social movements that seek to promote moral concern for all sentient beings have likewise emerged, such as (parts of) the effective altruism movement and the burgeoning movement of people who are united under the label of "sentientism". These developments suggest that it may be a strategic mistake to view the three broad issues outlined above as independent. Moreover, the significant commonalities between these issues probably have important implications for how we can best address them.

First, it seems likely that the people trying to address these distinct sources of suffering will have a lot to teach each other concerning which tactics have proven most successful. Second, a more unified and cohesive movement that can push for betterment for sentient beings in concert may be more effective than a more disjointed movement; and greater protections for one class of non-human beings might well pave the way for greater protections for others. Lastly, it seems that our efforts to reduce suffering for all sentient beings will generally be better if they reflect a more complete perspective of the problems and risks we are facing, including long-term risks of astronomical suffering (cf. Tomasik, 2011; Althaus & Gloor, 2016). Such a more complete perspective would likely update our priorities and strategies in crucial ways.

For instance, the importance of the long-term future has significant implications for how animal advocacy should ideally be done today (Animal Ethics, 2018; Baumann, 2020f). It means, among other things, that we should not lose sight of the bigger picture, despite the unspeakably severe and horrific urgencies of the present. Specifically, it means that we should be mindful of various risks of backlash that could potentially hurt not just non-human animals today, but also vast numbers of non-human beings in the future. Even if the risk of very bad outcomes due to backlash seems small, it is still very much worth reducing (cf. Baumann, 2017a).

There are strong reasons to think that the reduction of such risks requires us to adopt a highly cooperative approach. This not only implies a non-violent approach, but also the avoidance of needless controversy and antagonism (Vinding, 2020d). For even if we grant that alternative strategies can be justified in principle, the strategic reality is that highly antagonistic strategies will tend to be ineffective as a practical matter (Chenoweth & Stephan, 2011; Cochrane, 2018, 7.5). In the short term, unfriendly messaging is most likely to reduce people's receptivity. In the long term, it could well cause a growing resentment and a greater resistance to the cause than there would otherwise be. Such resentment and hostility could be a significant risk factor for worst-case outcomes (Baumann, 2019).

Thus, when we factor in risks of worst-case outcomes, we find even more strong reasons to pursue a cooperative approach that avoids antagonizing people. Yet such an approach is, to be clear, still compatible with being honest and assertive about the moral importance of non-human beings and their suffering (Taft, 2016, ch. 8; Vinding, 2020d).

10.9 Four Broad Strategies

Ideally, we should pursue actions that simultaneously address all three of the issues described above. Such broadly helpful actions might not always be the best way to reduce non-human suffering in practice, yet it probably makes sense to mostly pursue strategies that pertain to as many non-human beings as possible — not least considering the importance of the long-term future and the large number of non-human beings it will likely contain. Failing to take action to reduce the suffering of these many beings when we can is a missed opportunity.

Below are four broad strategies that may be helpful to this end, and which at the very least deserve further exploration.

10.9.1 Focusing on Anti-Speciesism

An approach centered on arguments against speciesism might be particularly effective for various reasons. First, there is the fact that the case against speciesism is surprisingly strong, indeed far stronger than even most animal advocates seem to realize. Virtually nobody would accept any of the commonly proposed counterarguments to defend discrimination in the case of human beings, regardless of these beings' traits or abilities, which reveals that most people do not in fact accept these counterarguments (cf. Horta, 2014). Animal advocates thus have a powerful tool on their hands that they mostly fail to utilize (cf. Horta, 2020, 9.10-16.40).

Beyond being remarkably strong, the case against speciesism also has the benefit of being exceptionally wide in its scope. It pertains to *all* non-human animals, both wild and domesticated, and it can readily be construed to pertain to all future non-human beings in general, as one may argue that novel kinds of sentient beings would themselves represent new species, even if they will not be biological.

A third consideration speaking in favor of an anti-speciesist approach is that it implies particularly *strong* moral duties toward individual non-human beings — again to a much greater extent than most animal advocates seem to appreciate. Specifically, it is widely accepted that we have moral duties toward human beings that go beyond not harming them, such as duties to help them in emergency situations, and the rejection of speciesism implies that we have similar duties toward non-human beings. That is, merely not harming them is not enough; we must actively help them when we can readily do so. To think otherwise is to engage in unjustified discrimination (Horta, 2010b; 2017b; Pearce, 2012; Vinding, 2015, ch. 5).

The case against speciesism thus suffices to establish that we should help wild animals when possible, and that we should work to reduce risks of future suffering for non-human beings. This goes far beyond the implications of the most common arguments employed by animal advocates, which tend to only pertain to animal exploitation in particular. And yet even if we were purely concerned with ending animal exploitation, there are tentative reasons to think that the anti-speciesist approach may in fact still be optimal.

For example, the organization Vegan Outreach conducted a randomized study (not peer-reviewed) in which they sought to examine diet change as a result of reading a variety of booklets with different messages. One booklet featured a case against speciesism, while the other booklets focused more on the cruelties of factory farming, or encouraged people to reduce their consumption of animal products. All the booklets caused a significant reduction in the amount of animal products people consumed, with the booklet focusing on speciesism leading to the greatest reduction on average, although the differences in the effects of the booklets were not statistically significant (Norris, 2016). Moreover, psychological research suggests that the rejection of speciesist beliefs is the main predictor of animal-free eating behaviors, implying that the best way to encourage such eating behaviors might be to challenge speciesist beliefs (Rosenfeld, 2019; Brockway, 2021).

Given the broad scope of anti-speciesist messaging, one could argue that we should generally pursue this approach even if it did significantly *worse* on the dimension of dietary change. So the fact that it seems to do about as well — and perhaps even better — on this dimension just serves to further support it (Vinding, 2016b; 2017). But it would be good if we had more empirical research on these matters, including on how best to increase concern for wild animals and future non-human beings more generally.

Two brief objections to the anti-speciesist approach are worth considering. The perhaps most common one is that (anti-)speciesism is just too abstract a concept for people to understand or to act on. This objection seems intuitively plausible, but there are a few reasons to think that it is not all that compelling. First, the Vegan Outreach study mentioned above suggests that the concept of speciesism is not in fact too abstract for people to follow, and that it may even be among the ideal notions to focus on when trying to motivate people to make concrete changes.

Second, in relation to the claim that anti-speciesism is too abstract for people to act on, it is worth noting that an anti-speciesist framing is wholly compatible with a wide range of concrete recommendations, such as recommending people to get politically engaged or to change certain behaviors, and hence this approach does not really represent an obstacle to providing concrete recommendations (cf. Horta, 2020, 9.10-16.40). Furthermore, there is the point that many forms of discrimination, such as racism and sexism, are not too abstract or alien to most people. On the contrary, these forms of discrimination are both highly concrete and well-known, suggesting that there is a solid template on which the case against speciesism can readily be built (Vinding, 2016b).

Lastly, various scholars have argued that the best way to change public opinion may be to change the views of elites, whose opinions have a disproportionate influence on society at large, suggesting that *even if* anti-speciesist messaging could only be followed by a relatively small group of influential elites (which there are strong reasons to doubt), it could still make strategic sense to adopt this approach so as to appeal to these elites (Zaller, 1992; Pinker, 2012; Taylor, 2015).

Another objection is that it would be better to instead choose a framing focused on sentiocentrism or sentientism, the view that sentience is what matters morally. This view is not necessarily different from anti-speciesism at the substantive level, but the framing is nonetheless different. Unlike speciesism, sentientism does not refer to a form of discrimination, and this may be a reason to adopt an explicitly anti-speciesist approach. As noted above, other forms of discrimination, such as racism and sexism, already have an important place in our moral and political discourse, meaning that there is considerable precedent for a concept such as speciesism to gain prominence (Vinding, 2016b; Bonnardel, 2020). Such concepts relating to discrimination have proven quite amenable to human psychology (cf. Section 8.6). Sentientism, on the other hand, has relatively little such precedent. The most similar concept in mainstream discourse might be humanism, which seems less widely known and less able to evoke a sense of injustice than do concepts relating directly to forms of discrimination.

It is by no means clear whether anti-speciesist messaging represents the best way to reduce the suffering of non-human beings, and the issue of whether other framings and strategies might be better is very much worth exploring further. Moreover, it should be noted that different strategies can be combined (e.g. an anti-speciesist framing can complement a sentientist framing), and the effectiveness of a given strategy and messaging tactic likely also depends on the audience one is addressing. Still, the considerations above do seem to recommend a greater emphasis on anti-speciesism in our moral and political endeavor to reduce the suffering of all sentient beings.

10.9.2 Focusing on Institutional Change

Another strategic point is that an approach centered on institutional change generally seems better than a focus on individual consumer change. So rather than chiefly framing the issue of non-human suffering in terms of individual food choices, as is common today, it seems more productive to mostly frame the issue in terms of what we need to do as a society, at the level of our collective norms and policies (Reese, 2016; 2018, ch. 7; 2020).

A line of evidence that supports this claim comes from historical case studies of other social movements seeking to create social change, such as the British anti-slavery movement. While it can be difficult to derive transferable lessons from the successes and failures of past social movements, it seems that these movements have generally had greater success with institutional framings and tactics (compared to a focus on individual consumer change), which does provide some reason to think that institutional tactics might be similarly helpful for creating positive change for non-human beings (Harris, 2021).

Another piece of evidence that supports an institutional framing comes from a 2017 survey that asked a representative sample of US adults various questions regarding non-human animals and food choices. Not surprisingly, more than 97 percent agreed with the statement that "to eat animals or be vegetarian is a personal choice, and nobody has the right to tell me which one they think I should do" (Sentience Institute, 2017). In contrast, when the issue was framed in institutional terms, such as "I support a ban on the factory farming of animals" and "I support a ban on slaughterhouses", almost half expressed at least a moderate degree of support for such significant changes (Sentience Institute, 2017; these findings were replicated independently in Norwood & Murray, 2018).

This suggests that animal advocates have hitherto been betting on precisely the wrong framing — the framing that leads almost everyone to oppose change, rather than the framing that leads a very large number of people to agree with quite radical policies that benefit non-human animals. The significance of this error is only magnified when we consider that sweeping institutional changes can in principle be brought about in electoral democracies when more than 50 percent of the population favors them. And the error appears graver still when we consider how the focus on individual food choices also seems likely to harm wild animals and future non-human beings more generally, as people would probably be more willing to support policies that help such beings if the case for considering non-human interests were not always made in the context of individual food choices, but instead made in terms of institutional change (Vinding, 2016b).

What does all this mean in more specific terms? For one, it suggests that political parties focused on reducing the suffering of non-human beings should limit their focus on individual consumer change. They should avoid calling themselves things like "The Vegan Party" or "The Vegetarian Party", names that focus on a select group of aspiring do-gooders whom other people are likely to display negative attitudes toward, a phenomenon known as "do-gooder derogation" (Minson & Monin, 2011). Instead, it seems more strategic to choose a name with broader appeal, like the uniquely successful

Dutch "Party for the Animals", a name that focuses on the beings whose interests the party is supposed to protect. By contrast, naming a party after the aspiring do-gooders themselves may appear somewhat self-centered and even off-putting, especially to outsiders.

It likewise seems better if these political parties mostly focus on institutional aims such as ending factory farming, shutting down slaughterhouses, and reducing wild-animal suffering — aims that can tap into a large reservoir of support that is unreachable when the issue is framed in terms of individual consumer change (cf. Sentience Institute, 2017; Ryder, 2018, 15.20-16.10).

To be clear, the point is not that there is no room for advocacy focused on individual actions and consumer change, but rather that messaging focused on institutional change likely should be given greater emphasis, and that people who care about non-human beings should organize around such institutional aims to a much greater extent (Reese, 2016; 2020; Harris, 2021).

10.9.3 Calling for the Abolition of Slaughterhouses

A specific form of institutional change that seems worth advocating for is the outlawing of slaughterhouses. This is supported by a number of arguments. First, the abolition of slaughterhouses represents a highly concrete policy aim, which might be helpful when seeking to create real-world change. Receivers will have little doubt about what a march to end slaughterhouses is calling for, whereas the aim of a generic animal rights march may be a lot less clear.

Second, the strategy finds support in the fact that a large number of people already endorse a ban on slaughterhouses: as mentioned above, almost half of the US population expressed support for such a ban (Sentience Institute, 2017; Norwood & Murray, 2018). This again stands in stark contrast to some generic animal rights march or message, especially when the focus is on personal consumption, which appears to lead the vast majority of people to support the status quo (Reese, 2020).

Relatedly, people may not feel particularly complicit in the horrors of slaughterhouses, which most people probably see as wrongdoings done by someone else, whereas a message focused on the consumption of animal products is likely to evoke much stronger feelings of complicity and guilt, and thus to reduce attitudes of receptivity and support (Pearce, 2020). This dynamic might help explain why people evaluate statements about personal consumption so differently from statements about institutional change, even when the ultimate implications of the respective statements are largely equivalent (cf. Sentience Institute, 2017).

Another important reason that speaks in favor of this strategy is that slaughterhouses are horrifying and shocking to most people. A focus on slaughterhouses effectively highlights the cruelty and brutality of animal agriculture, which helps undermine the wishful and self-deceived notions about idyllic and virtually painless animal lives that usually provide the core rationalization for this institution. A message focused on slaughter-houses forces people to confront the horrific violence, death, and suffering that is involved in the "animal industry" in a way that probably few other messages can. For this reason, most people also seem unlikely to strongly oppose a call for the end of slaughterhouses. As David Pearce notes, it is difficult to imagine rival "Save our slaughterhouses!" rallies (Pearce, 2020; stopabattoirs.org).

In pursuing this strategy, it would be important to ensure that fish are also mentioned very prominently, again since they are the vertebrates killed in by far the largest numbers, and arguably in the most horrific ways. Fish are usually not killed in traditional slaughterhouses, but the core message of opposing the needless slaughter and torment of other sentient beings — and thus opposing slaughterhouses in a broad sense of the term — would clearly still apply to them. Raising awareness about the horrors of fish slaughter may also be an effective way to communicate the cruelty and magnitude of the horrors humanity is currently perpetrating against non-human beings.

An objection to this strategy might be that the suffering of wild animals is much greater in scale and far more neglected than the suffering caused by animal agriculture, and hence that we should instead devote most of our marginal resources to the reduction of wild-animal suffering (cf. Vinding, 2020b). This is certainly a strong argument for not focusing *exclusively* on the abolition of slaughterhouses, and perhaps even to not *primarily* focus on this aim on the margin. But this point does not rule out that the abolition of slaughterhouses could still be an important component in our portfolio of strategies to reduce animal suffering, along with the other strategies mentioned in this section.

After all, different strategies need not be mutually exclusive: a general anti-speciesist approach is clearly compatible with a strategy of calling for the abolition of slaughterhouses, not least given that anti-speciesism itself directly implies the end of all slaughterhouses. Conversely, a focus on abolishing slaughterhouses might well be beneficial to the general cause of anti-speciesism — partly because it may be a potent strategy for igniting people's moral concern, as such concern often seems especially kindled by deliberate wrongs performed by perpetrators (Tomasik, 2013b; Schein & Gray, 2017; Vinding, 2020a, 7.7); and partly because the abolition of slaughterhouses may serve as a pivotal step for humanity toward helping rather than harming non-human beings (Pearce, 2020).

10.9.4 Making Our Concern for Non-Human Beings Common Knowledge

Two levels of knowledge are worth distinguishing in the context of human coordination (De Freitas et al., 2019):

- **Private knowledge:** "where each person knows something, but knows nothing about what anyone else knows"

- **Common knowledge:** "where everybody knows that everybody else knows it"

Common knowledge is often explained with the story of *The Emperor's New Clothes*, in which everyone had private knowledge that the emperor was naked (as far as they could see), but they could not be sure that others saw the same, and hence it was not common knowledge. But the moment a child exclaimed that the emperor wore no clothes, it soon became common knowledge, and eventually everyone shouted the child's words in unison.

This story makes a deep point about the importance of common knowledge for social coordination, as the child's exclamation did not merely change the state of knowledge of the onlookers, but also enabled them to coordinate, emboldening them to act in ways they would not have otherwise dared, such as laughing and shouting at the emperor. Indeed, not only do psychological studies show that people cooperate significantly more and better when they have common knowledge (Pinker, 2016; De Freitas et al., 2019), but there are also countless real-world examples of the importance of common knowledge for creating social change — and, conversely, how the suppression of common knowledge can *prevent* social change.

For instance, in Saudi Arabia, most young men are privately in favor of female labor force participation, but they will not say this until they are informed that most other young men think the same (Sunstein, 2019, p. 6). Likewise, all dictatorships, from Nazi Germany to contemporary North Korea, have made it a priority to suppress all expressions of dissent, as such expressions risk creating common knowledge about people's opposition to the rulers and their totalitarian policies (Mercier, 2020, p. 134). As one North Korean coal miner noted: "I know that our regime is to blame for our situation. My neighbor knows our regime is to blame. But we're not stupid enough to talk about it" (as quoted in Mercier, 2020, p. 134).

The relevance of this point to our moral and political neglect of non-human suffering is that the concern we have for non-human beings is not yet common knowledge. That is, most people care about non-human animals, but most people, including most animal advocates, do not realize the extent to which most people care about non-human animals (Anderson & Tyler, 2018, p. 8). This may help explain why surveys of public views on this matter consistently surprise us, as our privately held beliefs and ideals are far more compassionate than our actions might suggest.

For example, in the 2017 survey mentioned earlier, more than 80 percent of people expressed agreement with the statement that "farmed animals have roughly the same ability to feel pain and discomfort as humans", with about 30 percent agreeing strongly (Sentience Institute, 2017; Norwood & Murray, 2018). More than 60 percent of people agreed that "the factory farming of animals is one of the most important social issues in the world today", and around 40 percent of people said they would be at least somewhat likely to join a public demonstration against "the problems of factory farming" if asked by a friend (Sentience Institute, 2017; Norwood & Murray, 2018).

Another survey of more than 4,000 US adults found that 93 percent believed that chickens feel pain, 78 percent believed that fish feel pain, and a majority of respondents believed that insects such as honeybees (65 percent), ants (56 percent), and termites (52 percent) can feel pain. Among the minority of respondents who did not express agreement with the statement that these animals can experience pain, most expressed agnosticism rather than disagreement (Dullaghan et al., 2021, p. 3; see also Beggs & Anderson, 2020, pp. 10-11).

A similar survey conducted in the UK found that a majority agreed that honey bees (73 percent), shrimps (62 percent), caterpillars (58 percent), and flies (54 percent) can feel pain, and even more people thought that lobsters (83 percent), octopuses (80 percent), and crabs (78 percent) experience pain (Rethink Priorities, 2021).

Moreover, a US poll from 1996 found that 67 percent of people expressed at least some agreement with the statement that a "[non-human] animal's right to live free of suffering is just as important as a [human] person's right to live free of suffering", with 38 percent agreeing strongly (Deseret News, 1996).

A US Gallup poll from 2015 yielded similar results, with 32 percent of people indicating that, among three different statements, the one that came the closest to their view was that "[non-human] animals deserve the exact same rights as people to be free from harm and exploitation" (42 percent of female respondents agreed with the statement, as did 39 percent of Democrats). Meanwhile, 62 percent held that non-human animals deserve *some* protection from harm and exploitation, whereas only three percent thought that "animals don't need much protection from harm and exploitation" (Riffkin, 2015).

Additionally, a recent study in the UK found that most meat eaters consider vegetarianism and veganism to be ethical (77 percent and 72 percent, respectively) as well as healthy (more than 72 percent and 50 percent, respectively) (Bryant, 2019).

Making such beliefs and attitudes common knowledge should plausibly be a high priority: to simply document people's expressed views of non-human suffering and its moral importance, and to then publicize the results. This is important for two principal reasons. First, it makes it clear to politicians that the public actually *does* care about this issue, and that it wants to see legislators take this issue seriously (even if it is not most voters' primary concern). Second, it helps make the general public aware of the already widespread concern that exists for non-human animals, at least at the level of people's expressed ideals, which may in turn embolden them to stand by their values more firmly.

Indeed, making prevailing attitudes common knowledge might effectively reverse the social pressure: where people otherwise thought that public opinion went against their concern for non-human animals, and thus chose to hold back from expressing their views, the realization that a large fraction of the public shares these concerns may encourage them to speak up, suddenly giving them the feeling that the wind of social pressure is in their favor rather than against them. (And this would largely be true, as long as the problems and objectives are phrased in institutional terms.)

Furthermore, not only may people with sympathy for the cause feel more willing to speak up, but most people will likely also (slowly) increase their actual level of concern as they become aware of other people's pro-animal attitudes. After all, public attitudes and social pressure are among the strongest influences on people's views (cf. Haidt, 2001; Reese, 2018, ch. 6).

This is then another powerful tool that is not being employed to anywhere near its full capacity: continually broadcasting people's own stated attitudes — through popular articles, social media, documentaries, etc. — so as to make these attitudes common knowledge. And unlike in the case of oppressive dictatorships, there is really nobody who forcefully prevents us from employing this strategy. We are simply not choosing to use it, probably to the great detriment of non-human beings.

10.10 Plausible Proxies and Politics for All Sentient Beings

What do the three proxies outlined in the previous chapter imply for the political endeavor of reducing non-human suffering? Below is a brief exploration of each of them in turn. In many cases, they serve to further underscore key points made above.

10.10.1 Greater Levels of Cooperation

Recall that cooperation failures may be among the main risk factors for worst-case outcomes, both because they can cause immense suffering directly and because they can impede moral progress, implying that we should pursue a highly cooperative approach. Committing ourselves to this high road can admittedly be challenging in a context of continual violence against non-human beings on an immense scale. But a few considerations should make it clear that we owe it to non-human beings to make our best efforts in this regard.

First, there is the point that anything but a peaceful and cooperative approach most likely would be ineffective, indeed counterproductive, for the non-human beings suffering today (Chenoweth & Stephan, 2011; Cochrane, 2018, 7.5). Second, there is the consideration that an uncooperative approach likely increases the risk of worst-case outcomes with vast amounts of suffering for non-human beings in the future, whether they be farmed animals, wild animals, or new kinds of non-human beings (Tomasik, 2011; Baumann, 2017a; Vinding, 2020d).

Those who are strongly dedicated to reducing the suffering of non-human beings stand at a crossroads. They can either become a faction that wins people's (already quite sympathetic) hearts and minds through a cordial and cooperative approach, or they can become a faction that alienates the rest of society, and thereby risk reducing people's moral concern for non-human beings. Failing to adopt a cooperative approach would be a grave mistake at this critical juncture, especially when we consider the bigger picture and the risk of outcomes that are far worse than our current condition.

It is an open question how we can best promote a cooperative approach, but some key pieces of the puzzle probably include the avoidance of tribal us-them dynamics, the promotion of common knowledge about the extent to which concern for non-human beings is shared, and seeking to advance mutual understanding and win-win compromises when possible (cf. Tomasik, 2013a).

10.10.2 Better Values

Improving humanity's values is in a sense both a requirement for and the likely end result of greater political concern for non-human suffering. So this proxy is already quite strongly correlated with the broader political aim outlined in this chapter. Yet it is still worth asking *how* we can best steer toward such improvements in humanity's values. I have said quite a bit about this already, yet an additional point worth highlighting is that it is likely to involve a significant degree of pragmatism and incrementalism.

That is, significantly increasing humanity's concern for non-human beings will not happen in a flash, and to think that it will or could is probably counterproductive and apt to motivate suboptimal strategies. Instead, it seems wiser to seek to gradually increase humanity's concern for non-human beings, with concrete and realistic steps. This is not to say these steps must be unambitious — as noted above, anti-speciesism is highly ambitious and demanding in terms of its implications, and making the case against speciesism to the leaders and activists of tomorrow is both a concrete and realistic endeavor. What it does mean, however, is that we should adopt a long-term perspective and seek to make patient investments to the benefit of *all* sentient beings, including those who will exist in the future.

Especially important is that we avoid pushing people toward worse values, which is sadly a real risk, and potentially an extremely consequential one. This is yet another reason not to pursue some immediate change that is predictably unrealistic and unpopular: not only can it delay progress, but it also risks causing moral regress and backlash, the avoidance of which should be a high priority. Likewise, it is probably best to advance concern for non-human suffering in a non-partisan way — such as by highlighting that it is a shared concern among many prominent progressives, libertarians, and religious conservatives (see e.g. Nozick, 1974, p. 38; Singer, 1975; Scully, 2002; Linzey, 2009; Huemer, 2019; Nussbaum, 2022) — so as to prevent apathy for non-human suffering from becoming an entrenched and defining feature of any political faction.

10.10.3 Greater Capacity to Reduce Suffering

The third and final proxy — increasing our level of competence as moral agents — recommends a similarly gradualist approach. That is, to continuously build up the insights and resources that enable us to competently reduce the suffering of all sentient beings, such as by attracting promising minds and voices, and by pursuing relevant research.

Beyond increasing the competencies of the most dedicated agents of compassion (i.e. capacity-building at the marginal realist level), we also need to make our institutions at large better able to prevent the suffering of non-human beings. This not only involves legislation that protects non-human beings from suffering (Cochrane, 2018; 2020), but also the promotion of robust institutions that are able to steer us safely away from (novel) atrocities. After all, our institutions will probably be a key determinant of future outcomes, suggesting that compassionate agents should make it a priority to help improve the safety and worst-case resilience of our institutions (some proposals to this end are reviewed in Chapter 14).

10.11 Conclusion

There are three major problems when it comes to non-human suffering: wild-animal suffering, industrial animal exploitation, and the risk of creating new forms of suffering in the future. A crucial step toward addressing these problems is to inform ourselves and others about them, and to adopt a comprehensive approach that takes all of these problems into consideration.

Beyond that, there are various concrete policies and initiatives that we can support to push us in better directions in these respects, such as the development and employment of vaccines to help wild animals, progressively extensive bans on cruel and exploitative practices, and prohibitions against the creation of new forms of suffering.

In terms of more general strategies, there are good reasons to focus on anti-speciesism, to frame issues in institutional terms, to call for the end of slaughterhouses, and to make it common knowledge that people express both high levels of concern for non-human beings and high levels of support for institutional changes that benefit non-human beings.

The challenge of reducing suffering for all sentient beings can admittedly feel overwhelming. But the truth is that we *can* take real, incremental steps toward betterment and toward reducing the risk of worst-case outcomes. Our task is to ensure that we take the right such steps.

11

Liberty

The notion of liberty is perhaps the single most prominent notion in political philosophy. What does liberty entail? What, if any, are the legitimate limits to liberty? And of special relevance for our purposes: what are the optimal forms and degrees of liberty for reducing extreme suffering? These are the questions I will explore in this chapter.

11.1 Defining Liberty

Philosopher Isaiah Berlin famously defended the distinction between negative and positive liberty (Berlin, 1969). Negative liberty may be summarized as "freedom *from*", specifically freedom from coercion and interference by others. It is essentially the freedom to be left alone. (Berlin used the terms "freedom" and "liberty" interchangeably, and I will do the same here.) Positive liberty, on the other hand, may be summarized as "freedom *to*". Berlin specifically defined positive liberty as the freedom to overcome limits imposed by nature and to be one's own master, guided by one's own values and reasons rather than uncontrolled desires. That is, just as we can be free from enslavement and limitations imposed by other people (negative liberty), we can also be free from enslavement and limitations imposed by nature and by our own "unbridled passions" (Berlin, 1969, II). More broadly defined, positive liberty is the freedom to act on a wide range of choices in accordance with one's own will (Tuckness & Wolf, 2016, 2.28).

These two concepts of liberty are no doubt closely related. For example, if other people enslave us, or otherwise prevent us from developing our own values and capacities, then we obviously cannot be free in the sense of acting on our own values. A significant degree of negative liberty is a precondition for positive liberty. But it is also clear that negative liberty is not a *sufficient* condition for positive liberty — after all, people left completely to their own devices can still develop addictions that they themselves would prefer not to have, and a person stuck on a barren island with perfect negative liberty may nonetheless be unable to even survive (Tuckness & Wolf, 2016, 2.29).

Moreover, it might be that some limits to negative liberties will in turn increase positive liberties, and even increase negative liberties themselves (cf. Holmes & Sunstein, 1999; Konczal, 2021). For instance, if a foreign army threatens to conquer and enslave an entire society, it is at least conceivable that certain infringements on negative liberties, such as forced conscription and taxation, would be the only way to organize a sufficient defense against the aggressor, and against much greater infringements on liberty. This highlights some of the complexities and tradeoffs that can arise in the context of liberty, even when we talk about the same kind of liberty.

Many other varieties and definitions of liberty have been delineated. For instance, Milton Friedman distinguished three kinds of freedom: economic freedom (the freedom to buy and sell goods and services), civil freedom (e.g. freedom of expression and the freedom of peaceful assembly), and political freedom (e.g. the freedom to elect one's politicians). Friedman argued that these forms of freedom are also closely interrelated, as they tend to occur together, yet that they are nonetheless distinct, with British Hong Kong being an example of a society with significant economic and civil freedom, yet with no political freedom, as citizens of British Hong Kong could not vote for their leaders (Friedman, 1962, p. ix).

A similar variety of definitions exist when it comes to the term "liberalism". Philosopher Edwin van de Haar divides liberalism into three broad categories: classical liberalism, social liberalism, and libertarianism (van de Haar, 2015a; 2015b). These positions all place great importance on liberty, yet they tend to emphasize it in different ways. Classical liberalism favors limited government and is associated with negative liberty, while social liberalism favors a greater role for government in promoting positive liberties, while still protecting basic negative liberties. According to van de Haar, the main originators of classical liberalism are David Hume and Adam Smith, while social liberalism is strongly inspired by the views of John Stuart Mill, with John Rawls being an influential figure in the modern social liberal tradition.

Libertarianism, by comparison, regards negative liberty as even more absolute than does classical liberalism, and it is, according to van de Haar, sub-divided into two distinct positions. The first is anarcho-capitalism, the view that all institutions should be private and hence that there should be no coercive state, and the second is minarchism, the view that the state should only be responsible for functions such as the military, the police, and courts. (Anarcho-capitalists and minarchists mostly seem to have an empirical disagreement about whether negative liberties are best protected with or without a state.) Influential thinkers in the libertarian tradition include Herbert Spencer, Ayn Rand, and Murray Rothbard (van de Haar, 2015b).

Given the multitude of definitions of liberty — indeed, Isaiah Berlin claimed that historians of ideas have recorded more than 200 definitions of liberty (Berlin, 1969, I) — it makes little sense to simply talk about increasing or decreasing liberty as though it were an unambiguous and one-dimensional concept. We need to be more precise as to what kind of liberty we are talking about.

11.2 Preliminary Clarifications

To reiterate, a strong focus on reducing suffering is compatible with other values that one may consider intrinsically important, including liberties of various kinds. This means that there are two distinct questions worth asking here. The first is the moral question concerning which forms of liberty, if any, we consider intrinsically valuable or important, while the second is the empirical question of which liberties are optimal for minimizing suffering.

I will not say much on the first question here, beyond briefly noting why I primarily focus on the latter question. A relatively strong claim that has been advanced is that liberty is only good to the extent that it reduces suffering. This view has been defended by Richard Ryder, who further argues that liberty, both positive and negative, is highly conducive to reducing suffering (Ryder, 2001, pp. 92-97; 2006, pp. 22-26). John Stuart Mill similarly held that liberty is good purely because of its effects on the well-being of sentient individuals — "I regard utility as the ultimate appeal on all ethical questions" — and defended strong negative liberties on this basis (Mill, 1859, p. 9; 1863, ch. 5).

The following analysis is not predicated on these views, as it is wholly compatible with granting intrinsic value to liberty, of various kinds. I should note, however, that the moral view I myself endorse does entail that the reduction of extreme suffering always overrides the (purported) intrinsic value of any kind of liberty. That is, an action or policy that reduces extreme suffering — by which I mean suffering that the sufferer would find unbearable — is, in my view, morally right even if it fails to respect any given liberty (cf. Vinding, 2020a, ch. 4-5). This is why I am principally interested in the empirical question concerning which liberties are most conducive to reducing suffering: given my view of the moral importance of extreme suffering, further clarifications of the intrinsic importance of various forms of liberty will have limited practical significance.

Yet it is hardly critical whether one agrees with my particular view of the importance of extreme suffering, since the analysis that follows will likely still apply, in the main, to most views that entail a strong focus on reducing suffering. For example, if one holds that it takes *a certain amount* of extreme suffering to override a given liberty, the empirical analysis may still be largely convergent (cf. Enoch, 2021, pp. 8-10). (And I would argue that the more extreme suffering one is willing to allow for the sake of liberty per se — i.e. regardless of its consequences — the less plausible one's view of the intrinsic importance of liberty becomes, cf. Vinding, 2020a, ch. 4-5.)

I will primarily be concerned with questions pertaining to *human* liberty, and mostly set aside the issue of liberty for non-human animals; though this is not to say that I will ignore the effects that human liberty has on non-human animals, which will indeed be a central theme in this chapter.

11.3 The Case for Liberty Based on the Two-Step Ideal

Before diving into the case for or against liberty given the aim of reducing suffering, it is worth taking a step back to consider the two-step ideal proposed in the first chapter (i.e. clarifying our values and exploring how they can best be realized). Advancing this ideal is, after all, one of the core aims of this book, and honoring this ideal should, I submit, be considered important in itself as well (for reasons outlined in Section 1.3). And given that certain freedoms — especially freedom of expression and basic freedoms to live out one's values — are essential to the realization of the two-step ideal, the independent importance of this ideal seems to give us a *prima facie* reason to endorse such freedoms in practice, regardless of the specific moral view we may endorse.

And yet the case for liberty based on the two-step ideal is also relevant from the perspective of suffering-focused moral views in particular. For although reducing suffering might be the least controversial of moral aims, it is still, paradoxically, quite controversial to defend moral views that place a strong emphasis on this aim, and such views may be among the views that are at the greatest risk of being ignored or even suppressed. In other words, people with moral views that are neglected or at risk of being suppressed should be especially keen to endorse the two-step ideal and the case for free expression based on this ideal (Vinding, 2020c).

11.4 Reasons to Favor Liberty

It is worth noting that virtually every political thinker who has defended the reduction of suffering as a core political value has also been an avid defender of liberalism in some form. This includes John Stuart Mill and Henry Sidgwick in the utilitarian tradition, as well as Karl Popper and Judith Shklar, all of whom emphasized the centrality of individual freedom from oppression, and of free and open expression (Mill, 1859; Sidgwick, 1891; Popper, 1945; Shklar, 1989). The views of these philosophers should not, of course, be accepted on authority, yet their views still count as at least a weak reason to think that liberalism is conducive to the reduction of suffering.

More significant are the direct, object-level reasons in favor of liberty. Considering the issue from a marginal realist perspective, we see that there are strong reasons for any marginal political faction to endorse basic civil liberties, such as freedom of expression and freedom of assembly. Beyond the reasons mentioned in the previous section about the importance of being able to express one's moral views, there is also the simple fact that other people deeply value basic liberties to speak and act as they want, which strongly suggests that it would be a losing move for a political faction to oppose such liberties. For not only are these liberties highly regarded in liberal democracies as a cultural matter, but a preference for basic freedoms also seems to have deep roots in the human psyche.

Specifically, there is the phenomenon of psychological reactance: an unpleasant state experienced in the face of perceived restrictions of one's freedom to choose, which often leads to increased resistance and adverse reactions (Brehm & Brehm, 1981). Opposing others' freedoms may thus backfire by making people more hostile toward this anti-freedom faction itself, as well as by provoking people to endorse harmful values and practices in spite (cf. Vinding, 2020c, "Strategic reasons"). This is a strong reason for suffering-focused agents not to oppose others' civil liberties, and to make efforts to avoid even the *perception* of being opposed to others' liberties.

Yet the consideration above does not apply exclusively to political actors focused on reducing suffering. *Any* political faction that opposes the basic liberties of others may provoke reactance and hostility toward that particular faction, which is a reason to try to dissuade *any* political faction from opposing others' basic liberties, so as to reduce the risk of harmful political conflicts and reactance-motivated value regress in general, and to instead promote strong and widely shared norms in support of everyone's basic liberties.

Looking at the broad idealist level, we likewise find many reasons in favor of protecting and promoting basic civil liberties. One reason is that such liberties enable people to conduct what John Stuart Mill called "experiments in living" — i.e. to voluntarily test different ways of life. Such experiments can potentially benefit everyone by providing novel insights for anyone to use, both about the world in general and about how to live better lives in particular (Mill, 1859, ch. 4).

More fundamentally, there is the fact that people often suffer as a direct result of being deprived of basic freedoms and autonomy (Mill, 1859, ch. 3; Sumner, 1996, pp. 218-219; Ryder, 2006, pp. 22-23). For example, people trapped in North Korean concentration camps likely experience intense suffering even when they are not actively being tortured, due to their complete lack of control and fear of what will happen next. And North Korean individuals who are not currently trapped in concentration camps probably suffer for similar reasons, such as the pain of missing friends and relatives, not knowing what is happening to them, and the fear of being dragged away oneself.

A related reason to favor liberty, already gestured at in the previous chapter, is that the freedom to speak and criticize is a key element in enabling people to create common knowledge and to organize themselves against oppressive forces, such as totalitarian governments (cf. Section 10.9.4). Indeed, beyond already causing immense amounts of suffering today, totalitarian governments probably represent one of the main risk factors for worst-case outcomes with vast amounts of suffering (Caplan, 2008; Althaus & Baumann, 2020). Such risks of totalitarian outcomes constitute a compelling reason to endorse strong protections of the civil liberties of everyone, as a matter of firm principle.

Why of everyone? And why as a matter of firm principle? Because exceptions to this principle are precisely what can open the door to totalitarian oppression. Governments that suppress people's speech on the basis of case-by-case calculations cannot be trusted to make unbiased calculations, least of all when the speech they would like to suppress comes from their political opponents (Mayerfeld, 1999, p. 121). When basic liberties are not protected in a principled way, it is usually the least powerful who end up suffering for it (Strossen, 2018, ch. 7; Vinding, 2020c). This principled approach is not in tension with the view that the consequences are ultimately what matters — again, it is perfectly coherent, and indeed plausible, to think that a principled decision procedure is the best way to prevent bad outcomes, including totalitarian outcomes in particular (cf. Section 8.5; Bailey, 1997).

A more general reason to favor the protection of free speech is that it enables people to speak up about *any* neglected source and risk of suffering, and to challenge *any* potential wrongdoer, public or private. For example, if scientists or engineers are developing a new technology that they think the public ought to know about, it seems paramount that they be free to raise discussion about the issue, even if certain powerful people would prefer to silence them. Likewise, animal activists who simply inform the public about the actual cruelties performed by animal industries must be free to do so without facing violent threats or criminal charges. Protecting the free speech of those who raise such important issues — which is potentially everyone — seems essential for a society to be able to reduce suffering, whether ongoing or in the form of future risks.

Similar arguments apply to basic freedoms beyond free speech, such as the freedom to congregate, as well as the freedom to start an organization or a company. After all, the freedom of people to organize themselves as they want is just as important for curbing totalitarianism — and for addressing other problems — as is the freedom to speak up against these things. The freedom to use words is of limited value without the freedom to put action behind them.

If a government were to rob people of these basic freedoms, the question emerges as to what would prevent such a government from becoming totalitarian and tyrannical. So far, it seems that every government that has permanently removed these freedoms has become just that (cf. Roser, 2016; Gajic & Gamser, 2018).

11.5 Empirical Reasons to Favor Liberty

Looking more directly at the empirical literature, what appear to be the consequences of greater levels of freedom, such as free speech and economic freedom? One way to approach this question is to look at the countries that are the least free on these dimensions. For example, the countries that score lowest in terms of economic freedom — such as North Korea, Venezuela, Libya, Sudan, and Eritrea — are also the countries that score the lowest on measures of respect for human rights, which track the torture of humans, among other things (Gwartney et al., 2019, p. 9; Miller et al., 2021, p. 10;

Roser, 2016, "Human Rights Scores, 1946 to 2017"). Similar correlations exist between freedom of the press and human rights violations, with largely the same countries scoring the very lowest on these measures (Freedom House, 2017, p. 9; Reporters Without Borders, 2020).

Conversely, the countries that score highest on these measures of freedom also tend to score the highest in terms of respecting human rights. Specifically, the five countries with the greatest freedom of the press in 2020 according to Reporters Without Borders — Norway, Finland, Denmark, Sweden, and the Netherlands — are all ranked toward the very top in terms of respecting human rights in general, with one report ranking all these five countries within the top seven of human-rights-respecting countries (Reporters Without Borders, 2020; Gajic & Gamser, 2018, p. 22). Greater economic freedom is also correlated with greater respect for human rights, yet the correlation between respect for human rights and basic civil and political liberties appears considerably stronger (Gajic & Gamser, 2018, p. 14, p. 17).

Of course, respect for human rights is far from being a perfect measure of suffering. It does not, after all, measure suffering per se. Nor does it pertain to sentient individuals beyond humans — it only focuses on the 0.001 percent. Even so, measures of human rights violations probably do represent *some* meaningful proxy for suffering, and they arguably represent an even better proxy when it comes to risks of future suffering (cf. Baumann, 2017a).

Another point to keep in mind is that the correlations above do not strictly demonstrate a causal relationship between the associated factors, as these correlations could in principle be explained by underlying, confounding variables. But this point notwithstanding, the correlations above are still at least suggestive of a causal relationship between greater levels of freedom — including civil, political, and economic forms of freedom — and greater respect for human rights, and hence, plausibly, less future suffering.

This is also supported by a fairly credible theoretical explanation of *how* these liberties increase respect for human rights, especially in the case of civil and political liberties: freedom of speech, including freedom of the press in particular, empowers people to expose rights violations and oppressive tendencies, while genuine political freedom enables people to remove tyrannical leaders.

In the case of economic freedom, such a causal story is somewhat less clear (and as noted above, the correlation also seems weaker). Yet a possible causal story is that greater economic freedom generally leads to greater economic growth and per capita wealth — including among the poorest 10 percent of the population (Gwartney et al., 2019, pp. 18-20) — and greater wealth might in turn make people better able to stand up for their freedoms and resist human rights violations (Friedman, 2006a, p. 19).

The apparent link between economic freedom and economic growth may also speak in favor of economic freedom for another reason, which is that economic growth seems to be associated with greater tolerance of diversity and a greater commitment to fairness (Friedman, 2005, p. 4). Conversely, when people feel their economy is not doing well, zero-sum thinking and antipathy toward perceived outgroups seem to become more prevalent, which might in turn make victimization of and conflicts with such outgroups more likely (Friedman, 2005, p. 7, p. 128).

Thus, if greater economic freedom leads to greater economic growth — as it seems to (Gwartney et al., 2019, p. 18) — and if greater economic growth in turn increases tolerance and fairness, and reduces outgroup antipathy and risks of conflict, this may count as a reason to favor greater economic freedom. (Recall that conflicts might be among the main risk factors for worst-case outcomes, as argued in Section 9.3.1.) A related reason to favor economic freedom is that greater participation in commerce appears to increase cooperation and adherence to impartial norms, and more competitive markets tend to lead to greater trust and impersonal prosociality (Henrich, 2020, ch. 9-10).

There may, of course, be stronger reasons that count *against* greater economic freedom and growth, which we will explore shortly.

11.6 Liberty and Concern for Non-Human Beings

Given that non-human beings constitute the vast majority of sentient beings on the planet, it is crucial to consider the effects that greater liberties have on people's attitudes toward non-human animals. This is a difficult question to probe, and it is not made easier by the fact that we have rather limited cross-national data on human attitudes toward non-human animals.

Perhaps some of the most relevant data is found in the Animal Protection Index, which ranks the animal welfare legislation of 50 countries across the world. Specifically, the index tracks whether a country's legislation recognizes the sentience of non-human animals in law, the extent to which the infliction of pain on non-human animals is criminalized, and whether there are government bodies responsible and accountable for animal suffering (World Animal Protection, 2020).

The six countries that scored the highest on this combined measure are Austria, Denmark, the Netherlands, Sweden, Switzerland, and the United Kingdom. These are all countries that score relatively high on measures of civil and economic freedoms (see e.g. Gwartney et al., 2019, p. 8; Reporters Without Borders, 2020). On the other hand, the countries that scored the worst on the Animal Protection Index are, with the very worst scores, Azerbaijan and Iran, and with almost as bad scores, Algeria, Belarus, Egypt, Ethiopia, Morocco, Myanmar, and Vietnam (World Animal Protection, 2020). These, in contrast, are all countries that score low on measures of civil and economic freedoms (see e.g. Gwartney et al., 2019, p. 9; Reporters Without Borders, 2020).

Again, this association does not demonstrate a causal relationship. But the fact that high scores on the Animal Protection Index are only found in countries with high levels of civil and economic freedom, while the lowest scores on the Animal Protection Index are only found in countries with low levels of such freedoms, does suggest that greater civil and economic liberties have a positive effect on the legislative protection of non-human animals.

It must be noted, however, that even the countries with the highest ratings on the Animal Protection Index still allow egregious cruelties to be inflicted upon non-human animals on an enormous scale. For example, fish — the vast majority of vertebrates that humanity kills for consumption — can still legally be killed in horrific ways that cause extreme suffering (cf. Fishcount, 2014). And no country has yet banned the factories of agony and death we call slaughterhouses. Which is to say that we should not let these relative rankings deceive us about the absolute horrors that are still allowed, and indeed positively protected, by even the best of our so-called animal welfare laws.

Another set of relevant data points comes from a survey of attitudes toward farmed animals in Brazil, Russia, India, China, and the US. In Brazil, 79 percent of respondents expressed agreement with the claim that "animals used for food have approximately the same ability to feel pain and discomfort as humans". In Russia, India, and the US, roughly two thirds expressed agreement with that claim, while only 37 percent of Chinese respondents agreed with the statement (Anderson & Tyler, 2018, p. 6). Likewise, in response to the statement "low meat prices are more important than the well-being of animals used for food", 64 percent of Brazilian respondents disagreed; roughly half of the respondents disagreed in Russia, India, and the US; while only 24 percent of Chinese respondents disagreed (Anderson & Tyler, 2018, p. 7).

The overall picture emerging from this survey is that people in Brazil seem to show greater concern for farmed animals than do people in Russia, India, and the US, who in turn show considerably greater concern for farmed animals than do people in China. This picture is roughly consistent with the legislation of these countries as ranked in the Animal Protection Index, which scores the legislation of China the lowest among these countries, with Brazil, Russia, and the US scoring one notch higher, and with India a single notch higher still (on a seven-step rating system).

The attitudes documented in this survey are by no means perfectly correlated with greater civil and economic liberties. For instance, Brazilians expressed the greatest concern for non-human animals by a considerable margin among the five countries surveyed, yet Brazil scores significantly lower than the United States on measures of economic and civil liberties (Gwartney et al., 2019, p. 9; Reporters Without Borders, 2020).

However, we still find that people from the least free country in terms of civil liberties, i.e. China, are also the people who express the least concern for non-human animals, and their country similarly has the worst legislative protection for non-human animals among these five countries, which is consistent with — though by no means demonstrates — a correlation between civil liberties and greater concern and legislative protection for non-human animals (Anderson & Tyler, 2018, pp. 6-10; World Animal Protection, 2020; Reporters Without Borders, 2020). (Of course, it is possible for there to be a significant correlation, and even a causal relationship, between civil liberties and concern for non-human animals without civil liberties necessarily being the *main* predictor of such concern.)

A finding in this survey that represents some cause for optimism is that, when asked whether they would "oppose or support a law in [their country] that would require animals used for food to be treated more humanely", a majority of respondents in each of the five countries said that they would support it: 70 percent in Brazil, 62 percent in the US, and 51 to 53 percent in Russia, India, and China (Anderson & Tyler, 2018, pp. 9-10). In other words, even in the country where people expressed by far the least concern for non-human animals — the country where less than a quarter of people indicated that the well-being of animals is more important than the price of meat — a majority still supported legislation in favor of non-human animals. This lends further support to the institutional focus outlined in the previous chapter and elsewhere (Reese, 2018, ch. 7; 2020).

One can give a plausible account of how greater freedom can increase concern for non-human animals, and how it can foster moral progress more generally. In short, when free speech is protected, citizens are able to discuss moral issues, and to exchange views and arguments. And although we are often reluctant to hear and accept other people's arguments, it is still the case that we do listen to arguments to some extent, including moral arguments, and that we at least sometimes update our views when encountering new arguments (Huang et al., 2019; Lindauer et al., 2020; Mercier, 2020).

In contrast, this process of updating one's values based on arguments seems next to impossible in a society that does not allow public debate in the first place, whether on values or anything else — the thought of a strong animal rights movement emerging in authoritarian countries like Eritrea or North Korea seems fanciful. Indeed, regimes that suppress free expression appear to actively *worsen* people's values, such as by spreading xenophobic and conflict-oriented propaganda that serves to entrench the regime's power (cf. Käfer, 2018).

11.7 Reasons to Oppose Liberty

For this not to be a one-sided analysis, we also need to look at reasons to *reduce* the liberties discussed above. How might civil and economic liberties increase suffering and risks of worst-case outcomes? One possible way is by leading to greater economic growth, which can in turn increase our ability to cause harm. To be sure, economic growth is a double-edged sword: greater wealth and technological abilities give us the ability to both increase *and* reduce suffering (cf. Tomasik, 2011; 2013d; Pearce, 2017). But the default outcome may nonetheless be that greater wealth leads to more suffering, at least if the gain in wealth is not accompanied by significant moral progress.

Indeed, greater wealth may lead to more suffering for a group of beings even if it also increases moral concern for these beings. This is arguably what has happened in relation to non-human animals: wealthier countries with comparatively high levels of civil and economic freedom generally seem to show greater concern for non-human animals, both in terms of public attitudes and formal legislation, but they still tend to exploit, harm, and kill non-human animals in larger numbers per capita than do less wealthy and less free nations (Ritchie & Roser, 2017; 2019; OECD, 2022). This is probably mostly explained by the simple fact that people in wealthier countries can afford to buy more animal products, but the point still stands that greater wealth comes with risks of greatly increasing suffering, and that such risks have already materialized on a large scale.

However, it is also important not to overstate the extent to which wealth determines people's consumption of animal products. For example, Switzerland is one of the wealthiest nations in the world, yet the Swiss population still consumes less poultry meat per capita than does a considerably poorer and less free country like Vietnam — in fact, the Swiss consume less poultry meat per person than the global average (OECD, 2022). Likewise, China has the highest consumption of eggs per capita in the world, and China's per capita consumption of sea animals is also among the highest in the world, despite its per capita GDP being in the mid-range globally (Ritchie & Roser, 2017; 2019). So wealth is clearly not an all-important determinant of animal consumption.

It should further be noted that the consumption of animal products seems to have remained roughly constant in most liberal democracies over the last couple of decades, and that many democracies have seen a significant *decline* in animal consumption in the same period, even as these countries have become considerably wealthier (Ritchie & Roser, 2017; 2019). This suggests that greater wealth may, at a certain point, lead to *fewer* non-human animals exploited and killed (cf. Frank, 2008). But there are obviously many possible confounders here. For instance, it could just be that people have become better informed about the cruelties of factory farming, or about healthy alternatives, and these things might have little to do with individual wealth. On the other hand, one may argue that becoming informed in this way tends to require a certain level of freedom and economic development, and hence that a greater level of freedom and economic development is indeed required for a society to transition toward less harmful consumption patterns.

A related argument against liberty is that people may choose to do bad things with their freedoms, whether it be their freedom of speech or their economic freedom. This, too, is more than a mere theoretical notion. For example, some people use their freedom of speech to advocate for views that are harmful and immoral by any sensible standard, such as the view that the suffering of certain groups of individuals does not matter. And even more people use their economic freedom to buy products that cause immense harm, such as products from factory farms, or animals who are fried, boiled, or eaten alive. However, a significant complication here is that our anthropocentrism causes us to exclude non-human beings from our ordinary understanding of these freedoms. For example, inciting violence against humans is *not* protected by free speech as commonly understood, yet it generally *is* protected when the victims are non-human individuals. Likewise, buying and selling humans is considered obviously wrong and illegal, whereas buying and selling non-human beings is by and large considered unproblematic and a core part of our economic freedom.

So it seems relevant to distinguish arguments against free speech and economic freedom *in general* versus arguments against forms of free speech and economic freedom that morally exclude certain individuals. For instance, one can argue that notions of free speech and economic freedom that permit human slavery and incitements to violence against human slaves are wrong *because* they arbitrarily exclude certain individuals, while also maintaining that these freedoms are good as long as they are suitably construed. And similar arguments can be made regarding the moral exclusion of non-human beings in our current understanding of these freedoms (cf. Vinding, 2015).

But one may still argue that free speech and economic freedom are dangerous as a general matter, since we can never guarantee that things will not spiral out of control. Society's moral views might get worse as people exercise their freedom of expression, and economic freedom may lead to revolt-provoking inequality and coordination failures due to runaway capitalism: an unrestrained pursuit of profit that could, in the worst case, result in suffering on a vast scale. And some would argue that we currently find ourselves in just such a situation, or at least that we are headed firmly toward it (see e.g. Klein, 2014, p. 21).

11.8 Weighing the Arguments

What are we to make of these arguments against liberty? It seems undeniable that freedom of expression and economic freedom are associated with significant risks. But the question is what the remedy to these risks might be, and whether the supposed remedy is truly a better alternative. After all, that something is associated with risks does not imply that we should oppose it, since *everything* is associated with risks, and the alternative to a given principle or institution may well carry even greater risks. Specifically, in the case of freedom of expression and economic freedom, the question is whether a broad restriction of these freedoms is really a better option.

Moreover, there is the question of whether it makes *strategic* sense to oppose these freedoms. For even if we were to grant that restricting these liberties would be optimal at the broad idealist level, it is plausibly still strategically unwise to oppose them at the marginal realist level, both because restricting liberty to a sizable extent seems intractable, and because, as argued above, the most likely effect is to simply turn people against the self-declared opposers of freedom.

The case of animal exploitation is a good example of the strategic futility of framing one's views and advocacy in terms of opposition to liberty. *Ideally*, people should obviously not be free to pay others to mutilate and kill sentient individuals merely because these individuals happen not to have human bodies. But directly opposing people's economic freedom to do this is all but surely not the best way to help the billions of individuals that humanity systematically torments and kills. It seems much better to appeal to people's own agency and values, and to call for institutional changes that many more people would agree with, such as ending factory farming and closing slaughterhouses (Sentience Institute, 2017; Norwood & Murray, 2018; Reese, 2020).

Less strategic still is the opposition to *all* economic liberties on the basis that people support animal exploitation in particular, as that would be even less popular. It would also, of course, be a non sequitur. As noted above, it is possible in principle to reconcile economic freedom with a prohibition against buying and selling humans as property, and it is similarly possible to endorse a conception of economic freedom that does not permit the commodification and torment of non-human beings. This hints at the broader point that restricting liberty need not be a matter of all or nothing, a point that is also relevant to the two other arguments raised against liberty above: that free speech could lead to bad outcomes, and that runaway pursuits of profit may have catastrophic consequences.

In the case of free speech, it is widely accepted, both among democratic legal systems and democratic populations, that certain forms of speech indeed should be legally restricted, such as direct incitements to violence against humans. So prevailing conceptions of free speech do have safeguards against *some* bad outcomes. But the question is whether these safeguards and restrictions are ideal. Why not forbid the expression of dangerous viewpoints as well? This question has been debated at length, and an exhaustive discussion of it lies beyond the scope of this chapter. But in brief, while there are real risks associated with protecting the free expression of all viewpoints, it seems that the risks of allowing the suppression of certain viewpoints are generally much greater.

For instance, a risk one might worry about in a society that protects free speech is that it would protect and promote efforts to tyrannize vulnerable individuals. Yet departing from a firm protection of free speech may well increase rather than reduce this risk, since vulnerable groups, by virtue of being vulnerable, seem especially likely to have restrictions of free speech used against *their* speech (Strossen, 2018, ch. 7; Vinding, 2020c). Another way speech restrictions could aggravate these risks is through psychological reactance: people may become more motivated to express or develop harmful views if they feel such views are being suppressed, and those who publicly express such suppressed views may come to be seen as free speech martyrs (cf. Conway et al., 2017; Strossen, 2018, ch. 7; Vinding, 2020c).

Such dynamics might have played out in pre-Nazi Germany, which had anti-hate laws that among other things forbade antisemitic speech (Strossen, 2018, pp. 134-136). Contemporary France may be another example, as France has similar laws that might inadvertently have increased antisemitism (Strossen, 2018, pp. 136-138). Yet even if not actively harmful, anti-hate laws still appear largely ineffective, whereas alternative strategies for combating harmful speech, not least publicly challenging it, generally seem more effective (Strossen, 2018, ch. 7-8).

Thus, not only do restrictions to free speech that ban the expression of certain viewpoints come with increased risks of *other* dangers (e.g. totalitarian developments), but they also seem ineffective at addressing the very risks commonly used to justify such restrictions. In light of these considerations, as well as other considerations reviewed in previous sections and elsewhere, there is good reason to think that those seeking to reduce suffering should favor a principled protection of the legal freedom to express any viewpoint (more elaborate arguments for this claim are found in Strossen, 2018; Vinding, 2020c).

Similar points apply to worst-case risks caused by economic freedom and rampant pursuits of profit, at least in that we must distinguish severe restrictions of freedom in general from delimited restrictions aimed to address particular risks. For instance, just as we can have laws specifically against speech that stirs up violence, we can also have laws that effectively guard against concrete problems and risks associated with economic freedom — laws against pollution may be cited as an example. And it seems plausible that the best way to reduce worst-case risks stemming from economic freedom is to push for such specific restrictions that prevent particular harms rather than to oppose economic freedom wholesale. Why? First of all because, as hinted above, severely restricting people's economic freedom appears both an unpopular and intractable aim to push for on the margin; policies that address specific problems seem significantly more tractable. Second, because restricting economic freedom in general to reduce particular risks is a blunt instrument that might fail to target the risks in question, and it may in any case be *less* effective than more specific solutions. And third, because sweeping restrictions on economic freedom seem likely to result in worse outcomes, such as by disempowering people and increasing risks of totalitarianism.

In sum, both in the case of freedom of expression and economic freedom, pushing for broad restrictions on individual freedom appears highly ill-advised. Indeed, it seems that we should generally endorse and protect these basic freedoms, not least because the alternative — i.e. people *not* having these basic freedoms — seems to be associated with significantly greater risks. Yet it must be stressed that upholding these basic liberties is still compatible with more specific restrictions that prevent actions that harm other individuals. And such restrictions are especially warranted when the harms in question involve extreme suffering.

11.9 Freedom From a State?

A foundational question in political philosophy is what, if anything, can justify the existence of a state. This question deserves considerable attention, not only because of its unique prominence in political philosophy, but also because various thinkers have argued that basic liberty and "common sense morality" ultimately imply that states should not exist (see e.g. Rothbard, 1973; 1982; Huemer, 2013).

A famous attempt to provide a justification for the state comes from Thomas Hobbes, who argued that a sovereign government was required to avoid the "natural condition of mankind", which he thought entailed a perpetual war of all against all (Hobbes, 1651, ch. 13). Hence, Hobbes argued, people have created and submitted themselves to a government so as to avoid this violent state of nature, and this agreement, or social contract, is what legitimizes the state according to Hobbes (Hobbes, 1651, ch. 14). To be clear, the sovereign state envisioned by Hobbes was not a democratic one, and it entailed no separation of powers. Yet similar arguments have been made to justify the legitimacy of modern democratic states (see e.g. Weale, 2020).

Some scholars argue that there is empirical support for the Hobbesian view of the state's influence on violence. For example, Steven Pinker contends that the state monopoly on physical force has, through various mechanisms, caused violence to decline sharply over the last few centuries (Pinker, 2011, ch. 2). One of the most important of these mechanisms, Pinker argues, is that state institutions such as the police and courts serve as an impartial bystander in conflicts between citizens, which enable these institutions to limit incentives both to aggress and to retaliate. There is, for instance, less of a need to aggress upon others to signal one's defensive strength to potential aggressors, because it is common knowledge that defending all citizens against aggressors is the task of the police. And there is less of an incentive to retaliate, since ensuring punishment is likewise recognized to be the duty of the police and the courts, and because retaliation itself is illegal (Pinker, 2011, p. 35).

The legitimacy of the state has nonetheless been questioned by anarchist thinkers (the term "anarchy" is here simply defined as the absence of government). These include Mikhail Bakunin and Pyotr Kropotkin, who defended collectivist anarchism, as well as David Friedman and Michael Huemer, who defend anarchism of an individualist variant (Bakunin, 1873; Kropotkin, 1892; Friedman, 1973; Huemer, 2013). Distinct as anarchist thinkers are, they tend to agree that states are unjust, and that there are better ways to arrange society without a state, relying on purely voluntary institutions.

Before diving into a discussion of anarchism, it is worth noting that virtually everything I have said in this book would apply to an anarchist society as well, since such a society would still have a public discourse, and would still need to make collective decisions of various kinds.

Another preliminary point worth highlighting is that we should not underestimate the degree to which societal structures might change in the future. For while it may be tempting to think that modern liberal democracy represents the "end of history" (cf. Fukuyama, 1992), the truth is that liberal democracy is an exceedingly recent phenomenon on historical timescales. Most democracies in the world are less than 40 years old, and as of 2015, only 11 democracies were more than 100 years old (Roser & Herre, 2013/2019). The continued existence of such a recent system is by no means certain, and hence discussions about anarchism, or other alternatives to contemporary democracy, are probably less fanciful than many of us are inclined to think (Huemer, 2013, 13.1). After all, modern democracy was made possible by various inventions, such as the printing press and mass education, and we now have many new inventions — such as the Internet and blockchain technologies — that may similarly pave the way for new and better institutions. It is worth exploring what those potentially better institutions might be.

The question of whether a state can be justified is, relative to the values I am exploring here, chiefly a matter of consequentialist analysis. Specifically, the main defense of a state, or of anarchist alternatives, would by and large need to be cashed out in terms of the effects on suffering, particularly on extreme suffering (cf. Vinding, 2020a, ch. 4-5; Enoch, 2021). If the best anarchist system that is feasible resulted in significantly *more* extreme suffering, then a state — at least one that resulted in less extreme suffering — would be justified. Conversely, if the best anarchist system would lead to significantly *less* extreme suffering, then this form of anarchy would be justified.

11.10 For and Against Anarchy

The suffering of non-human beings represents one of the most relevant and neglected issues in discussions of the justification for the state versus anarchy. (Indeed, while many anarchists claim to uphold the non-aggression principle, NAP, the truth is that they only tend to endorse an extremely restricted version of this principle, namely the *anthropocentric* non-aggression principle, ANAP, which excludes all sentient beings that are not human.) Given that non-human beings constitute the vast majority of sentient individuals, it is vital that we explicitly ask which system best reduces extreme suffering for *all* beings. This is no doubt a difficult question to answer, and it is only made more difficult by the fact that there are various dimensions to it: there is suffering due to animal farming, suffering in nature, and risks of suffering in future beings to consider.

Considering the first, animal farming, it seems difficult to have top-down legislation to protect non-human animals from egregious harms in a stateless society. To be sure, existing "animal welfare" laws are in many ways profoundly ineffectual, as they can and do allow atrocious horrors, but it still seems better to have *some* such laws than to have none. On the other hand, states also subsidize animal agriculture with vast sums of money, which significantly increases the number of beings who are exploited, suffering, and killed by the hands of these industries. Such subsidies are unlikely to exist in any stateless society.

In both these cases, one could argue that there are *some* versions of the respective institutions that avoid these pitfalls. An anarchist society *could* have laws protecting farmed animals, and a state *could* avoid subsidizing animal farming, the latter arguably being the more realistic of these proposals; New Zealand is an example of a developed economy in which the government does not provide subsidies for agriculture (St Clair, 2002). But it is in any case clear that both systems have some significant pitfalls to which the other system is less vulnerable.

In relation to wild-animal suffering, it likewise seems more realistic to see large-scale interventions to reduce such suffering performed by governmental institutions than by private ones. Yet governmental institutions also appear somewhat more likely to spread and increase suffering, such as through so-called rewilding efforts and by pursuing environmentalist policies that harm wild animals (cf. Animal Ethics, 2014; Horta, 2018; Faria & Paez, 2019). So in this respect, too, it is not wholly obvious whether statist or anarchist societies would be best for reducing non-human suffering.

Third, there is the risk of creating novel forms of suffering (Metzinger, 2021). Here, states may be double-edged as well, in that they might be uniquely able to enforce laws against the creation of such suffering, yet they might also be more likely to develop novel forms of suffering in the first place, given their large budgets and their track record for funding extensive research and engineering projects for which there is no immediate demand. Moreover, the larger budgets commanded by states may enable them to create significantly larger amounts of such suffering than people would or could in an anarchic society (assuming novel forms of suffering had already been developed), though the presumably reduced ability to prohibit the creation of such suffering in an anarchic society renders it unclear which system is optimal in this regard.

The risk of large-scale conflicts and atrocities is another crucial factor to consider (cf. Section 9.3.1). Naively, it would seem that statist societies are more likely to cause such conflicts and atrocities, given their ability to concentrate large amounts of resources that may be devoted to war. Yet whether this has been the case historically is somewhat unclear. For instance, Matthew White argues that "chaos is deadlier than tyranny", and that more large-scale atrocities have resulted from "the breakdown of authority rather than the exercise of authority" (White, 2011, p. xvii). On the other hand, the three deadliest atrocities in history, according to White, have all been caused by states or empires — World War II, Genghis Khan's conquests, and the rule of Mao Zedong. And many of the "chaotic" atrocities and civil wars listed by White were likewise conflicts between different military leaders and dynasties, and hence they were not really conflicts absent of authority, as opposed to being absent of an *overarching* authority. Whether stateless societies with anarchic institutions would be at greater risk of succumbing to such warring rulers stands as an open question.

Note that we also need to account for the risk that worse states might emerge. For instance, if a democracy that transitions to anarchy is at great risk of eventually devolving into a malevolent autocracy, such as if certain private corporations create a new de facto state without any separation of powers, then this would seem considerably worse than if the society had stayed democratic. Of course, anarchists might argue that democratic states are at greater risk of such developments, but it remains true that such risks must be accounted for either way.

Similar points apply to the dynamics between different kinds of societies. There are, after all, many possible combinations of societies, and one could well imagine there being anarchic, democratic, and totalitarian societies all at the same time, and the likely consequences of such conditions would also be necessary to account for. For instance, if anarchic societies would be more vulnerable to invasion from totalitarian states than would democratic states (e.g. because anarchic societies tend to invest less money into tanks and fighter jets), then it could be that having a democratic state is better than an anarchic society in a world that contains large and aggressive totalitarian states, even if anarchic societies happened to be better otherwise. (Some anarchists indeed consider defense against foreign aggressors to be "the hard problem" for anarchy, Friedman, 1973, ch. 34.) The global context is thus also critical to these discussions (cf. Huemer, 2013, pp. 330-331).

The considerations raised above are admittedly superficial and speculative for the most part. My main purpose in reviewing them has not been to settle these issues, but rather to highlight some of the key questions we need to ask in these discussions, and to demonstrate that the answers to such questions are unlikely to be simple or easy to find. Again: What are the likely effects on non-human suffering? What are the likely effects on the risk of conflicts and atrocities, particularly those that would result in a lot of suffering? And what kind of society seems optimal given the actual global context in which we find ourselves?

11.11 Marginal Realist Upshots on Anarchism vs. Statism

Fortunately, the practical implications at the marginal realist level are relatively clear, even as the answers to the broad idealist questions raised above may not be. And the marginal realist level is arguably also the most relevant one at which to draw practical conclusions at this point.

A plausible thing to push for is to raise the epistemic standards of discussions concerning the state versus anarchy. Specifically, it would be good to reduce overconfidence — on *all* sides — about the outcomes of various institutions, which appears to be one of the main problems in contemporary discussions. Defenders of statism tend to be highly confident that anarchist institutions could never work, while anarchists tend to be highly confident that they *could* work, despite the fact that the institutions in question have never been tested in a modern context.

Another sensible step is to highlight some of the biases and blind spots that plague people's thinking about this issue. One of these blind spots is our tendency to unquestioningly obey (perceived) authorities, including when they give unreasonable or even starkly unethical commands. For example, a person wearing a made-up uniform is significantly better able to get strangers to follow commands on the streets (Bushman, 1988). And in various versions of the famous Milgram experiment, a majority of people were willing, even if reluctantly, to obey instructions to electrocute an innocent person, or rather an actor who pretended to receive electric shocks (Milgram, 1963; 1974). (Milgram has been criticized for the methodology of his experiment and for overstating his results, see e.g. Perry, 2012, yet recent variations of the experiment have yielded largely the same results, Burger, 2009; Dolinski et al., 2017).

These findings have important implications for how we think about authority, and the extent to which we should trust our authority-related intuitions (Huemer, 2013, ch. 6). On the other hand, some scholars argue that we tend to underestimate the good that governments do, because it is rarely visible to us, which may also bias our view of government (Holmes & Sunstein, 1999; Amy, 2011; Hacker & Pierson, 2016). Of course, anarchists might argue that we are even more prone to overlook and underestimate the *bad* things that governments do (cf. Huemer, 2013, 9.4). But it holds true regardless that our immediate evaluations of government are likely to be flawed and worthy of skepticism.

The causal opacity of (many of) our institutions is another potential pitfall to be aware of (cf. Section 5.2). It implies that clever ideas for novel institutions that look good on the drawing board nevertheless have a real risk of failing in practice. Such ideas may, for instance, overlook the effects that various institutions have on people's psychology, or overlook other second-order effects that are difficult to predict in advance (cf. Henrich, 2020). Again, this is not to say that radical institutional change is necessarily impossible or undesirable, but it does mean that we should be careful not to be too confident in purely theoretical arguments. As anarchist David Friedman writes: "Human beings and human societies are far too complicated for us to have confidence in a priori predictions about how institutions that have never been tried would work" (Friedman, 1973, "Interlude").

Worth keeping in mind, too, is the risk of suspicious convergence (cf. Lewis, 2016). That is, if we have strong intuitions that lead us to endorse, say, maximal personal freedom, and if we favor a particular political system on these grounds, we should be highly skeptical that this political system *also* happens to produce optimal outcomes relative to very different aims, such as reducing suffering, as that would be a remarkable coincidence. This kind of wishful thinking appears common when we have different values that we want to satisfy — as we usually do — and hence we should be careful not to fall for it.

Beyond a greater awareness of biases, it seems worth pushing for a greater focus on suffering reduction in discussions of this issue. I already raised some specific questions above that have not gained sufficient attention, but besides raising such questions, there is the more general aim of getting people to view the entire issue of statism versus anarchism more from the perspective of reducing suffering and increasing robustness against worst-case outcomes. Getting a suffering-focused perspective included to a greater degree might itself be among the best contributions we can make on the margin today, both in this particular discussion and in our political discourse in general, to ensure that people in the future will take it into account.

Contrary to our inclinations toward position-taking, there is hardly a need to rush to take a strong stance on the issue of statism versus anarchism, least of all at this point where we know so little. If there is anything we *should* take a strong stance on, it is the need to know more, especially in terms of the likely consequences of different institutions. Another reason not to champion a strong position on this issue, beyond our current ignorance, is that it seems more tractable and effective to focus on other issues, such as those outlined in the previous chapter. Put differently, the opportunity cost may be too high.

To the extent that one does engage with the issue of anarchism versus statism, the best thing one can do on the margin is probably not to join the tug of war by strongly favoring one side over the other, as opposed to "pulling the rope sideways" (Hanson, 2007). The above-mentioned proposals to try to increase awareness of biases and to ensure that the aim of reducing suffering is given greater consideration both count as good examples of such strategic sideways-tugging, as these are things nobody strongly opposes, and which most people indeed likely favor on reflection (cf. Tomasik, 2015b; Future of Life Institute, 2017; Caviola et al., 2022).

11.12 Plausible Proxies and Liberty

Turning to the plausible proxies outlined in Chapter 9, we again find that these proxies help to elaborate on some of the points made above.

11.12.1 Greater Levels of Cooperation

The proxy aim of increasing cooperation generally seems to favor respecting, indeed protecting, the liberty and autonomy of others, as such mutual respect appears more conducive to cooperation and conflict resolution than does its absence. In theoretical terms, it seems that individuals who respect each other's personal freedom and autonomy will have less of an incentive to engage in conflict, and that they will be less prone to psychological reactance. In empirical terms, it seems that societies that have higher levels of civil and economic freedom tend to be significantly more peaceful and less conflict-prone (see e.g. Gajic & Gamser, 2018, pp. 19-31; Gwartney et al., 2019, pp. 8-9; Institute for Economics & Peace, 2021, pp. 9-10).

It is true that respect for individual freedom will imply significant differences in how people view the world and how they choose to live their lives. Yet such differences only underscore the need to strive for what John Rawls called a "reasonable pluralism", where people with different views and ways of living can nevertheless respect each other in peaceful co-existence (Rawls, 1993, pp. xviii-xix).

The aim of securing cooperation also underscores the need for certain restrictions on liberty, such as laws that prevent conflicts and harms to others. These restrictions mostly appear to be prohibitions against acts of aggression that are typically thought to fall outside the domain of legitimate liberty, yet it is conceivable that they include more than that. For instance, it may be warranted to have laws that require nations and other large-scale actors to negotiate and seek compromises, even before any acts of aggression have occurred, provided such laws help prevent conflicts.

11.12.2 Better Values

As noted earlier, liberty is a precondition for having an open-ended conversation on values, and thus seems indispensable for improving our values. Yes, there is the risk that free expression will lead to worse values, but as argued above and elsewhere, the risk of value deterioration generally appears greater in the case of draconian restrictions on free speech (Strossen, 2018, ch. 7-8; Vinding, 2020c). Moreover, if we take a broad look at the empirical record of liberal democracy and free speech, in terms of their effects on the development of human values, it seems that their effects have been mostly positive.

For example, in relation to humans, the last three hundred years have witnessed the abolition of legal slavery; the end of public torture; and significant changes in attitudes toward discrimination based on sex, race, sexuality, and other morally irrelevant characteristics (Pinker, 2011, ch. 4; 2012; Huemer, 2013, 13.1). Likewise, public torture of non-human animals, such as cat-burning, is no longer considered an acceptable form of entertainment in most countries, and many such public forms of animal cruelty — though by no means all — are now illegal in democratic countries. As liberty has increased, most countries have gone from having no legislation against animal cruelty to having at least some such laws (although they are often not enforced).

Overall, the emergence of liberal democracy seems to have coincided with moral progress, and some scholars argue that this progress is partly attributable to liberal values such as free speech (see e.g. Pinker, 2011, ch. 4; 2018, pp. 4-6, p. 28). Conversely, there appears to be little evidence for the claim that free speech and other civil liberties have generally made our values worse. Indeed, the cases where values have deteriorated in catastrophic ways in modern times — such as Nazi Germany, Fascist Italy, and the Soviet Union — have all been characterized by a forceful *suppression* of liberty.

It is true, however, that a framework of laws and norms that merely protect our liberties is not sufficient in relation to the aim of improving our values. We also need to cultivate norms of actively using our precious liberties to discuss, reflect on, and develop our values. Such norms should not be promoted in an intrusive way, of course, but simply by appealing to the sensible notion that few things could be more important and more worthy of the exercise of our freedom than the further development of our values.

11.12.3 Greater Capacity to Reduce Suffering

It is almost tautological to say that we cannot advance our ability to reduce suffering without the freedom to do so. In this regard, the paramount importance of freedom is obvious, especially the freedom of the moral advocate that many people would like to suppress. The danger, of course, is that greater freedom in general may also pave the way for a greater ability to cause harm. As argued above, the solution to this problem is not to push for sweeping restrictions on liberty, since such restrictions likely have worse consequences overall.

A better policy, again, is to push for solutions that address specific problems, such as norms that favor disproportionately advancing our wisdom and our ability to cooperate (Tomasik, 2013d). Likewise, one can push for norms against pursuing particularly harmful research, as well as laws against experiments that have a high risk of causing harm (cf. Bostrom, 2011; Metzinger, 2021).

Ideally, we should increase our capacity to reduce suffering within a framework of reasonable pluralism, meaning that we should expand our collective capacity to achieve a plurality of reasonable goals, and advance our ability to create gainful compromises when possible (cf. Tomasik, 2013a).

11.13 Conclusion

The aim of reducing suffering strongly recommends that we endorse and protect basic liberties, especially civil liberties such as free speech. To address the risks associated with such freedoms, it seems that we should push for narrowly targeted norms and laws that help guard against those risks. Not only does such general freedom combined with certain sensible restrictions appear optimal from a broad idealist perspective, but it is also by far the most feasible position to promote on the margin. This is not to say that it is easy to protect civil liberties, or to identify and institute the right norms and laws to prevent particular risks, but merely that it is the best and most realistic option.

It must again be stressed that this has not been an exhaustive or definitive exploration. Even if we accept the broad conclusions drawn above, there is still much research to be done in terms of clarifying which freedom-restricting norms and laws best prevent suffering — though it is safe to say that a critical step in this regard is to expand our existing such norms and laws so that they include all sentient beings. We should not have the legal freedom to impose intense suffering on non-human beings, as we sadly do in many ways today. The same applies at the level of our norms and general ethical principles pertaining to freedom. For instance, the harm principle, which says that our actions should only be limited for the purpose of preventing harm to others, must be construed such that "others" means *all* sentient beings (Cavalieri, 1991). In this respect, we need to push for a radical revision of our conception of freedom and its legitimate limits.

Finally, it seems that one of the most effective things we can do on the margin today is to "pull the rope sideways" in political discussions, such as by trying to raise the overall quality and epistemic standards of the conversation (e.g. promoting intellectual humility and a greater awareness of biases), and not least by working to ensure that suffering — the suffering of *all* sentient beings — is given significant and explicit consideration in people's discussions and evaluations of political policies going forward.

12

Equality

Equality, like liberty, is among the most prominent notions in political philosophy. And like liberty, the notion of equality raises many foundational questions. These include conceptual questions about what we understand by equality, normative questions about the importance of different kinds of equality, as well as the empirical question that will be the primary focus of this chapter: what are the optimal forms and degrees of equality for reducing extreme suffering?

12.1 Equality of What? — Different Notions of Equality

To simply talk of equality without first specifying what kind of equality we have in mind is about as vague and meaningless as is talking about liberty without further specification. There are, after all, countless things there could be an equality of, and many of these things and accompanying forms of equality have little direct bearing on each other. Indeed, equality of some kinds, such as equal hourly wages, will inevitably give rise to *in*equality of other kinds, such as unequal pay checks for those who work a different number of hours.

One kind of equality is the equal consideration of interests (Singer, 1979, p. 20). This form of equality entails, for instance, that the same suffering should be given equal consideration regardless of who is experiencing it — i.e. regardless of an individual's sexuality, race, sex, or species. Sadly, this kind of equality, particularly its extension beyond the human species, has received relatively little attention in political philosophy (some exceptions include Garner, 2005; Cochrane, 2010; 2018).

Another form of equality is equality before the law, or legal equality. This is usually taken to mean that laws should be written and enforced in a way that does not discriminate against any individual or group of individuals (though in this context the term "individual" is often understood such that it excludes both non-human animals and foreigners). The law should, as it were, be blind and impartial. Such legal equality is a common ideal in liberal democracies, at least for domestic humans (Tuckness & Wolf, 2016, 3.63).

Closely related is the concept of political equality, which usually refers to ideals of equal political influence, such as "one person, one vote" — ideals that are also common in liberal democracies, yet which are difficult to fully satisfy (Dahl, 2006; Tuckness & Wolf, 2016, 5.6-5.7). (Political equality is usually construed in purely anthropocentric terms, with one vote to every *human* person, but a non-anthropocentric alternative is presented in Cochrane, 2018, ch. 3-4; 2020, ch. 6.)

A frequently drawn distinction in discussions of equality is that between equality of *opportunity* and equality of *outcome*. Yet these respective notions of equality are also rather vague and underspecified as they stand. For instance, equality of opportunity is often defined as having a "level playing field", but what this means is hardly self-evident. Do two individuals who grow up in households with very different levels of wealth and social support have equal opportunities as long as the law and society at large do not discriminate against either of them?

This hints at two distinct definitions of equality of opportunity delineated by John Roemer. One is a nondiscrimination principle, which says that equality of opportunity involves judging individuals based purely on their qualifications when evaluating them for a given position. The other is a more demanding notion of equality, according to which equality of opportunity requires society to actively level the playing field among people in their formative years as well, so that everyone has (more of) an equal opportunity to realize their potential — what John Rawls called "fair equality of opportunity" (Roemer, 1998, p. 1; Rawls, 1971, p. 73).

Definitions of equality of outcome are also numerous, indeed at least as numerous as the different kinds of outcomes we might care about. For example, we may care about equal outcomes in terms of wealth, income, misery, or burdens. And equality along one of these dimensions need not imply equality along the others. Moreover, there are many ways to define equality of outcomes even *within* these respective dimensions. In terms of wealth, for instance, we may look at people's share of wealth across an entire lifetime or at a single point in time, and these perspectives may differ greatly (cf. Temkin, 1993, ch. 8).

A final point worth making is that equality almost always comes in degrees. This is worth stressing since ideals of equality are sometimes dismissed with the claim that perfect equality is impossible or undesirable, or both. But even if perfect equality is neither possible nor desirable, it does not follow that the same is true of *a greater degree* of equality, which is often what advocates of equality are in fact supporting, and which tends to be more difficult to dismiss.

12.2 Preliminary Clarifications

Once again, a few clarifying notes on values seem in order. Some philosophers defend the view that equality, of various kinds, is *intrinsically* good (Temkin, 1993; Parfit, 1995). Others, in contrast, argue that all forms of equality are merely good as means to an end, such as reducing suffering or increasing happiness (Mill, 1859, p. 9; Ryder, 2006, pp. 26-29). The *prima facie* duty to reduce suffering I explore here does not commit us to any of these respective views, and is compatible with both of them.

I should note, however, that the values I myself endorse do entail that the reduction of extreme suffering is always more important than equality in itself, of *any* kind (Vinding, 2020a, ch. 4-5). And I would further argue that the more extreme suffering a given view would permit for the sake of any kind of equality per se, the less plausible that view becomes. But again, the analysis that follows should still apply to virtually any view that entails a strong *prima facie* duty to reduce suffering, including views that sometimes prioritize other things higher than the reduction of extreme suffering.

12.3 Extending "Equal Consideration of Equal Interests"

T. M. Scanlon writes that basic moral equality — "the idea that everyone counts morally" — is "perhaps the most important form of moral progress over the [past] centuries" (Scanlon, 2018, p. 4). Unfortunately, he fails to realize that the same holds true of the moral progress that lies ahead of us, as we have yet to extend this "now widely accepted" idea about counting everyone morally so that it includes non-human beings as well. Specifically, we have yet to apply the basic principle of equal consideration of equal interests to *all* sentient beings (Singer, 1979, p. 20; Vinding, 2015; Cochrane, 2018, ch. 2).

Indeed, humanity's disregard of non-human beings — i.e. our complete failure to apply anything close to equal consideration of equal interests — is probably the most important form of inequality to address by far if our aim is to reduce suffering. Unfortunately, this massive inequality is often neglected even by supposed champions of equality, despite the fact that egalitarian views imply we should be *especially* concerned about non-human animals (Faria, 2014; Horta, 2016). As Oscar Horta argues, since other animals are generally worse off in comparison to humans, "egalitarianism prescribes giving priority to the interests of non-human animals" (Horta, 2016, abstract).

The same plausibly applies to all impartial views concerned with the reduction of suffering. That is, giving equal consideration to all suffering will likely mean prioritizing non-human suffering on the margin, partly because non-human beings are so numerous, partly because their suffering is often extremely intense, and partly because their suffering is uniquely neglected — especially the suffering occurring on factory farms, in the fishing industry, and in nature; three of the biggest screaming elephants in the room of modern political discourse.

A serious complication is that many people will be inclined to oppose such priorities, and hence extending the principle of equal consideration of equal interests to non-human animals would be difficult on a broader political level. While this is true, it is also important not to overstate this resistance. Recall that most people in countries like Brazil, India, Russia, and the US agree that "animals used for food have approximately the same ability to feel pain and discomfort as humans", and that around a third of US citizens seem to agree that human and non-human beings deserve the same rights as far as the avoidance of harm and exploitation is concerned (Riffkin, 2015; Anderson & Tyler, 2018, p. 6).

Of course, people mostly fail to act in accordance with these beliefs, but this is largely true of all of us — we *all* routinely fail to live up to the values we claim to hold. And one may argue that the point of our political institutions is precisely to realize our ideals better and more consistently than we ourselves can as uncoordinated individuals (cf. Cochrane, 2018, p. 4).

It remains true, however, that we are far from extending equal consideration of equal interests to non-human animals at the level of public attitudes, let alone public policy. And this surely does necessitate a lot of strategic wisdom on behalf of those who are trying to advance society's values toward recognizing this most basic form of equality. One of the prime mistakes animal advocates have made in this endeavor, I submit, is to have the conversation focus mostly on diet and social identity rather than on institutional change and the ethics of species discrimination. (Again, the main strategies I would recommend in this regard, as well as the reasoning behind them, were outlined in Section 10.9.)

12.4 Reasons to Favor Less Economic Inequality

Most discussions of inequality seem to be concerned with economic inequality in particular, such as inequalities of wealth and income. The rest of this chapter will mostly focus on this issue. Worth clarifying in this regard is that the issue of economic inequality is distinct from the problem of poverty, even if the two are related (Frankfurt, 2015). A society with high levels of inequality may still have less poverty than a more equal society. Indeed, John Rawls famously argued that economic inequality would be good to the extent that it helps the least advantaged (Rawls, 1971, p. 83).

That being said, a standard utilitarian argument in favor of greater economic equality is that it would reduce the misery of those who have the least. In particular, the diminishing marginal utility of money means that an additional thousand dollars would help a poor person more than it would help, say, a billionaire, and hence it would be better, all else equal, if the poor person got an additional thousand dollars (Shapiro, 2003, pp. 27-28).

This argument would support a highly equal distribution of wealth, at least other things being equal. However, as utilitarian philosopher Jeremy Bentham argued, other things would most likely *not* be equal, one reason being that strong incentives to work would seem incompatible with an equal distribution of wealth in the real world. Hence Bentham, like Rawls, did not endorse perfect economic equality in practice, but rather the degree of "practical equality" that would be best from a utilitarian perspective (though he did not say much about what this optimal level of equality would be, Shapiro, 2003, pp. 29-30).

Another reason it might be good to have less economic inequality has to do with the human psychology of social comparison. Large differences in wealth and income can lead to large differences in people's perceived social status, which may in turn cause those who have the least to feel inferior, humiliated, and miserable in other ways (Payne, 2017, ch. 1; Scanlon, 2018, ch. 3). Note that this dynamic can be independent of absolute levels of income: even if those who earn the least in a given group are not poor in absolute terms, their social status might still be painfully low if everyone around them earns significantly more than they do. And studies have indeed found that people's relative *rank* of income in a wealthy society is a stronger predictor of life satisfaction, mental health, and physical health than is income itself (Boyce et al., 2010; Wood et al., 2012; Daly et al., 2014).

One may take these results about relative rank to mean that inequality does not matter much, since there would still be a relative rank of income in a society with low levels of inequality (Hanson, 2018). However, another interpretation is that these studies simply show that people are highly concerned about their relative status, which is consistent with thinking that greater differences in income will tend to exacerbate such status concerns. Indeed, there is considerable evidence that greater economic inequality increases status anxiety and social comparison (Buttrick et al., 2017; Quispe-Torreblanca et al., 2021, pp. 534-535).

None of this suggests that absolute levels of income are at all irrelevant to measures of human life satisfaction and health, as they surely are not (Ortiz-Ospina & Roser, 2013). The point is simply that high levels of inequality can have significant negative effects on people's well-being, even when those who feel like they are at the lower end of the status hierarchy are not poor in absolute terms (Payne, 2017, ch. 1). And empirical data likewise suggests that lower levels of income inequality lead to greater nationwide happiness for humans when the wealth of a nation is held constant (Oishi & Kesebir, 2015).

Beyond the effects that economic inequality can have on people's well-being, we also need to consider how it influences our behavior. An important finding in this regard is that greater economic inequality significantly reduces interpersonal trust in wealthy societies (Jordahl, 2007; Barone & Mocetti, 2016). Studies have also linked economic inequality to lower social cohesion, weaker rule of law, greater sociopolitical instability, more academic cheating, and higher crime rates (Fajnzylber et al., 2002; Choe, 2008; Neville, 2012; Buttrick & Oishi, 2017). All of these factors are plausibly quite negative relative to the aim of reducing suffering and of reducing risks of conflict in particular.

Moreover, there is evidence that greater inequality can trigger antisocial behavior, especially when transparent cues of inequality are present. One study analyzed incidents of air rage from more than a million flights, to test whether planes with a first-class section provoke more episodes of aggressive behavior, and found that such class-divided planes were almost four times as likely to have incidents of air rage. The study also found that class-divided flights that had people board from the front of the plane — where people would be confronted with unequal status — provoked more than twice as many air-rage episodes among economy-class passengers, and almost 12 times as many episodes among first-class passengers, compared to class-divided flights that had people board from the middle (DeCelles & Norton, 2016).

In addition to showing a clear link between perceptions of inequality and aggressive behavior, these findings suggest that environmental design and *signals* of inequality may be more important than economic inequality per se when it comes to ameliorating the downsides of inequality.

12.5 Institutional Reasons to Favor Less Economic Inequality

Another class of arguments in support of less economic inequality is that it has negative effects on our institutions at large (Scanlon, 2018, ch. 6). For instance, a number of political scientists argue that public policy in the US is disproportionately influenced by the wealthiest people (Gilens, 2005; Page et al., 2013). This may be especially true of the richest one percent, a group that one study called "extremely politically active", and which appears markedly more conservative than the average US citizen (Page et al., 2013, p. 51).

Indeed, beyond influencing incumbent politicians, wealthier people also seem in a much better position to become politicians themselves, not least given the costs of running successful campaigns (Scanlon, 2018, p. 94). As a case in point, most of the Democratic candidates running for nomination in the 2020 US presidential election were millionaires, and two out of the last eight candidates were billionaires, which means that billionaires were 10,000 times more prevalent among this group of candidates than among the general population; not to mention that the incumbent president was a billionaire as well (Center for Responsive Politics, 2020; Forbes, 2020).

Such a skewed influence exerted by the wealthy may be considered problematic based on normative views that deem equal opportunities for political influence to be intrinsically important (Rawls, 1971, pp. 221-228; Scanlon, 2018, ch. 6). But there are also reasons to think that it would be bad from a perspective concerned with the reduction of suffering.

One reason is that large disparities in wealth and power seem likely to create similar disparities in the air time and attention devoted to the voices of those who have the least (Scanlon, 2018, p. 91). Thus, not only may economic inequality distort the political process at the formal level, but it may also distort our public discourse in general, such as by enabling a relatively small number of wealthy people to have a strong influence on the popular media. Indeed, given that attention is limited, and given that money can buy attention, such as in the form of advocacy campaigns on large platforms, it follows that greater disparities in the amount of money people have can lead to greater disparities in the attention that different groups of people are able to bring to their respective issues of concern. And this point about relative overbidding for limited attention again holds true even if those who have the least are not poor in absolute terms.

Such an underrepresentation of the voices of those who have the least is plausibly also bad for others. As Scanlon argues, "By narrowing the range of viewpoints represented in public discourse it puts everyone in a less good position to decide what policies to favor" (Scanlon, 2018, p. 91). This argument can be made both from the perspective of the two-step ideal in general, from which we should like to consider a broad range of moral outlooks and opinions, as well as from a suffering-focused perspective in particular, from which we should consider a wide variety of policy proposals and empirical views.

Furthermore, studies have found that greater levels of income inequality are associated with lower levels of civic engagement, and less civic engagement likewise seems suboptimal relative to the aim of hearing a wide range of perspectives (Uslaner & Brown, 2005; Lancee & van de Werfhorst, 2012).

It must again be stressed that the point made above is not that disparities in influence can be eliminated entirely, or that this is necessarily desirable, but rather that reducing economic inequality may be a way to reduce such disparities in influence, and that this is plausibly beneficial on the margin — at least in light of the reasons reviewed above.

12.6 Reasons Not to Favor Less Economic Inequality

Again, for this not to be a one-sided analysis, we must also consider reasons why less economic inequality might be bad. There may, after all, be tradeoffs between reducing inequality and increasing other things, and perhaps inequality itself has beneficial effects that are more significant than the potential downsides mentioned above.

One argument might be that greater inequality increases the incentive for people to create prosperity and economic growth (cf. Conard, 2016, ch. 3; Lacalle, 2020, ch. 7). If outcomes were going to be more equal, people would be less motivated to create goods and services that help others. Yet the evidence does not seem to support this argument. That is, empirical analyses do not find that greater equality reduces economic growth (on the margin) in modern market economies (Neves et al., 2016). Moreover, as hinted in the previous chapter, it is not clear whether greater economic growth is even a good thing relative to the aim of reducing suffering, as it may disproportionally advance our technology and our ability to do harm compared to our wisdom (Tomasik, 2011; 2013d; 2013e).

Another argument might be that wealthier people invest their money more patiently, including when it comes to altruistic investments (cf. Trammell, 2021), and perhaps less economic inequality would result in fewer such patient investments, which could be a bad thing overall. This seems a more plausible argument in favor of greater economic inequality from a suffering-focused perspective, though it is still questionable on various levels. First, it is unclear whether greater economic inequality indeed increases patient investments on the current margin — especially as far as altruistic investments are concerned, since economic inequality appears to increase people's perceived need to gain money for themselves (Payne et al., 2017).

Second, even if we grant that greater inequality does lead to more patient investments from the wealthiest people, one can still doubt whether the patient investments that the wealthiest people will be inclined to make are generally better than the investments that would be made in a more equal society; partly because the patient investments by the wealthiest might mostly be self-serving and relatively frivolous, and partly because the investments that would be made in a more equal society, such as greater investments in health and education by those who have the least, might themselves count as decent long-term investments.

Alternatively, one may argue that people tend to vastly overestimate the significance of economic inequality per se, and hence that we give far too much attention to this issue compared to other things we should devote greater attention to. This argument seems largely correct. For instance, many debates focus on economic inequality per se, especially within wealthy nations, when abject human poverty on a global scale accounts for far more human misery that could be alleviated at a relatively low cost (cf. GiveWell,

2014). (Again, while economic inequality and poverty are related, they are by no means the same.) And as mentioned above, the form of inequality that accounts for most suffering by far is the radically unequal regard — indeed the violent *disregard* — that humans display toward the interests of non-human beings. So there is no doubt a strong case for prioritizing other things higher than the reduction of human economic inequality.

But note that this is not an argument in favor of high levels of economic inequality, nor a repudiation of the claim that less economic inequality would generally be a good thing in modern market economies. In other words, this argument amounts to an opportunity cost argument for prioritizing other things from a marginal realist perspective; it is not an argument against lower levels of economic inequality at the broad idealist level. At this level, the evidence reviewed above still seems to suggest that less economic inequality would generally be better in relation to the aim of reducing suffering, even if it is not the most important thing to focus on.

12.7 What to Do About Economic Inequality? — A Complex Question

Whether a high level of economic inequality is generally a bad thing is different from the question of what, if anything, should be done about it. Thus, the claim that it would be better if economic inequality were markedly reduced does not necessarily imply that, say, taxes should ideally be raised, even as this is a commonly assumed implication. The truth is that there is a wide range of means that may be used to reduce economic inequality, each of which must be considered in terms of its respective upsides and downsides.

Worth noting is that most people actually seem to agree that lower levels of economic inequality would generally be better than the current state of inequality. For instance, one survey study found that Americans on average thought that the wealthiest top 20 percent should ideally own just over 30 percent of total US wealth, while they in fact owned more than 80 percent (Norton & Ariely, 2011).

The study also asked respondents whether they preferred a more equal wealth distribution (what was in fact the wealth distribution of Sweden) or a less equal distribution (what was in fact the wealth distribution of the US), and found that 92 percent favored the Swedish distribution. Even among people who earned more than $100,000 a year (the income bracket with the least egalitarian attitudes), around 90 percent deemed the more equal wealth distribution more desirable (Norton & Ariely, 2011, p. 10).

While there is likely significant cultural variation in how people would respond to these questions, the results above still suggest that a majority of people would prefer a more equal distribution of wealth over a less equal one (in terms of actual wealth distributions found in modern market economies). The more controversial question is what kind of means, if any, are acceptable for achieving less economic inequality.

Another issue worth exploring before jumping to policy proposals is what the overall trend is when it comes to economic inequality. After all, it seems necessary to understand the actual state and trajectory of economic inequality if we are to have an informed view of how we should respond to it. If we look at global income inequality, it turns out that inequality has in fact been declining on some measures over the past 20 years. For example, while the income share of the top 10 percent rose to 57.7 percent in 2000, it has since steadily declined to an estimated 52.3 percent in 2020. Likewise, the share of income of the bottom 50 percent has risen from 6.2 percent in 1980 to 8.4 percent in 2020 (World Inequality Database, 2020).

This is obviously not to say that the current state of affairs is anything close to ideal, but it does suggest that the global trend is at least moving in a more equal direction as far as income is concerned. And this in turn does raise the standards we should have for policy proposals to reduce economic inequality, as it means that improving the current trajectory is not as easy as one might naively have thought.

Another issue to consider is that some policies may reduce economic inequality locally while nonetheless increasing it globally — e.g. if a policy increases the income of the lower middle class in a wealthy country (who are still among the richest people globally) while it fails to increase, or even marginally reduces, the income of the poorest people globally (cf. Roser & Ortiz-Ospina, 2013a).

Such tradeoffs raise the question of whether it is more important to reduce inequality at the national or the global level. (To be sure, one can likely endorse policies that reduce both local and global inequality, but these respective aims probably still face significant tradeoffs, cf. Lewis, 2016.) Many of the reasons in favor of reducing inequality reviewed above seem to apply most strongly at the local level, yet global inequality might nevertheless be the more pressing issue. For not only may global inequalities come to feel increasingly local in an ever more globalized world, in which case many of the points mentioned above could apply globally as well, but global inequality may also be important for other reasons, such as for securing international stability and cooperation (Rogoff, 2021).

Moreover, global inequality may be more important given that its scope is greater, both in that it involves more people and because human poverty is far more severe among the global poor than among the poorest within wealthy nations. For example, of the 730 million people who lived in extreme poverty in 2015 (defined as living on less than $1.90 a day), the vast majority lived either in Sub-Saharan Africa or South Asia (Roser & Ortiz-Ospina, 2013b/2017).

A complete picture of global poverty and economic inequality must also include non-human beings, who may be considered victims of the most extreme forms of poverty and economic inequality (cf. Carlier & Treich, 2020). After all, the vast majority of non-human beings do not have the most basic of means (e.g. shelter and food) to fend off misery and premature death. And there is indeed no justification for ignoring this suffering and destitution in discussions about economic inequality and what to do about it (cf. Vinding, 2015; Johannsen, 2020). (The extreme poverty of wild animals may also help explain why economists have been among the leading figures drawing attention to the problem of wild-animal suffering, see e.g. Ng, 1995; Cowen, 2003.)

The points raised above highlight some of the many complexities involved in attempts to reduce economic inequality. How confident are we that our favored policies will in fact reduce economic inequality, and how confident are we that they will address the *most relevant* forms of economic inequality, rather than exacerbate them? This is yet another case in which we must make an effort to suspend our political overconfidence, and instead look at policy proposals and the empirical data with humility.

12.8 Reducing Economic Inequality Through Social Norms?

The idea of reducing economic inequality via norms may sound naive, until we realize that it actually has considerable precedent. For example, the early centuries of Christianity saw a campaign to make it admirable to donate to help the needy, which caused the rich to compete to see who could give the most to the poor (Henrich, 2015, pp. 128-129). Similar dynamics have played out in recent times, such as with Warren Buffett's Giving Pledge, which asks extremely wealthy people to give away at least half of their wealth to charity, with total pledges amounting to $600 billion. Such donations by the prestigious can inspire others to give (because of our tendency to imitate the prestigious, cf. Section 5.1) and can themselves serve as signals of status and prestige, which may further motivate charitable giving (Henrich, 2015, pp. 128-129).

Joe Henrich conjectures that there is an evolutionary logic to charitable and prosocial actions from the highly prestigious: since people tend to copy the behaviors of the most prestigious, it makes sense for prestigious people to lead by example with acts that establish norms of prosocial generosity, thereby inspiring the entire group to act in more prosocial ways toward everyone, including the prestigious themselves. This eventual payback of generous behavior was presumably more direct and visible when humans lived in small tribes — and Henrich acknowledges that this dynamic of conspicuous generosity is not so prevalent in modern societies. Yet examples such as the charitable norms of early Christianity reveal that similar dynamics can be realized in larger societies as well (Henrich, 2015, pp. 128-129).

Indeed, data suggests that the amount of money people donate to charity has increased significantly in recent years, which lends additional support to the feasibility of strong donation norms in a modern society. For instance, charitable donations in the US have risen from $150 billion in 1978 to around $450 billion in 2019 (in inflation-adjusted 2019 US dollars). These donations have also become more secular over time, as the fraction of charitable donations devoted to religious institutions has fallen from more than 50 percent in the mid-1980s to less than 30 percent in 2019 (Bellafiore, 2020).

Another clue to the power of social norms is that rich Asian countries such as Japan, South Korea, and Taiwan have relatively low levels of inequality at the level of market incomes, i.e. incomes before taxation (Milanovic, 2016, pp. 219-220). This low level of inequality probably has many causes, but an indication that norms and attitudes play an important role is that people in Japan express significantly greater approval of egalitarian income distributions, as well as a greater egalitarian orientation in general, compared to people in the West (Chiavacci, 2005, p. 109). Economist Thomas Piketty likewise suggests that recent changes in social norms regarding compensation rates have contributed to growing income inequality in countries such as the US and the UK (Piketty, 2013, pp. 419-420).

As mentioned above, the negative psychological effects associated with economic inequality may primarily be due to strong *signals* of inequality rather than inequality per se. Such signals, too, are clearly subject to norms. An anecdotal example might be the implicit dress codes and dressing norms that appear to prevail in, say, Italy versus Denmark. Whereas being dressed in a highly fashionable way is generally a positive thing in Italy, and perhaps even a must in order not to appear careless, the situation seems rather different in Denmark, where being dressed fancy in daily life is completely fine, but not important, and generally not something that gives status points; if anything, it might be read as a sign of insecurity or a lack of solidarity. (One should be careful not to overgeneralize, of course, but in broad terms, this cultural difference does seem real and significant.) Similar attitudes appear prevalent in Swedish culture, where the notion of "lagom" plays a prominent role. Lagom roughly means "in moderation" or "suitable", and is also associated with fairness, solidarity, and there being "enough for everyone".

Cultural norms can clearly influence the extent to which cues of inequality are magnified or muted in everyday life. How, then, can we move toward norms that encourage fewer overt displays of inequality as well as fewer status races of the kind that increase status anxiety and aggression? This stands as an open question. But a sensible proposal might be to make it common knowledge that many modern pursuits of relative status are mostly zero-sum, whereas this is not true of pursuits of status that have positive externalities, such as competing to donate the largest amount of money to the best charities, or "competing" to have the most low-key and most friendly demeanor.

After all, what counts as high-status depends heavily on the context, especially on the values and knowledge in people's heads. Just as smoking was cool until people came to know about its health consequences, conspicuous displays of economic inequality that involve zero-sum or even negative-sum dynamics may likewise come to be seen as uncool and embarrassingly uninformed — at least provided that it becomes common knowledge that prosocial, positive-sum signaling norms represent a superior equilibrium.

Such a change in norms may sound hopelessly ambitious and naive, yet note that among wealthy elites trying to impress other elites, the main thing that would need to change is "merely" what those other elites consider impressive and prestigious. And even a relatively small group of elites who decide to devote a substantial fraction of their money to effective charities rather than to absurd extravagances can still make a significant difference on the margin.

To be clear, nothing I have said above implies that better norms are necessarily the *only* or even the *main* way to reduce economic inequality and increase beneficent behavior. But it seems that it can at least be a significant factor to this end, and one that is far from being fully utilized. Note also that social norms would not involve any force, which renders them a uniquely agreeable tool to a broad range of political perspectives, from those that emphasize social solidarity to those that emphasize voluntarism.

12.9 Taxation

Few political subjects are more controversial than that of taxation. Indeed, it seems that much of the controversy over whether inequality is good or bad stems from underlying assumptions regarding the tax policies that are thought to follow from a given view of inequality. If one is strongly opposed to higher taxes for the wealthy, one will likely be more inclined to resist the notion that inequality has significant negative effects. Conversely, if one does support higher taxes for the wealthy, one will likely be inclined to overstate the negative effects of inequality (cf. Weeden & Kurzban, 2014, pp. 154-156).

It is worth noting that taxation is much less of an obvious good than some progressives seem to assume, as tax revenues are often spent on extremely harmful things. These include massive subsidies to factory farms and the fishing industry, as well as other forms of "corporate welfare" that plausibly serve to exacerbate economic inequality (Jansa, 2019). The roughly two trillion dollars that humanity spends each year on state militaries is another example (SIPRI, 2021). And beyond transparently harmful things, government budgets are also spent on things that are of questionable value, or at least things that are difficult to justify seizing people's money to buy, such as sports stadiums and art galleries.

One may argue that tax revenues should ideally not be spent on such harmful or frivolous things, but the reality is that they in fact *are* in today's world, and hence that increasing tax revenues likely would increase the budget spent on these things. That governments spend tax revenues on harmful things does not, of course, establish that taxes are generally harmful all things considered, or even that taxes should generally be reduced. But it does make it *less clear* than one might naively suppose that increasing tax revenues is necessarily a good thing, and it does raise the bar considerably for any argument seeking to establish a conclusion to that effect.

The truth is that taxation, like economic inequality, is a complex issue that involves many distinct dimensions. There are questions concerning *what*, if anything, should be taxed — e.g. income, wealth, or consumption. There are questions, often quite neglected, concerning *how* tax revenues should be spent. And there are questions about which policies are politically feasible in the real world.

None of these questions are simple. And a further complication is that the answers may vary depending on the *level* at which we approach these questions. For just as we can approach economic inequality from both local and global perspectives, questions about tax policy and spending can likewise be analyzed from various frames of reference. A policy that appears optimal when we consider only the local effects might nonetheless have bad consequences when we take its global effects into account.

Any claim depicting "the" optimal tax policy as a straightforward matter is thus clearly a case of political overconfidence and oversimplification — at least relative to values that give strong weight to the reduction of suffering. High confidence on these matters can hardly be warranted given the inherent uncertainty of economic systems. It is in this spirit that any tax proposal should ideally be considered: as a tentative suggestion that calls for further exploration. This is also true of the proposal outlined below.

12.10 A Negative Income Tax?

The idea of a negative income tax has some unique advantages that make it worth considering. The basic idea is that people who earn below a certain level of income will *receive* rather than pay money in taxes, where the amount paid is gradually reduced as the income increases. A benefit of the negative income tax is that it reduces inequality by directly helping those who earn the least money. And a benefit compared to existing welfare programs is that a negative income tax does not strongly reduce the incentive to work, unlike welfare checks that are suddenly no longer received the moment one earns a certain amount of money. Many existing welfare programs effectively perpetuate poverty in this way, by strongly disincentivizing higher earnings among the poorest, whereas a negative income tax would mean that tax recipients always end up with more money as their earnings increase.

Another advantage is that a negative income tax seems to have broad appeal among different political factions. The appeal among progressives should be obvious, yet many of those who have defended a negative income tax (and similar policies) most fervently have in fact been free-market libertarians (see e.g. Friedman, 1962; Murray, 2006; Zwolinski, 2014; Hemel & Fleischer, 2017). This potentially wide support may be among the main reasons to push for a negative income tax, since most other policies for reducing poverty and inequality seem unlikely to gain similarly wide support.

What might be the benefit of a negative income tax compared to a basic income paid to everyone? This is not an entirely straightforward question, since a universal basic income can be wholly equivalent to a negative income tax, provided that the tax rate is adjusted accordingly (Tondani, 2009, p. 247). But if we compare a negative income tax to a basic income that is paid to everyone tax-free, without the changes in tax rates that would render the two policies equivalent, the main benefit is that a negative income tax would be much cheaper, since far fewer people would be paid any money. And fewer still would be paid the full negative income tax that one would get at zero income. This may render a negative income tax more commonsensical, as it is provided only to those who need it, and roughly to the extent that they need it, which might in turn make a negative income tax more politically feasible.

Indeed, some proponents of a negative income tax are strongly opposed to a universal basic income (see e.g. Lacalle, 2020, ch. 11). By contrast, proponents of a universal basic income seem (more) likely to also support a negative income tax (as it can be seen as a step toward a universal basic income), which is a reason to think that a negative income tax would find broader support. On the other hand, the idea of a negative income tax seems less intuitive and less "sticky" than does the simpler idea of a basic income, which could be an impediment to the approval and eventual enactment of a negative income tax (cf. Heath & Heath, 2007).

One might object that a negative income tax in a wealthy nation would fail to help the poorest people who need money the most, i.e. the global poor, and that it would fail to address the most significant form of economic inequality, namely global inequality. This is a sensible objection, at least in relation to the claim that a negative income tax in a wealthy nation is the best way to reduce poverty and economic inequality from a broad idealist perspective.

Yet given that highly cosmopolitan policies are unlikely to be feasible in the near term, and hence that politics is likely to remain mostly local in all wealthy countries in the foreseeable future, it could be the case that a merely local negative income tax is among the best *feasible* policies for reducing poverty and economic inequality at this point.

Second, in terms of cosmopolitan policies, it seems that something like a negative income tax might also be among the more promising ways to provide foreign aid. For instance, richer countries could increase foreign aid budgets, or even reallocate current foreign aid budgets, such that they finance a negative income tax in the poorest countries (cf. Carter & Huston, 2018). Wealthy countries could thus coordinate so as to "cover" the poorest countries with a minimum income support for those who have the very least. And such a negative income tax in the poorest countries would indeed — provided it can be implemented — be relatively cheap to finance, since a low negative income tax by the standards of a wealthy nation could go very far in the poorest countries. A global program of this kind could also be implemented in gradual steps, starting with the very poorest countries, and then gradually expanding it to cover the somewhat less poor countries.

One can further speculate that the two forms of negative income tax discussed above — i.e. national and (more) cosmopolitan ones — could each, if implemented, make the other one more likely to be realized (cf. Aveek, 2012). Relatedly, it may be that a negative income tax would help entrench the idea that we should help those who are worst off, both economically and otherwise, which might have positive effects for suffering reduction in general.

But these points are rather speculative. Indeed, none of what I have said above should be read as a case for thinking that a negative income tax is necessarily the ideal tax policy, at any level. Rather, what I have outlined in this section are merely some reasons to think that a negative income tax *might* be a promising policy, and hence something that merits further consideration. Yet there is admittedly great uncertainty on this matter. After all, even if a negative income tax happened to be the best policy for reducing both poverty *and* economic inequality among humans, both locally *and* globally, it could still be suboptimal for other reasons. It could, for instance, increase the number of non-human beings exploited and tormented by humanity, since more people would be able to buy the products of such harmful practices (cf. Section 11.7; Holness-Tofts, 2020). This again underscores how tax policy is a deeply complicated issue, and that deeper investigations are required before strong recommendations can be justified.

12.11 The Debate on Inequality

12.11.1 Distortions and Overstatements

As an aside, it is worth noting how the debate on economic inequality exemplifies many of the points reviewed in Part II. For instance, in line with Jonathan Haidt's social intuitionist model — "intuitions come first, strategic reasoning second" — it seems that many people's views of inequality are based mostly on their immediate intuitions, which then motivate tendentious framings, cherry-picking, and a disregard of complexities (cf. Haidt, 2012, Part I; Sychev & Protasova, 2020).

These strong intuitions and failures of epistemic integrity are probably only amplified by dynamics of loyalty signaling, which give people an added incentive to engage in motivated reasoning and to posture with overconfident statements in favor of one side over the other, in effect pushing the debate toward unreasonable extremes (cf. Simler, 2016). At one extreme, there are those who claim that economic inequality is the single most important problem of all, and at the other, there are those who claim that economic inequality is not a problem in the least.

Those who claim that inequality is unimportant are often economists who appear unaware of, or otherwise downplay, the literature in social psychology that documents the psychological effects of inequality. Conversely, those who claim that economic inequality is the single most important problem we face are often social psychologists who seem unaware of, or otherwise downplay, the complexities and tradeoffs of modern economic systems, and who thus gloss over the opportunity costs and potential drawbacks of making the reduction of economic inequality our greatest priority.

This should not be all that surprising, as people readily see the world through the theoretical and cultural glasses they have been trained to use. And other forces likely also conspire to push the public debate on inequality toward an exchange of extreme positions. For example, it is generally to be expected that there is a selection effect of sorts when it comes to strong positions on contentious issues, since those who have the strongest and least mainstream views often get disproportionate media coverage compared to those who hold more moderate views. This may in turn distort our perception of the overall distribution of views on a given issue, a distribution that is probably more moderate than our public discourse tends to suggest — recall that most people characterize their political views as being close to the center of the traditional left-right spectrum (Tuschman, 2013, ch. 2).

12.11.2 The Overlooked Compatibility of Freedom and Equality

Similar points apply to debates on economic systems in general, and the potential tradeoffs between liberty and equality. Here, too, it is common to see a clash of overstated extremes that are hardly representative of most people's views, and which obscure the fact that one can be in favor of both liberty and greater economic equality at the same time. The social liberal views of John Stuart Mill and John Rawls are obvious examples of this, as both thinkers strongly endorsed and defended liberty, especially civil liberties, while also supporting policies that would reduce poverty and increase equality of opportunity (Mill, 1859; Rawls, 1971, pp. 73-78, ch. IV-V; Jensen, 2001).

Indeed, most people would probably endorse both liberty and (some level of) economic equality, and accept certain compromises between these values (cf. Norton & Ariely, 2011). And all modern democracies can likewise be said to exhibit such compromises to a significant degree, although the particular ways in which these respective values are accommodated clearly differ from country to country.

The notion that freedom and high levels of economic equality are irreconcilable is further undermined by the fact that many of the countries with the highest levels of freedom are also among the most economically equal countries. For instance, the five biggest Nordic countries — Denmark, Finland, Iceland, Norway, and Sweden — are all in the top 20 of both the Fraser Institute's rankings of the world's freest countries *and* the World Bank's rankings of the most economically equal countries (Roser & Ortiz-Ospina, 2013a, "Income inequality around the world"; Vásquez & McMahon, 2020, p. 5).

High levels of freedom thus clearly do not stand in an inverse relation to high levels of economic equality (even as there can be tradeoffs between them), which shows how many either-or debates on inequality are poorly framed.

12.11.3 False Choices and "Tail-End Awareness"

Debates on inequality are not unique in this regard, of course. Our political debates often set up such false conflicts, and present us with false choices between extreme positions. Balanced middle positions and compromises are usually possible, and probably widely supported. Yet such positions may be difficult to brand as a distinctive signal of political identity, in addition to being difficult to communicate in a single sentence, which might make these positions less visible (relative to their actual level of support).

This dynamic can be harmful not only by preventing nuanced and balanced positions from being discussed, but also by increasing political antipathy and strife. For if we feel that a lot of people hold certain extreme views — e.g. because these views are often presented in various media — a natural reaction may be to move somewhat toward the opposite extreme, so as to compensate for the perceived extremism (Vinding, 2020c).

A skewed representation of the overall political environment could thus contribute to a self-reinforcing spiral of polarization. This is a good reason to cultivate a political "tail-end awareness" — i.e. an awareness that the extreme views we encounter on various media are not representative of the overall distribution of political views, but rather the views of a minority found at the tail-ends of this distribution.

12.12 Plausible Proxies and Inequality

The proxies outlined in Chapter 9 again help to highlight and supplement some of the points made earlier.

12.12.1 Greater Levels of Cooperation

As mentioned above, greater economic inequality has been found to reduce interpersonal trust in wealthy countries, and to be associated with lower social cohesion, weaker rule of law, and more crime (Fajnzylber et al., 2002; Jordahl, 2007; Choe, 2008; Buttrick & Oishi, 2017). Some historical analyses have likewise found greater economic inequality to be associated with greater political instability and more violent conflicts, at least within the US (Turchin, 2013a; 2013b; 2016).

These findings suggest that the reduction of economic inequality is helpful for increasing cooperation and reducing the risk of conflict in the future, other things being equal. As one study summarized its findings on economic inequality and trust in wealthy countries:

> According to our preferred estimation, a 1 percentage point increase in the Gini index [a standard measure of inequality] leads to a decrease of approximately 2 percentage points in the share of individuals who believe that most people can be trusted. (Barone & Mocetti, 2016, p. 795)

This implies that even marginal reductions of economic inequality can have significant effects on levels of interpersonal trust, and hence on cooperation. Indeed, experiments suggest that interpersonal trust is crucial for overcoming partisan biases and political zero-sum mindsets, and for facilitating cross-partisan cooperation (Carlin & Love, 2013).

Similar findings have been reported for poverty in particular, which has been found to predict not which political wing people support, but rather political extremism in general, both on the left and the right (Tuschman, 2013, pp. 36-41). Reducing poverty thus also seems important for increasing cooperation and reducing the risk of political conflict.

These patterns make sense in theoretical terms. For just as "low-status, unmarried men" are more willing to engage in risky behaviors — because they have relatively little to lose and much to gain in biological terms (Henrich et al., 2012) — it makes sense that people who are poor, as well as people who perceive that they have much less than others, are willing to engage in more extreme and more risky behaviors, since they may instinctively feel that they have little to lose and much to gain. And studies indeed suggest that greater economic inequality increases risk-taking behaviors — even as the more risky choices in question had a lower expected value — which might help explain why greater inequality is associated with higher crime rates (Payne et al., 2017).

Thus, on theoretical and empirical grounds, we have reason to think that lower levels of economic inequality and lower levels of poverty are both conducive to greater cooperation and reduced risks of conflict, other things being equal.

12.12.2 Better Values

One way in which lower levels of economic inequality might be helpful for improving our values falls almost directly out of the point made above: if less inequality helps promote trust and cooperation (Jordahl, 2007), and in turn helps reduce partisan biases and zero-sum thinking (Carlin & Love, 2013), then it likely also enables us to have better conversations about values and compromises, and to advance our values together, rather than getting stuck in disagreements or ending up in conflicts over them.

The previous point represents a way in which equality might serve as a *means* of improving our values. Yet incorporating a greater degree of equality into our values themselves would also represent a great step toward better values. In particular, granting equal consideration to equal suffering in our moral and political deliberations may well be the single greatest value improvement we can make today. And even if instituting equal consideration of equal suffering is not currently politically realistic, we can still take steps toward instituting such equality to a greater extent.

12.12.3 Greater Capacity to Reduce Suffering

It seems likely that lower levels of economic inequality (relative to current levels in most wealthy countries) are also generally good for improving our capacity to reduce suffering, other things being equal. The positive effect that lower inequality has on interpersonal trust represents one reason to think so, as greater trust likely facilitates a greater capacity to work toward shared moral aims, including the aim of reducing suffering.

The association between lower levels of inequality and less risky and criminal behavior is another reason to think that less economic inequality is beneficial (Payne et al., 2017). For not only may a greater propensity to risky behavior impede our capacity to reduce suffering by weakening co-operation, but it may also be antithetical to the patient build-up of insights and resources that is necessary for reducing suffering in the long term (cf. Baumann, 2021).

Lastly, less economic inequality could be helpful for our capacity to reduce suffering given that high levels of economic inequality plausibly lead to a skewed and limited representation of viewpoints — recall that greater economic inequality is associated with reduced civic engagement (Uslaner & Brown, 2005). Consequently, we have tentative reasons to expect that less economic inequality would result in a wider range of views represented in our public discourse, which seems helpful for our overall ability to reduce suffering (cf. Scanlon, 2018, p. 91).

12.13 Conclusion

Many kinds of (in)equality are relevant to the reduction of suffering. The kind of equality that seems most important is the equal consideration of equal interests — extending this basic equality to *all* sentient beings, so that we count equal suffering equally. This is the equality conversation we need to have above everything else, and contributing to this conversation in sensible ways is plausibly the best marginal contribution we can make as far as equality is concerned.

Economic inequality among humans is also relevant, and seems worth reducing for a wide range of reasons. Yet what, if anything, we should do to achieve less economic inequality is a highly uncertain matter, both because of the difficulty of predicting the ultimate outcomes of various policies, and because of the potential tradeoffs with other aims that may be similarly or even more important than the reduction of economic inequality.

Perhaps one of the best contributions we can make in this regard, from a marginal realist perspective, is to help make the conversation about economic inequality more measured and nuanced. In particular, we can highlight that less economic inequality generally seems better (relative to current levels), but that further research is necessary to clarify which policies best satisfy both this aim and other aims relevant to reducing suffering. More broadly, it seems good to ensure that a consequentialist concern for suffering is featured prominently in the public conversation about inequality, such that future decisions reflect this concern to a greater extent.

13

Justice

Many views in political philosophy aim for justice above all else. But what does justice mean? What is the relationship between reducing suffering and justice? And which conceptions of justice should we endorse so as to best reduce suffering? These are some of the central questions of this chapter.

13.1 Definitions of Justice

The term "justice" is often used in rather different ways. One definition of justice simply treats it as synonymous with moral rightness in general — i.e. what is ethically right to do (Miller, 2017, 1). A more specific and perhaps more common conception of justice defines it as *institutional* moral rightness in particular. On this definition, justice primarily concerns what is morally right at the level of our laws and norms, yet does not necessarily pertain to all aspects of our personal lives. A similar and reportedly widely shared definition of justice understands it as "the minimal requirements that apply to us", and sees justice as essentially being about respecting the rights of others (Tuckness & Wolf, 2016, 4.1).

Other general definitions of justice include impartiality, equity, fairness, and "everyone getting what they deserve" (see e.g. the entry on justice in the Merriam-Webster Dictionary; Miller, 2017, 1). Some of these definitions of justice, such as equity and fairness, are problematic since definitions of these terms themselves often include the quality of being "just", which renders these definitions of justice somewhat circular. What is clear, however, is that "justice" is an ambiguous term, and hence that it is a term whose meaning we must specify before using it.

In contrast to these general conceptions of justice, there are also more narrow forms of justice, including criminal justice, distributive justice, and procedural justice. These terms, too, have been defined in various ways, yet their meaning is at least somewhat clearer. Criminal justice usually refers to legitimate practices and institutions relating to crime and punishment. Distributive justice is usually about how resources ought to be distributed (an issue that was explored at some length in the previous chapter). And procedural justice usually concerns legitimate procedures for institutional decision-making, such as when writing and enforcing laws (an issue that will be explored to some extent in the next chapter).

13.2 Reframing Justice, Reframing Suffering Reduction

Justice has hitherto rarely been framed explicitly in terms of reducing suffering. But if we understand justice as moral rightness — whether as a general matter or as a matter of *institutional* moral rightness in particular — then this failure to connect justice and suffering reduction is a mistake, in two distinct ways. First, as argued in Chapter 7, the reduction of suffering must at the very least be considered a critical component of moral rightness, and hence of justice in this synonymous sense. Again, this is not to say that justice (as moral rightness) is necessarily *only* about reducing suffering. But it is to say that the aim of reducing suffering must be given first-rate prominence in our conception of justice (Mayerfeld, 1999; Vinding, 2020a, Part I).

Second, our failure to frame the reduction of suffering as a matter of justice probably represents a mistake from the converse perspective as well. That is, we have not only made a mistake when talking about justice without connecting it explicitly with the reduction of suffering, but we have also, it seems, made a mistake when talking about the reduction of suffering without framing it more in terms of justice. The latter mistake is more a strategic mistake than it is a mistake at the level of normative theory — a strategic mistake that relates to the point made earlier about moral software amenable to the human mind (see Section 8.6). In particular, framing things in terms of justice appears to have some unique advantages compared to framing things purely in terms of ethics. As noted above, justice often has strong connotations of *institutional* and *collective* moral rightness, whereas ethics often has more personal connotations — i.e. ethics often seems more concerned with what *individual* agents ought to do than does justice. This might render sound precepts less motivating when they are phrased in ethical terms, and perhaps make them feel less imperative, compared to equivalent precepts and principles framed in terms of justice, at least to many people.

It may thus be wise, for instance, to translate a strong *prima facie* duty to reduce suffering into the claim that, other things being equal, a society is more just the less intense suffering it entails. And the suffering-focused conception of justice — or at least the suffering-focused *component* of justice — might likewise be usefully communicated in pithy statements, such as "justice as the prevention of extreme suffering", or simply "justice as effective compassion".

To clarify, the point I am making is not that all or even most discussions about suffering-focused ethics should be reframed in terms of justice; after all, the ethics framing also has unique benefits, such as being more precise and more familiar to certain audiences. The point is merely that the complete neglect of the justice framing likely represents a missed opportunity, and hence that there ideally should be considerably *more* talk of suffering reduction in terms of justice, especially in political discussions.

13.3 Criminal Justice as Effective Harm Prevention

Justice in general is strongly associated with *criminal* justice in particular, indeed so much so that the term "justice" is often used synonymously with criminal justice. What would a criminal justice system look like if it were strongly animated by "justice as the prevention of extreme suffering"? This is a vast and complicated issue, of course, but we can at least outline some of the main answers to the question in broad idealist terms.

13.3.1 Expanding the Scope: Truly Impartial Criminal Justice

First, and perhaps most important, the scope of criminal justice should be radically expanded such that it includes all sentient beings. Deliberately causing intense suffering to *any* sentient being should be considered a serious crime, and the prevention of such crimes should be a key objective of the criminal justice system. This obviously applies to corporations just as much as to individual citizens: all deliberate impositions of serious harm for mere pleasure, convenience, or profits should be outlawed, which would effectively imply a ban on factory farming, slaughterhouses, and the fishing industry (Cochrane, 2012, ch. 4).

13.3.2 Preventive Rather than Retributive Justice

Another key point is that the criminal justice system should be forward-looking, aimed at the *prevention* of suffering, rather than backward-looking and aimed at retribution. In other words, harm reduction should be the primary aim of the institutions that constitute our criminal justice system. Laws, the police, courts, prisons, and rehabilitation centers — all of them should be set up such that they prevent people from causing intense suffering and other serious harms, e.g. by deterring, containing, and rehabilitating criminals. And these institutions should also take the suffering of criminals themselves into account, regarding this suffering as something to be reduced as well (within the constraints of the need to create deterrence). After all, a ruthless criminal justice system can itself be a major source of extreme suffering, such as by sanctioning the torture of criminals, and in some cases the torture of mere suspects (cf. Hajjar, 2013).

Such a concern for the suffering of criminals may invite the objection that a justice system aimed at suffering prevention would be dangerously soft on crime. Yet this does not follow. After all, a justice system that seeks to reduce suffering would be as keen as any to prevent, say, sadistic criminals from causing extreme suffering, and should therefore be willing to employ the means necessary to prevent such horrors.

It is an open question which means are in fact optimal for such crime prevention, but some degree of proportionality of punishments relative to the severity of a crime is likely required, one reason being basic compatibility with human psychology — if a justice system *feels* extremely unfair to everyone's intuitions, it is hardly optimal all things considered (cf. Section 8.4; Boyer & Petersen, 2012, p. 9, pp. 16-17).

On the other hand, while ordinary intuitions about crime and punishment should not be wholly disregarded, they should also not be trusted uncritically. An effective criminal justice system ultimately needs to be guided by what in fact works, as opposed to what merely feels right to our most immediate intuitions.

Worth noting in this regard is that beliefs about the effectiveness of punishment — a strictly *empirical* question — are strongly influenced by people's political persuasions. For example, conservatives tend to consider punishment more effective than do liberals, and also tend to think that a lenient criminal justice system will encourage more crime (Tuschman, 2013, p. 248; Silver & Silver, 2017). Yet our political attitudes should obviously not determine our views on these purely empirical matters. We should ideally be acutely aware of, and seek to control for, such biasing influences, whatever our intuitive inclinations may be.

In terms of what seems to work for effective crime and harm prevention, it is worth highlighting the success of the Norwegian criminal justice system in particular, which can be considered highly forward-looking. For instance, the criminal justice system in Norway has a strong focus on rehabilitating prisoners, and makes an active effort to make them functional members of society after prison. It grants prisoners roughly the same access to education and health care services as the rest of the population, and the prisons are considered among the most comfortable prisons in the world (Dorjsuren, 2020; Kriminalomsorgen, 2021). These factors may help explain why Norway has among the lowest crime and incarceration rates in the world — its incarceration rate is 13 times lower than that of the United States — and possibly the single lowest recidivism rate in the world (World Population Review, 2021a; 2021b).

Of course, the justice system itself is not the only factor that determines these outcomes. As we saw in the previous chapter, broader factors such as economic inequality can also influence crime rates, and these broader factors, too, are worth considering in efforts to reduce crime (Fajnzylber et al., 2002; Choe, 2008). Yet the success of justice systems that focus more on rehabilitation, such as the justice systems of Norway and other Nordic countries, along with a meta-analysis of the effectiveness of restorative justice practices, do suggest that such forward-looking alternatives to traditional retribution are indeed more effective at preventing crime (Latimer et al., 2005; see also World Health Organization, 2010). In terms of specific interventions, there is evidence that cognitive-behavioral therapy can significantly reduce the recidivism rates of criminal offenders (Lipsey et al., 2001; Illescas & Genovés, 2008).

13.3.3 Special Attention to Crimes of Extreme Cruelty

Certain forms of crime are especially worthy of priority for a justice system that gives chief importance to the prevention of intense suffering. Sadistic crime, both against human and non-human beings, is one such class of especially serious crimes, as sadistic criminals are often motivated to cause suffering of extreme intensities. In particular, sadistic slaughterhouse and factory farm workers currently represent a significant source of extreme suffering, and uncovering and preventing such large-scale sadism should be an urgent priority of the criminal justice system (cf. Eisnitz, 2009, Part Two; Wilson, 2014). (Of course, it should be an urgent priority to end *all* the horrors of slaughterhouses and factory farms, yet exposing and bringing to trial the worst cruelties of these institutions seems more tractable in the near term, and may also be a uniquely promising way to bring greater attention to the broader problem of non-human suffering, cf. Section 10.9.3.)

Another important class of crimes to prevent is vengeful crime, and largely for the same reason: these crimes often involve especially severe suffering. Indeed, vengeful crime may be considered a form of sadistic crime, though one that is triggered by a perceived wrongdoing rather than a general enjoyment of the infliction of suffering. And while vengefulness is far more common than unprovoked sadism — according to psychologist David Chester, revenge is the most common motive behind violent and aggressive behavior — it turns out that sadistic people are far more likely to pursue vengeful acts (McNeill, 2017; Chester & DeWall, 2018). This suggests that sadism is a crucial risk factor to screen for and ideally prevent when seeking to minimize extreme crimes of various kinds.

How these crimes can best be prevented again stands as an open question. One proposal might be to ensure that people who commit crimes of extreme sadism or vindictiveness are not granted the freedom to cause extreme suffering again. That is, people who have deliberately inflicted extreme suffering on others should perhaps be imprisoned for life without parole, on the grounds that they pose an unacceptably high risk.

It also seems important to take strong *proactive* steps to prevent these crimes. One such proactive step could be to develop reliable screening procedures for traits of extreme sadism and vindictiveness among people charged with violent crime, and to then use such screenings to inform decisions on whether a given prisoner should be released (cf. Milgram, 2014). Other steps might be to explore treatments for these extreme traits that people could undergo voluntarily, and to search for interventions that can help prevent such traits from developing in the first place (cf. Althaus & Baumann, 2020).

13.3.4 Rejecting Victimless "Crime"

A forward-looking criminal justice system motivated strongly by "justice as the prevention of extreme suffering" would not only imply significant *expansions* of our conception of criminal justice (e.g. ensuring that it includes all sentient beings). It would also imply the *shrinkage* and eventual *elimination* of prevailing excesses of criminal justice systems around the world. In particular, it would imply the legalization of things that are currently considered criminal in various countries, yet which do not impose suffering on anyone. Obvious examples include homosexuality, which is still illegal in many countries, as well as any sexual act between consenting adults that does not impinge on others. Intolerance toward such relationships and activities is difficult to justify based on a concern for suffering, which indeed rarely, if ever, seems the basis for such intolerance, let alone the criminalization of these consensual activities. On the contrary, a strong concern for the prevention of suffering would most likely imply that we vigorously *affirm* tolerance toward such consensual activities, and that we actively *protect* people's right to engage in them — not just at the level of our laws, but also at the level of our culture at large.

Likewise, there are strong reasons to think that people who are undergoing intense suffering should have the legal right to end their own lives, and to get assistance to this end — something that has indeed been legal for several years in Belgium, Canada, Colombia, Luxembourg, and the Netherlands.

There is considerable evidence that these laws help reduce intense suffering. For example, in Belgium, where voluntary euthanasia was legalized in 2002, the euthanasia law has enabled thousands of terminally ill patients — mostly cancer patients — to be relieved from intense suffering that they preferred not to endure (Dierickx et al., 2016). Moreover, a large survey study found that 90 percent of Belgian physicians expressed approval for voluntary euthanasia for terminal patients, while a significant majority, 66 percent, further thought that Belgium's euthanasia law "contributes to the carefulness of physicians' medical behavior at the end of life" (Smets et al., 2011).

There are, to be sure, legitimate worries about negative secondary effects of legalizing voluntary euthanasia (see e.g. the objection raised in the following section). And the risk of such negative effects is certainly worth actively exploring and reducing, not least by instituting safeguards against abuse. However, we should also not lose sight of the potential *positive* secondary effects, such as moving our laws and culture at large in a direction of showing greater concern for suffering, which is probably the overall direction that a suffering-focused conception of justice would recommend. (For an in-depth exploration of this complicated moral and legal issue, see Sumner, 2011.)

Drugs and drug laws represent another controversial issue in this regard. While a thorough treatment of this subject lies beyond the scope of this chapter, it is worth noting how prevailing drug laws cause unnecessary suffering in numerous ways. For one, they fuel drug cartels, which in many cases perpetrate crimes that involve extreme suffering, such as the torturous murders performed by drug gangs in Mexico, and the horrors of the Mexican drug war in general, which is among the deadliest ongoing conflicts in the world (Agren, 2020; Zorzut, 2021). Second, prevailing drug laws often lead to dangerously potent and impure drugs, which increases the risk that the drugs cause severe suffering and death (Cowles, 2019, ch. 21).

Third, the criminalization of safe and private drug use results in judicial processes and imprisonments that waste public resources — resources that could otherwise be used to reduce intense suffering — while seriously harming drug users who have caused no harm to others (Earp et al., 2021). For example, it is estimated that around 40,000 people are imprisoned for cannabis offenses in the US, the problematic nature of which is all the more striking given that cannabis is now legal in many states (Oleck, 2020).

Fourth, prevailing drug laws prevent the alleviation of certain forms of extreme suffering for which various illegal substances show great promise. For example, cluster headaches, also known as suicide headaches, are among the most extreme forms of pain known to medicine, and psychedelic substances such as psilocybin show unique promise in reducing, and in some cases even completely preventing, cluster headaches (Leighton, 2020). Our drug laws thus effectively force such patients to endure some of the most extreme forms of suffering. Similar points apply to other painful conditions — including PTSD, depression, and anxiety — for which psychedelic substances likewise show great potential, yet a potential that prevailing drug laws have largely suppressed, by which these laws have also caused much suffering (Krediet et al., 2020; Goldberg et al., 2020; Vargas et al., 2020). (Additional problems caused by prevailing drug laws are reviewed in Rorheim & Roll Spinnangr, 2016, pp. 2-5.)

There is room for reasonable debate about which regulations of drugs, if any, are optimal for reducing suffering. Yet it seems safe to say that significant steps toward drug liberalization are recommendable in any case, including various policies that have already been successfully implemented in a number of countries. For instance, in 2001, Portugal decriminalized the use of all drugs (though not the sale of drugs), and switched from an approach of punishing to one of treating people with drug dependence. Beyond solving the problem of wasting resources to imprison harmless drug users, this reform was followed by a more than 70 percent decline in annual HIV infections among people with drug dependence (a gradual decline from 2000 to 2006), a more than 50 percent reduction in annual deaths due to opiates (e.g. heroin), and more than a doubling of the number of people seeking treatment for drug addiction (Greenwald, 2009, pp. 15-17; Hughes & Stevens, 2010). Other countries, such as the Netherlands and Switzerland, have likewise had great success with measures focused on assisting rather than punishing people with drug dependence, including the provision of heroin-assisted treatment facilities. This approach, too, has significantly reduced HIV infections and opiate-related deaths (Blanken et al., 2010; Smart, 2018; Knopf, 2019).

It also seems safe to recommend that research into the medical potential of psychedelic substances should be legalized, and that sufferers whose pain can be alleviated by certain drugs should be allowed to use these drugs. Both of these steps have already been taken to some extent in many countries. Yet despite recent progress, current drug laws are still responsible for vast amounts of extreme suffering, by barring access to effective pain relief and prevention — e.g. morphine for terminally ill patients who endure intense pain, and psilocybin for those who suffer from cluster headaches (Leighton, 2018; 2020). Reforming laws to help these sufferers of extreme pain could be a relatively easy victory, as such reforms are likely to face much less opposition than more radical drug reforms.

Regardless of how radically liberal our drug laws should ultimately be, the most promising changes to push for at this stage are probably fairly moderate and gradual in nature. These changes plausibly include the legalization of specific substances that are already legal in some countries, e.g. marijuana and psilocybin mushrooms, as well as decriminalization policies of the kind adopted by Portugal — policies whose widespread adoption is also supported by mainstream organizations such as Human Rights Watch and the International Federation of Red Cross (Cowles, 2019, ch. 21-23; Rorheim & Roll Spinnangr, 2016, pp. 5-7).

13.3.5 What About the Opacity of Institutions?

An objection to these arguments about victimless crime might be to invoke the point that our institutions often function in opaque ways, and hence that we should be careful about overruling existing laws (cf. Section 6.4).

This is indeed a reason to be cautious about the arguments outlined above. However, a couple of things are worth noting.

First, this objection applies most strongly to aspects of our culture that reflect deep trial-and-error adaptations, and many of the laws mentioned above, including our current drug laws, do not appear to reflect such a process. The so-called "War on Drugs", for instance, is only about a century old, prior to which prohibitions against drugs were much less prevalent. Indeed, in the early 20th century, the US government regulated the production and distribution of cocaine (History, 2017). Yet many drugs were then completely banned, including alcohol, which was banned in the US in 1920, and in various other countries around the same time.

In the case of alcohol, however, people were relatively quick to realize that the prohibition policy was a disaster, as it greatly increased organized crime and the consumption of dangerously impure alcohol, e.g. liquor containing the potentially lethal compound methanol (Thornton, 1991). The prohibition on alcohol was lifted in the US in 1933, with countries such as Iceland, Finland, and Norway revoking similar bans around the same time. And one may argue that these respective revocations are unique in the history of modern drug laws, in that they *did* reflect a trial-and-error process of seeing what works and legislating accordingly. Bans on other drugs, in contrast, have generally persisted despite the bans having largely the same deleterious effects.

In other words, it seems that one could just as well make the opposite argument to the one raised in the objection above, at least regarding drug laws: our prevailing policy of extensive prohibition is a novelty that has not been thoroughly tested, and in the relatively few cases where we have genuinely scrutinized this policy, it appears that the outcome has been revocation rather than recommendation. Of course, this argument does not imply that it would be ideal to legalize all drugs, but it does at least cast serious doubt on the idea that the opacity of institutions necessarily favors our current drug laws. And such doubts appear further supported by the consequences and lessons that are now emerging from these laws, as it seems increasingly clear that the "War on Drugs" is a failed policy — a policy that is indeed now slowly being revoked in many parts of the world (History, 2017; Cowles, 2019).

Another point worth emphasizing is that the opacity of our institutions merely represents a *provisional* reason to be *cautious* about radical reforms. It is by no means a decisive reason against change. Thus, when a change in existing laws can be supported by strong reasons — e.g. that it could prevent extreme suffering for people who prefer to end their lives (in the case of legalized euthanasia) — it is not a sufficient counterargument to simply invoke the opacity of institutions in the abstract. A plausible argument must be presented as to *why*, in more specific terms, the proposed policy is bad, despite the strong reasons that favor it. And such arguments are more difficult to make when other countries have already implemented similar policies with what appear to be overall positive effects, as in the case of the drug harm reduction policies of the Netherlands, Portugal, and Switzerland, or the euthanasia policies of Belgium, Luxembourg, the Netherlands, and other countries.

So while it is true that there are serious complications associated with the policies discussed in the previous section, these complications alone are hardly a sufficient reason to support the status quo. Indeed, we should be careful to control for status quo bias when thinking about these matters — that is, our tendency to prefer things as they are simply because that is the way they are (Bostrom & Ord, 2006). Specifically, it is worth asking whether our evaluations of a given policy change would be different if it had already been implemented.

For example, while we might feel intuitively opposed to changing the law so as to decriminalize drug use, the issue may seem wholly different if we think about it in the Portuguese context, where this change has *already* been implemented and followed by significant reductions in HIV infections and opiate-related deaths. When considered from this perspective, it seems highly *un*reasonable to support a change back to the previous condition. And there indeed appears to be no serious political effort to return to the previous approach in Portugal at this point (cf. Greenwald, 2009, p. 28; Ferreira, 2017).

13.4 Practical Steps Toward "Criminal Justice as Effective Harm Prevention"

The points made in the previous sections mostly pertain to the broad idealist level. But what can we do today, at the marginal realist level, to move toward a criminal justice system that helps prevent suffering more effectively? It seems there are two broad strategies.

First, we can make the general case that criminal justice should be aimed at the prevention of intense suffering, or at least that suffering reduction should be a foremost aim of the criminal justice system. This includes conveying the points above regarding how the criminal justice system ought to protect all sentient beings, how it should be forward-looking and take the suffering of criminals into account, and how it should give special priority to preventing crimes of extreme cruelty against any sentient being. Working to increase support for these ideals of criminal justice — especially among policy-makers and other influential elites — is likely among the best ways to eventually realize them (cf. Pinker, 2012; Taylor, 2015; Harris, 2021).

Second, we can further explore which specific policies and laws would be recommended by these ideals, including which policies represent the best steps toward a more effectively compassionate justice system. This may include laws that incrementally increase and extend punishments for animal abuse, many forms of which are currently legal, as well as policies that ensure a greater enforcement of laws against animal abuse, which is woefully lacking in current legal systems (Sunstein, 2009, II.A-B; Shooster, 2018). Other promising steps may include reforms that gradually advance a more forward-looking approach to criminal justice, such as laws that require prisons to offer evidence-based therapy programs to all prisoners (cf. Lipsey et al., 2001; Latimer et al., 2005).

Such explorations of specific policies would neatly complement the first strategy outlined above, by providing a clearer sense of the practical recommendations of a compassionate and forward-looking approach to criminal justice. In general, one of the best steps we can take today, on the margin, is likely to promote more of an empirical approach to criminal justice, whereby we gradually update our justice system based on the best available evidence, especially with an eye to the expected consequences for suffering reduction.

13.5 Plausible Proxies and Justice

The proxies outlined in Chapter 9 help underscore an important point that has been largely neglected so far in this discussion, both as it pertains to justice in general and criminal justice in particular. The point being that institutions that give strong weight to the reduction of suffering should not always focus on reducing suffering in very direct ways. Instead, it is often more important to focus on indirect and supportive aims, such as ensuring the safety and stability of our institutions — aims that serve as preconditions for any successful endeavor to reduce suffering, yet which can be tempting to overlook from a naive consequentialist perspective. This means that even if we were to orient all our laws and policies *purely* toward the reduction of suffering, they would in many ways still be less radical than one might intuitively expect (cf. Vinding, 2020a, 9.3-9.6).

13.5.1 Greater Levels of Cooperation

As we have seen, securing cooperation seems a key aim for suffering reduction, even if it is not the first thing that comes to mind when we think about optimal ways to reduce suffering (cf. Section 9.3.1). Consequently, the search algorithm for identifying the ideal justice system in relation to suffering reduction should likely focus strongly on the question, "How can we best secure cooperation and minimize conflict?"

In more specific terms, this likely implies a focus on predictability, trust-building, and de-escalation mechanisms for potential conflicts, both at the level of domestic and international law (cf. Tomasik, 2013f). How these aims can best be achieved is an open question worthy of further exploration. Yet the two broad strategies outlined in the previous section again seem reasonable: 1) increasing the level of support for the general aim of promoting cooperation and compromise, such as by explaining the many reasons why it is even more important than common sense suggests (Tomasik, 2013a; Vinding, 2020d). And 2) investigating which particular policies appear best suited to this end — an endeavor that seems a high priority from a marginal realist perspective (Tomasik, 2014a; 2014b).

13.5.2 Better Values

The positive proxy of improving humanity's values has similar implications, in that it recommends a justice system that secures certain *preconditions* for suffering reduction rather than always focusing on this aim directly. In particular, it underscores the importance of protecting free speech, so that moral and empirical views can be openly discussed, and so that the voices of activists and the powerless will not be silenced (cf. Sections 11.4, 11.8, & 11.12.2). This not only means securing people's right to speak without interference from governments, but also the freedom to speak without being subjected to violent threats from private actors.

Other preconditions for improving our values likely include impartial and reliable institutions, at every level of our criminal justice system, such that these institutions avoid breeding mistrust and conspiracies, and instead help foster a public environment in which we can have good-faith dialogues among opposing parties. Again, strong protections of free speech and trustworthy institutions may not be among the first things we think about when considering the ideal justice system for reducing suffering, yet a closer examination strongly suggests that these broader factors are critical indeed.

13.5.3 Greater Capacity to Reduce Suffering

In order to improve our overall capacity to reduce suffering — e.g. accumulating useful insights, competences, and resources — we likewise need a criminal justice system that helps secure the stability and incentives that are required for this project to succeed. Institutions that fail to provide safety against violence and theft in the near term will likewise fail at fostering long-term investments toward humanity's future capacity to reduce suffering, and toward our capacity to steer away from bad outcomes in general. The positive proxy of increasing our capacity to reduce suffering thus also lends support to many of the common-sense aims of criminal justice, including the provision of safety and stability.

13.6 Conclusion

It is a mistake that justice is not more strongly associated with the reduction of extreme suffering. Those concerned with justice make a serious normative mistake when they fail to connect justice strongly and explicitly with the reduction of intense suffering, whereas those concerned with the reduction of suffering probably make a strategic mistake by not framing this moral aim (more) in terms of justice.

With respect to criminal justice in particular, we can point to a number of key changes that would be recommended by "justice as the prevention of extreme suffering". The criminal justice system should seek to minimize harm in a forward-looking way; it should expand its scope so as to become truly impartial, striving to protect *all* sentient beings from deliberate harm; and it should give special priority to preventing crimes of extreme cruelty. Moreover, it should stop criminalizing victimless "crime", and thus stop creating or perpetuating intense suffering where there otherwise would be none.

Yet the criminal justice system should clearly do more than just seek to prevent extreme suffering directly, even if reducing suffering were its sole aim. It must also support cooperation and help secure a condition in which we can improve our values and our capacity to reduce suffering, all of which implies dependable and sensible laws that do not flagrantly violate the moral intuitions of most people.

The best marginal steps we can take to push the criminal justice system in these directions probably include defending this general approach — or at least defending effective harm prevention as being *among* the foremost aims of criminal justice — as well as further exploring and conveying which specific policies and laws appear most recommendable within this framework.

14

Democracy

The last prominent notion of political philosophy I will explore is democracy. What does democracy entail? How can we improve existing democratic systems? And are there better alternatives to modern liberal democracy? These questions are important to investigate, not least in our complacently democratized age. After all, liberal democracy is a relatively new invention that has gone from being virtually non-existent to encompassing roughly half the human population in just two centuries, during which our understanding of democracy has likewise undergone significant shifts. This changeful history suggests that we could soon be headed for similarly significant changes in our understanding and practice of democracy, and perhaps new forms of governance altogether. What those future systems will look like may be up to us to decide.

14.1 The Meaning of Democracy

The word "democracy" derives from the Greek words *demos*, "the people", and *kratia*, "rule", which together capture the general and widely accepted definition of democracy: "rule by the people". But beyond this general definition, the concept of democracy is in fact quite ambiguous and carries rather diverse meanings, as illustrated by the history of democracy itself.

For instance, the democracy of ancient Athens would only grant political influence to adult, "free-born" men who owned land, and a large fraction of its human population were slaves. The same was true for much of the history of the United States, which is often considered the oldest existing democracy: it allowed human slavery for almost a full century after its founding, and like most democracies in the early modern age, it did not give women the right to vote until the 20th century (Tuckness & Wolf, 2016, 5.4).

So while these democracies amounted to "rule by the people" in one sense, they were clearly quite far from being "democratic" in the standard, contemporary sense of the word, given how many people they denied political influence. Yet the question of who gets to be included or represented in the political process is merely one among many dimensions along which democracies can vary. For example, democratic systems can take radically different forms (e.g. direct vs. representational), use different methods for casting and aggregating votes (e.g. ranked choice vs. first-past-the-post), and have different constitutional designs (e.g. parliamentary vs. presidential).

Worth noting, too, is that democracy has come to entail a wide range of principles and institutions that go beyond mere political decision procedures. These include the protection of civil liberties and property rights, as well as principles such as the rule of law and equality before the law. Such principles are among the cornerstones of democracy in the modern sense of the word, what is also known as liberal democracy. (The alternative, "illiberal democracy", is commonly considered undemocratic, and is sometimes referred to as "electoral authoritarianism", Zakaria, 2003, ch. 3; Schedler, 2006.)

That democracy has come to cover such a broad range of principles is worth keeping in mind when discussing the merits of democracy and potential ways to improve it. After all, one may criticize specific decision procedures that prevail in modern democracies without necessarily questioning some of the core principles associated with liberal democracy, such as civil liberties and equality before the law. This also highlights how democracy — in its broad, modern sense — cannot be separated from the general issues of liberty, equality, and justice. Since I have already discussed many of the key questions and principles related to these general issues, I will not re-examine them here. Instead, this chapter will focus on specific governance structures and how these can be improved. (Though to be sure, certain governance structures are, as we shall see, both dependent on and conducive to the realization of broader "democratic" principles and rights, such as civil liberties.)

14.2 Preliminary Clarifications

Several scholars have argued that democratic decision procedures are desirable independently of their consequences (even if the consequences also matter). For instance, some have argued that people have a right to self-government, from which a right to democratic participation is claimed to follow, while others have argued that democracy is desirable because it is implied by certain forms of equality that are intrinsically good. These views stand in contrast to instrumentalist views of democracy, which hold that the desirability (or undesirability) of democracy depends *purely* on its consequences (Christiano & Sameer, 2006, 2.1-2.2).

The *prima facie* duty to reduce suffering that I explore here does not commit us to a particular view of the value of democratic decision procedures, and can indeed be compatible with any of them, even as it does imply a strong consequentialist focus on suffering reduction. My own view is that democracy should be evaluated chiefly based on how conducive it is to reducing extreme suffering (compared to alternative forms of government). But as in the case of the previous chapters, the thrust of the following analysis should still apply to virtually all views that entail a strong *prima facie* duty to reduce suffering, including views that sometimes give greater priority to other things.

14.3 Democracy vs. Other Tried Systems of Government

Let us start by exploring how democracy compares with existing alternatives across a number of key parameters.

14.3.1 Securing Liberty

An important metric we can use to evaluate different forms of government is their respective propensity to protect basic liberties. Indeed, this metric is important both to the two-step ideal, for which free expression serves as a precondition, and to the aim of reducing suffering (see Chapter 11).

It turns out that there is a significant correlation between civil liberties and democratic decision procedures. For example, the Democracy Index published by the Economist Intelligence Unit ranks countries on a scale from 0 to 10 in terms of how well they protect civil liberties and how democratic their electoral processes are, respectively. And the correlation between these two factors is striking. The 21 countries that scored above 8.8 on civil liberties all happened to score above 9 on democratic electoral processes, while the countries that scored below 1 on civil liberties all scored 0.08 or below on their electoral processes. Conversely, all of the 24 countries that scored 0 on electoral processes scored below 3.6 on civil liberties, with most of them scoring below 1.5. And a similar correlation is evident at the intermediate stages of these respective measures (Economist Intelligence Unit, 2021, pp. 8-13).

In other words, when looking at existing forms of government, it seems that societies with proper democratic elections tend to strongly protect civil liberties, whereas societies without democratic elections tend to suppress civil liberties. (In light of this close association between democratic elections and civil liberties, it should not be surprising that many of the most relevant considerations pertaining to democracy, including some of those made below, happen to mirror some of the most relevant considerations pertaining to civil liberties reviewed in Chapter 11.)

14.3.2 Protection of Human Rights

Another relevant factor to consider is human rights protection, which includes protection against human torture, political imprisonment, and government killing. Democracies also prove consistently better than existing alternatives in this regard. For example, when ranking the world's political regimes on a scale from –10 (full autocracy) to 10 (full democracy) and plotting them against a "human rights protection score" ranging from around –3.8 to around 5.4, only the countries that score 8 or above on the democracy scale manage to score above 2 on the human rights protection score (Roser & Herre, 2013). To be clear, democracy is not a *sufficient* condition for the protection of human rights, as evidenced by various democratic states that score low on human rights protection (e.g. India, Mexico, and Kenya). But democratic states still tend to be much better than non-democratic states at protecting basic human rights (Roser & Herre, 2013).

14.3.3 Animal Protection Laws

Democracies also tend to have better (or rather, "less bad") legal protections for non-human animals, with the most democratic nations generally scoring the highest, and the least democratic nations generally scoring the lowest on ratings of their respective animal protection legislation, to the extent that the latter have such legislation at all (World Animal Protection, 2020). However, it must be stressed that *all* countries continue to allow the existence of factory farms and slaughterhouses, and that we should not allow these rankings to deceive us about the unthinkable horrors that are still being inflicted on non-human beings in all countries, democratic or not. (For some additional qualifications and further discussion, see Sections 11.6-11.8.)

14.3.4 Securing Peace

Another relevant factor to consider is the frequency with which governments of different kinds engage in violent conflict (cf. Section 9.3.1). "Democratic peace theory" holds that democracies are reluctant to wage war against each other, in part because voters generally prefer to avoid wars. While democratic peace theory has some critics (Layne, 1994; Rosato, 2003) — for instance, some question whether the relationship between democracy and peace is causal — it nonetheless appears widely accepted that war between democratic nations is uniquely rare. And various studies suggest that the relationship is indeed a causal one, running from democracy to peace (Mousseau & Shi, 1999; Gelpi & Griesdorf, 2001; Imai & Lo, 2021). As one analysis concluded:

Overturning the negative association between democracy and conflict would require a confounder that is forty-seven times more prevalent in democratic dyads than in other dyads. To put this number in context, the relationship between democracy and peace is at least five times as robust as that between smoking and lung cancer. (Imai & Lo, 2021, abstract)

It is important to note that these conclusions pertain to conflicts in democracy-democracy dyads in particular, as distinct from conflicts between democratic nations and non-democratic nations, so-called "monadic conflicts", which are considerably more common. However, some studies suggest that democracies are also significantly less likely to initiate monadic conflicts compared to non-democracies (Souva & Prins, 2006; Caprioli & Trumbore, 2006). And this conclusion seems to apply more strongly to democracies of certain kinds. As one study concluded, "a country's electoral system turns out to be the most important institutional factor that dampens war involvement" — in particular, "democracies with a proportionate-representation system [i.e. a system in which political parties gain seats in proportion to the number of votes they receive] tend to have significantly less such involvement according to three alternative measures" (Leblang & Chan, 2003, abstract).

Taken together, the evidence pertaining to democratic peace theory suggests that greater democratization at the expense of authoritarianism will tend to reduce the risk of war, which holds true even if we only grant the dyadic version of the democratic peace theory (while assuming, in line with the evidence cited above, that greater democratization at least does not make conflicts with non-democratic nations *more* likely).

A similar pattern is found in measures that take domestic peace (in relation to humans) into account, such as the Global Peace Index. In addition to a country's tendency to engage in international conflicts, the Global Peace Index scores countries on internal metrics such as crime rates, violent demonstrations, terrorist acts, and political stability. The pattern is again strikingly consistent: the most peaceful countries are generally highly democratic ones — the top five in 2021 were Iceland, New Zealand, Denmark,

Portugal, and Slovenia — whereas the least peaceful countries tend to be highly authoritarian ones; among the most violent countries are North Korea, Russia, Iraq, Syria, and Afghanistan (Institute for Economics & Peace, 2021, pp. 9-10; see also Christiano, 2011, III).

14.3.5 Convergent Conclusions

On each of the key issues reviewed above — civil liberties, protection of human rights, animal protection laws, and proneness to conflict and violence — democracy seems markedly better than the existing alternatives, i.e. variations on authoritarianism. This is hardly a controversial claim. Indeed, the view that liberal democracy is superior to authoritarian alternatives is shared by authors of a wide range of moral persuasions, including those concerned with the reduction of suffering (see e.g. Mill, 1861; Popper, 1945; Sen, 1999, ch. 6; Ryder, 2006, p. 33; Christiano, 2011; Mayerfeld, 2016; Enoch, 2021, sec. 5).

Even critics of democracy tend to agree that liberal democracy is significantly better than all other systems tried to date. (E.g. anarchist Michael Huemer: "In large and obvious ways, [democracy] is superior to all other known forms of government" Huemer, 2013, p. 79; Jason Brennan: "[Democracy is] great, it's the best system we have so far" Illing, 2018.)

Modern liberal democracy seems better than authoritarian alternatives — both for reducing suffering and for realizing the two-step ideal — not necessarily because modern democracy is in itself so great and unimprovable, but mostly because the hitherto tried alternatives are so terrible: they suppress free speech, stifle moral progress, fail to secure peace, torture people, and provide even worse legal protections for non-human animals than do democracies. Compared to this, liberal democracy does appear the lesser evil overall, despite the crimes against sentience that it continues to commit in all of its contemporary manifestations.

14.4 Better Alternatives?

To say that liberal democracy in its modern form seems significantly better than the existing alternatives is obviously not to say that it is the best system possible. In fact, it would be highly surprising if even the best functioning liberal democracies of today happened to be optimal (relative to a given set of plausible values), especially considering how much change such democracies have undergone recently. So it is only natural, and indeed paramount, to ask whether there might be better systems on offer.

Worth noting in this regard is that many proposed alternatives to modern democracy are in fact, in the great scheme of things, still quite democratic in nature, and hence they arguably count more as significant *revisions* of democracy than as new systems altogether. To be sure, this is not true of anarchist proposals, which would do away with governments altogether (for a discussion of anarchy, see Sections 11.9-11.11). But it does seem true of most proposed alternatives that maintain a ruling government, including proposals such as futarchy and epistocracy, which we will explore below.

14.4.1 Futarchy

The hypothetical form of government known as futarchy was first proposed by Robin Hanson, who summarizes it as "vote on values, but bet on beliefs" (Hanson, 2013). The core idea is to divide policy decisions into two steps that mirror the respective steps in the two-step ideal: a step in which we choose values and a step in which we sort out empirical beliefs. At the level of the first step, Hanson's proposal entails that we keep the democratic status quo, by having people vote on their preferred values. Then, in the second step, the idea is to use a betting market to predict which policies best realize these democratically chosen values (Hanson, 2013, IX).

Hanson leaves it open as to how exactly these respective steps can best be carried out, which is something that could be refined over time. But he outlines the following as a potential way it might be done. First, in terms of voting on values, one could have voters elect representatives whose task will be to construct an overall value measure — what Hanson calls "national welfare", although it could in principle reflect wholly cosmopolitan values. This might include measures of human health, GDP, and animal suffering, all weighted so as to reflect the collective values of voters (Hanson, 2013, III, IX, XI). A betting market would then be used to determine which policies have the best effects in terms of increasing this overall value measure, provided that the policies abide by constitutional constraints (Hanson, 2013, IX).

For example, if a new policy has been proposed, people will be able to bet on the effects that the policy would have on the voter-based value measure. The policy will then be adopted if it is estimated to increase the value measure relative to the status quo; otherwise, it will be rejected. If the policy is rejected, people who have bet on its effects will get their money back. If it is implemented, people will gain or lose money depending on how accurate their predictions turn out to be in future assessments of the overall value measure. (This is a highly simplified summary; for more details, see Hanson, 2013, IX.)

Perhaps the most common objection to futarchy is that some people, such as wealthy individuals and corporations, might attempt to manipulate the market. Hanson argues that attempts to manipulate betting markets generally do not reduce their accuracy, and cites empirical evidence in favor of this claim (Wolfers & Zitzewitz, 2004; Hanson et al., 2006; Hanson, 2013, II). Yet one can doubt whether this will also apply to betting markets pertaining to the most consequential decisions, where manipulators may be incentivized to engage in elaborate manipulation schemes.

Another criticism relates more to the psychological feasibility of the institution (cf. Boyer & Petersen, 2012; Bøggild & Petersen, 2016). For example, futarchy lacks certain features that people might be intuitively drawn toward, such as the ability to hold elected leaders accountable for their policy decisions — a betting market cannot be held accountable in the same way leaders can. It is, to be sure, by no means obvious that this represents a fatal problem for futarchy. Yet nor is it obvious that it does not. After all, there is some evidence that the *feeling* of participating in and influencing policy decisions is a significant contributor to people's well-being in democracies (Frey & Stutzer, 2000, 4.7). And while futarchy does allow people to vote on values, it may still fail to provide nearly the same feeling of influence as do contemporary democracies, even if the ultimate level of influence is roughly the same. (Additional objections to futarchy are explored in Vaintrob, 2021.)

In any case, Hanson does not recommend futarchy as something to be instituted right away, but rather recommends testing it on smaller scales, and then tweaking and scaling it up gradually, provided that it works well on those smaller scales (Hanson, 2013, XIV). He likewise acknowledges that there are many potential problems with futarchy, yet argues that it might still be better and less subject to problems than existing alternatives (Hanson, 2013, XIII).

14.4.2 Epistocracy

Another form of government that has been put forward is epistocracy, which can roughly be defined as "rule by the knowledgeable" (Brennan, 2016, ch. 8). There are many proposed versions of epistocracy, all of which can be seen as more or less radical revisions of democracy. One example is a plural voting system in which everyone is granted at least one vote, but where additional votes are granted to people who have proven themselves more knowledgeable in a test of political knowledge. Additional votes may then either be granted to everyone who scores above a certain threshold, or in proportion to the test score (Brennan, 2016, p. 15).

A more controversial version is restricted suffrage, which would entail that voting rights are granted only to those who prove themselves sufficiently knowledgeable on political matters. Such a system would still have a (more or less) representative government, and would still grant widespread voting rights, although these rights would be significantly less widespread than in liberal democracies as we know them (Brennan, 2016, p. 15).

An argument in favor of epistocracy is that existing democracies already exclude people under a certain age from voting, with the rationale that people who are under a certain age are not sufficiently competent to vote. Hence, the criterion of competence is already accepted in some form, and defenders of epistocracy may argue that their criterion — i.e. people's actual level of knowledge as revealed by a test — is significantly less arbitrary than a crude age limit (Brennan, 2016, pp. 148-149). After all, an epistocratic system could offer its test of competence to *all* citizens, regardless of age, and thus in principle exclude no one from the opportunity to gain political influence. A related argument is that requiring people to demonstrate a minimum level of competence in order to vote is similar to requiring people to have a driving license in order to drive a car. In both cases, the argument goes, incompetent people are likely to make bad decisions that harm others in significant ways (Brennan, 2016, ch. 8).

An objection to epistocracy is that it seems difficult to devise tests of political competence that are fair and free from bias. Who is to construct these tests, and which criteria should we use to determine what counts as relevant political knowledge? A possible response is that we could use democracy itself to decide what should be included in the test. For example, one could crowdsource suggestions for topics to test voters on, and then have people vote on these suggestions such that, say, the 30 most popular suggestions end up going on the test (Illing, 2018).

Another objection is that the people who would do well on these tests are likely to have different interests from the population at large. For instance, it seems that such tests would select for people who belong to the cognitive elite, people who are probably significantly wealthier and more resourceful than average, which could make such people less likely to favor policies that would help those who are worse off. (Recall the influence self-interest can have on political attitudes, reviewed in Section 2.5.)

A worry might thus be that epistocracy risks sliding toward a (greater) neglect of the weakest and neediest in society, which may undo whatever would be gained by having more informed voters. After all, the fact that one scores well on a knowledge test does not imply that one will endorse, let alone personify, values that are more advanced than the values of people who score lower on such tests.

Lastly, epistocracy might be difficult to implement for psychological reasons similar to those reviewed above in relation to futarchy (cf. Boyer & Petersen, 2012). For example, epistocracy appears strongly at odds with the egalitarian ethos that prevails in modern democracies, at least as far as political equality (for adult humans) is concerned — an ethos that arguably has ancient evolutionary roots (cf. Boehm, 1999). It does not seem far-fetched that people who consistently fail in epistocratic tests of political knowledge would come to feel disempowered and frustrated, and that they might eventually revolt. The political turmoil and polarization we are currently witnessing may be mild compared to what an epistocratic society would induce.

However, supporters of epistocracy tend to make recommendations similar to those made by Hanson with regard to futarchy: rather than rushing to implement it on a large scale, they recommend testing it out on smaller scales, and then tweaking and scaling it up if it is successful on those smaller scales (Brennan, 2016, ch. 8).

14.4.3 Sortition

Democracy is often considered synonymous with elections, and elections are indeed a defining feature of all modern democracies. Yet there is an alternative form of democracy that involves neither elections nor politicians as we know them, namely sortition: governance by randomly selected citizens, also known as lottocracy. While this idea may appear unrealistic on its face, it has in fact been used in various places throughout history, including in the democracy of ancient Athens, not to mention that many countries already use random selection when choosing jurors for jury trials, which serve consequential roles as well. Moreover, interest in sortition as a serious alternative to elective democracies has been rising in recent years, and it has been defended by an increasing number of scholars (see e.g. Burnheim, 1985; O'Leary, 2006; Dowlen, 2008; Delannoi & Dowlen, 2010; Guerrero, 2014; Van Reybrouck, 2016; Hennig, 2017; Landemore, 2020).

Sortition can take many different forms. An example might be a system in which a country's laws are created by a citizens' assembly consisting of, say, 500 randomly selected citizens who will serve for a few years. Participation in this assembly could be made wholly voluntary, such that citizens may decline the offer if they prefer. It could also offer each participant a good compensation and extensive education so that they have the time and resources required to deliberate thoroughly on the relevant issues.

One of the main arguments in favor of sortition is that it would avoid much of what seems bad about politics today. It could allow political decision-makers to focus on studying and deciding on the relevant issues rather than worrying about sending the right signals to optimize their election prospects. Besides, it could enable these public decision-makers to collaborate in ways that are often difficult for party politicians, as it seems easier for decision-makers to openly change their minds and to collaborate with opponents when no one is tied by party coalitions. Resources devoted to zero-sum pursuits, such as election campaigns and lobbies that fund opposing politicians, could instead be devoted to positive-sum endeavors.

In terms of the broader cultural effects, sortition might likewise reduce political factionalism and polarization among the population at large, as the presentation of politics in the media would be less centered on a zero-sum competition for votes between opposing politicians and parties (cf. Hannon, 2021, sec. 2). For instance, it seems unlikely that the current state of political polarization in the United States would be nearly as intense if there were no politicians or parties vying for power, and if policy issues were no longer viewed through the stupefying identity lenses of "Democrats versus Republicans" (cf. Drutman, 2021).

A common critique of sortition is that it fails to select people based on their expertise, and hence risks giving too much power to ignorant or incompetent people. This may be a legitimate concern. However, one could argue that elective democracies are vulnerable to similar critiques, as politicians in such democracies are hardly elected based on their expertise in policy-making either, as opposed to their ability to appeal to voters and donors. But even if we grant that the average politician in elective democracies has significantly more policy expertise than the average citizen who accepts lottocratic selection, it may still be the case that lottocratic systems will tend to produce better collective decisions than do elective systems, e.g. in terms of being more cooperative and more successful in achieving widely shared aims, such as reducing suffering.

Another concern might be that sortition, like futarchy, could fail to give people the *feeling* of influencing policy to the same extent as an elective system would, and hence that people might feel unhappy and powerless in a lottocratic system, even if such a system were better at satisfying their idealized policy preferences (cf. Boyer & Petersen, 2012). This worry may be mitigated somewhat by the fact that a lottocratic system truly gives everyone an equal chance of becoming a political decision-maker — something that is decidedly not the case in elective democracies — which might make the lottocratic system seem more fair and more representative. Yet it could still be the case that a tiny chance of being randomly selected is too psychologically unsatisfying compared to the more palpable experience of casting a vote, and of being included in *some* way, even if each person's vote has a similarly tiny chance of altering the election results.

Again, as in the case of futarchy and epistocracy, it is hardly advisable to rush to implement sortition-based institutions in a sweeping manner. In the words of sortition proponent Alex Guerrero, "a piecemeal, small-steps, small-scale approach to introducing any such institutions would be wise" (Guerrero, 2014, p. 178).

14.4.4 Algorithmic Governance: Replacing Politicians with Software

On the more futuristic end of suggested alternatives to existing democracies, there is the class of proposals that would have us automate our political system to a much greater extent, toward "algorithmic governance" (Hughes, 2017).

One such proposal is what César Hidalgo calls "Augmented Democracy", which entails (eventually) replacing politicians with software agents that represent each voter based on the voter's preferences. Rather than casting a single vote, each voter would feed their representative software program with detailed information about their policy preferences, and the software agent should then be able to optimize for those policy preferences more competently than any human politician could, at least when compared to a human politician who is simultaneously representing thousands or millions of other people who also voted for them (Hidalgo, 2019a; 2019b; see also Sætra, 2020).

An argument in favor of applying advanced software in politics to a greater extent, and to perhaps even let it replace politicians eventually, is that such software systems can make decisions based on superhuman amounts of data and calculations, and hence, the argument goes, these decisions can be expected to become increasingly superior to human decisions in virtually all domains. Just as advanced software systems handily beat even the best humans at chess today, so they might eventually come to beat humans at making good political decisions.

Yet these competences also represent one of the main arguments *against* having advanced software in power: handing over all political power to software programs, or even just granting them significantly *more* power, might increase the risk of catastrophic outcomes driven by advanced software. After all, such software systems could be extremely competent in a technical sense without necessarily reflecting the best of human values, or even a minimal concern for suffering. (This theme is explored in Bostrom, 2014, ch. 7. Note that Bostrom's particular conception of a localized "intelligence explosion" has been discussed and criticized in Hanson & Yudkowsky, 2013; Vinding, 2016a. However, the point that competent software systems might fail to embody sensible values stands regardless.)

Some proponents of algorithmic governance acknowledge these and other risks of technological innovation and empowerment, while also arguing that a greater integration of advanced software in our political decisions ultimately represents the best way to address these risks (Hughes, 2017).

Other objections relate to the lack of transparency of powerful software systems, risks of algorithmic biases, and a lack of accountability. These are all potentially serious objections, yet defenders of algorithmic governance argue that existing political systems might in fact be worse in these regards, and that these objections are in any case not strong enough to undermine the case for algorithmic governance (Sætra, 2020, sec. 4).

Algorithmic governance is in many ways (even) less developed than the proposals explored above. But it still seems an idea worthy of further exploration and development. In particular, it seems a priority to further clarify the risks and opportunities associated with algorithmic governance, and to gain greater insight into which forms of algorithmic governance appear most promising (cf. Danaher et al., 2017).

14.5 Improving Democracy

The four broad proposals outlined above represent alternatives to modern liberal democracy. But there are also proposals that count more as *improvements* of modern democracy rather than as outright alternatives (though again, there is no clear line between what counts as "an alternative to" versus "an improvement of" present-day democracy; it is obviously a spectrum).

Below are some proposals that could all be pursued squarely *within* the core framework of liberal democracy as we know it.

14.5.1 Sentiocracy: Granting Political Representation to All Sentient Beings

One such proposed improvement that is compatible with prevailing ideals of political rights and participation, and arguably even entailed by these ideals, is to grant democratic representation to non-human animals — what Alasdair Cochrane calls a "sentientist democracy" (Cochrane, 2018, ch. 3). This can be seen as yet another step away from political discrimination against historically marginalized groups, and toward a more just society that excludes no sentient being from moral and political consideration.

The core argument for granting political representation to non-human animals is essentially the same as the core argument for granting them *moral* consideration: sentient non-human beings have interests, such as the interest not to suffer, and the mere fact that these beings belong to a different species cannot justify that we disregard or exclude them or their interests — neither morally nor politically. (For more elaborate arguments, see Garner, 2017; Cochrane, 2018, ch. 3; Hooley, 2018, ch. 3.) Likewise, on an instrumental level, it seems reasonable to expect that a society that grants political representation to non-human beings would in fact be better at respecting the interests of these beings, and that such a society would prioritize the alleviation of non-human suffering to a greater extent.

Similar arguments can be made in favor of granting (stronger) political representation to human children, which is also worth supporting (cf. Ryder, 2001, pp. 83-84). Yet given that most parents partly vote based on the interests of their children, and given that human children are already granted extensive legal protection in modern democracies (even if inadequately enforced), this seems comparatively less urgent than does the need to grant *some* minimal representation to the most numerous and most tormented group of beings among us (cf. Hooley, 2018, p. 62).

There are various ways in which political representation of non-human beings could be realized. A concrete proposal advanced by Cochrane is to have representatives whose sole task is to represent the interests of non-human beings in the political process. Cochrane suggests that such representatives could be appointed by a randomly selected citizens' assembly, and argues that these representatives ought to represent all non-human beings, both domestic and wild, living within their jurisdiction (Cochrane, 2018, ch. 3). (Additional proposals are explored in Hooley, 2018, ch. 8.)

Tentative steps have in fact already been taken toward greater political representation of non-human beings (cf. Chaney et al., 2021). For example, a recently proposed animal welfare bill that is to be considered in the parliament of the United Kingdom would create an "animal sentience committee" — a committee that would advise the government on how its policies might harm non-human animals "as sentient beings" (Goldsmith, 2021, p. 1). The passing of this bill could be a significant step toward greater representation of non-human interests in the political process, and a step that might set the precedent for still greater consideration and representation of non-human beings in the future.

Just as we no longer consider societies that disenfranchise certain groups of (domestic) humans to be truly democratic, there may come a time in which a democracy that does not grant political representation to non-human beings will likewise be considered unacceptably regressive and inconsistent with the most basic notions of political equality and fairness.

14.5.2 More or Less Direct Democracy?

Various scholars argue that it is undesirable to have a pure direct democracy in which *every* legislative decision is made by popular vote, without any representative politicians involved (see e.g. Achen & Bartels, 2016, ch. 3; Landemore, 2020, ch. 3). A common argument for this conclusion is that a pure direct democracy would require too much time and effort on the part of ordinary citizens. Most voters are already ignorant and unmotivated to learn about things that concern major voting decisions made every few years, and being confronted with countless voting decisions — often of a highly technical nature — seems likely to just compound this problem (cf. Caplan, 2007, ch. 5). Indeed, this is a key difference between a pure direct democracy and a lottocracy with a limited number of randomly selected decision-makers: in the latter case, the decision-makers will have time to learn about the relevant issues, and be better able to discuss and coordinate their decisions. (Lottocracy is sometimes considered a form of direct democracy, yet what I mean by direct democracy in the discussion below is direct democracy in the standard sense of giving *every* citizen a vote on *all* political decisions.)

Perhaps a more interesting question is whether modern liberal democracies should generally have *more* or *less* direct democracy compared to what they have today. Should most democracies strive to be more like Switzerland, with its many referendums, or should democracies generally strive to have even *less* popular influence on the margin?

Some scholars have argued that the latter would be better in many cases, as direct democracy is prone to overruling expert judgments in ways that lead to bad consequences (Zakaria, 2003, ch. 5; Achen & Bartels, 2016, ch. 3; Jones, 2020). One example of this was a popular vote in California in 1978 that effectively closed a number of firefighting companies in an area at high risk of fires; 13 years later, a large fire broke out and destroyed 3,000 houses and killed 25 people and an untold number of non-human animals. Contrary to the recommendations of fire professionals, direct democracy chose to reduce safety and emergency measures (Achen & Bartels, 2016, p. 84).

Direct democracy also seems to have hampered moral progress in several cases. For instance, women in Switzerland were only given the right to vote at the national level in 1971. And in the Swiss canton of Appenzell Innerrhoden, arguably the canton with the highest level of direct democracy, women had to wait until 1991 before they got the right to vote in local elections, a right that was only secured due to a ruling of the Swiss Supreme Court (Foulkes, 2001). The use of popular referenda was likewise the reason that Lichtenstein was the last country in Europe to grant women the right to vote in national elections, which happened in 1984, by a narrow margin (51.3 percent) in an all-male national referendum — 66 years after neighboring Austria granted suffrage to women (Gesley, 2021).

On the other hand, there may also be considerable upsides to greater levels of direct democracy (Matsusaka, 2005). For example, among the 26 cantons of Switzerland, there is some evidence that citizens in cantons with greater levels of direct democracy generally report higher levels of subjective well-being (Frey & Stutzer, 2000). Moreover, while direct democracy can impede moral progress, it may also have the potential to accelerate it. A case in point might be the popular initiative to ban factory farming in Switzerland that was proposed in 2019, and which managed to receive the 100,000 signatures required to bring the initiative to a public referendum (SWI, 2019). While it remains to be seen whether this initiative will be successful, the fact that citizen activists are able to put such a pressing issue on the mainstream political agenda is itself likely a positive feature of a relatively high degree of direct democracy.

It seems unclear whether it is generally better to have more or less direct democracy. Perhaps it is desirable to preserve and promote certain aspects of direct democracy, such as the right to launch ballot initiatives (cf. Schukraft, 2020), while not requiring the broader public to decide on, say, technical issues that require security expertise. More research on the effects and possible variations of direct democracy seems warranted. Yet the mixed considerations and literatures cited above do cast doubt on the notion that "more versus less direct democracy" is among the most promising dimensions to focus on in political efforts to reduce suffering.

14.5.3 Parliamentarism vs. Presidentialism

Among modern democracies, one can broadly distinguish two different systems of government: parliamentarism and presidentialism. In a parliamentary system, the executive branch of government is appointed by — and may also be dismissed by — the legislative branch, and the ministers of the government carry a collective responsibility. In a presidential system, by contrast, the head of government, i.e. the president, is elected directly by citizens. The president has the power to appoint and dismiss ministers, and is responsible for the entire executive branch (Santos, 2020, p. 2).

A number of scholars have argued that parliamentarism has proved superior to presidentialism across a wide range of important metrics. In the words of political scientist and diplomat Tiago Santos, "political science analysis of the different systems is close to a consensus on the superiority of parliamentarism, economic models almost unanimously point in the same direction, and empirical evidence supports it" (Santos, 2020, p. xii).

In particular, countries with parliamentary systems are generally better at protecting individual liberties, including freedom of the press, and income inequality is 12-24 percent higher in presidential countries compared to parliamentarist ones (McManus & Ozkan, 2018; Santos, 2020, p. 1, p. 11). Parliamentary systems appear to have significantly lower levels of political polarization, and are generally more stable, more peaceful, and less prone to coups (Santos, 2020, p. 1, ch. 1; Casal Bértoa & Rama, 2021). They also tend to have "better corruption control, bureaucratic quality, rule of law, [...] and literacy" (Gerring et al., 2009; Santos, 2020, p. 47).

In terms of more general measures, parliamentarist states generally have higher scores on the UN Development Program's Inequality-Adjusted Development Index, which tracks the overall level of human health, education, and income of more than 150 nations. For instance, only parliamentary countries are found in the top 20 of this index, despite the fact that presidential countries are about as numerous as parliamentary ones (Santos, 2020, p. 2, p. 11).

Evidence pertaining to corporations and local governance likewise supports the overall effectiveness of parliamentary models over presidential ones. In terms of corporate governance, most corporations choose a structure similar to parliamentarism, whereas virtually none opt for a presidentialist structure, which suggests that parliamentarist structures have considerable advantages for effective and adaptive governance (Santos, 2020, 1.2.2).

At the level of local government, it turns out that cities that opt for more parliamentary structures, such as by electing a city council that appoints a council manager, tend to do better on various measures compared to cities that opt for a more presidential structure, such as a "strong mayor" model in which a city mayor and council are elected separately. For example, cities with the council manager model tend to have less corruption and less conflict among senior officials (Carr, 2015; Nelson & Afonso, 2019; Santos, 2020, 1.2.3).

What might account for this apparent superiority of parliamentarist structures compared to presidentialist ones? Santos argues that the difference can be thought of as a general algorithmic difference: parliamentarist systems implement a decision algorithm that is generally better suited for making good decisions (Santos, 2021b). By design, parliamentary systems tend to have a relatively high level of alignment between the government and the legislature, as the latter appoints the former. Presidential systems, in contrast, have no mechanism for aligning the majority of the legislature with the head of government, which means that the president is likely to diverge in significant ways from a majority of the legislature. In addition, parliamentary systems can more easily replace incompetent leaders, and tend to have less concentration of power, which may likewise support better decision-making (Linz, 1990; Santos, 2020, 1.1.1).

If there is indeed such a strong case in favor of parliamentarism over presidentialism, across so many relevant measures, should we not expect parliamentarism to be more popular? First, parliamentarism arguably *is* quite popular, especially among political scientists, as hinted by Santos above, and as evidenced by an elaborate literature defending its superiority compared to presidentialism (see e.g. Linz & Valenzuela, 1994; Riggs, 1997; Selinger, 2019; Santos, 2020).

Second, it is not surprising if parliamentarism has a difficult time gaining widespread popularity, in part because the case for parliamentarism can sound vaguely technical and boring, and in part because any vision to advance parliamentarist change is unlikely to stir our primal political motivations. It fails to inspire a struggle against a political outgroup — there is no clear "anti-parliamentarist" coalition to oppose — and hence being in favor of parliamentarism fails to signal any clear partisan loyalties, just as it fails to be a signal of altruistic traits. (Recall the difference between *showing* that we care versus *actually* reducing suffering, and how we are plausibly often secretly motivated to do the former, even when we are sincere about actually reducing suffering, cf. Section 8.10; Simler & Hanson, 2018, ch. 12.)

That said, it must be acknowledged that, as always, there is considerable uncertainty. For even if we grant that the case for parliamentarism over presidentialism is convincing, it still remains an open question how parliamentarism can best be promoted (Santos, 2020, ch. 6), and not least whether the promotion of parliamentarism is indeed among the best things we can push for on the margin, compared to some of the other potential changes explored in this chapter. (We shall return to the latter question in Section 14.7.)

14.5.4 Voting Reform

Democracies vary greatly in terms of the voting systems they use, which raises the question of whether some voting systems are better than others. One example of a voting method is single-winner plurality voting, the system used in the US and the UK, where voters each cast a single vote for a candidate or party, and the one that gets the most votes (e.g. in a local district or state) wins the entire vote.

There are many alternatives to single-winner plurality voting, such as ranked-choice voting (voters rank their preferred candidates); approval voting (voters mark each of the candidates they approve of); or simply giving each voter a single vote in a proportional, multi-winner voting system where different parties gain influence in rough proportion to the number of votes they receive — a voting system used in many European and South American countries.

Replacing single-winner plurality voting seems desirable for a number of reasons. One reason is that plurality voting, due to its winner-take-all nature, tends to produce a political system with fewer parties — often just two, as exemplified by the Democrat-Republican duopoly in US politics (Duverger, 1954). This appears to have various bad effects (Drutman, 2020, Part II).

In theory, a two-party system seems at a greater risk of producing excessive political polarization, in that it forces voters to unite around two antagonistic poles, as opposed to having a spectrum of parties that allows for the expression of more fine-grained preferences and compromises. And empirical evidence supports this story: voters in multiparty, proportional democracies tend to display significantly less animosity toward opposing parties — as well as a greater affinity for their preferred party — than do voters in democracies with fewer parties and low proportionality (Drutman, 2021).

The polarization and partisan animosity of contemporary US politics is a salient case in point. For example, a poll from 2014 found that 27 percent of Democrats and 36 percent of Republicans saw the other party as "a threat to the nation's well-being" (Pew Research Center, 2014). Such high levels of polarization and animosity seem antithetical to the aim of securing cooperation and improving our values through open-ended dialogue (cf. Sections 9.3.1-9.3.2).

Another reason a system with low proportionality and few parties might be bad is that it risks leading voters to feel disempowered, as any voting preference that departs from the few dominant parties is likely to feel wasted. In general, having fewer political options to choose from likely leads voters to feel a lower "political fit" with their preferred party — a conjecture that seems supported by the above-mentioned finding that voters in multiparty systems tend to express a greater affinity for their preferred party (Drutman, 2021). Lastly, replacing plurality voting with a more proportionate system appears desirable given that democracies with a proportionate voting system have significantly less war involvement compared to democracies that do not (Leblang & Chan, 2003).

It is widely agreed among voting experts that single-winner plurality voting ought to be superseded in democratic elections. A step recommended by various voting experts in this regard is to instead use approval voting or ranked-choice voting (Laslier, 2011; see also electionscience.org and fairvote.org).

These alternatives likely represent a better voting system. However, the benefits of moving from plurality voting to these alternative systems seem quite limited as long as one maintains a single-winner voting system — that is, if voters continue to elect a single winner in each district, only now through ranked-choice voting or approval voting. After all, such alternatives would still largely fail to bring about proportional representation and its associated benefits reviewed above (cf. Drutman & Strano, 2021). To fully achieve these benefits, one will arguably need to promote a parliamentarist system (with multi-winner districts) over a presidentialist one, given the inherent winner-take-all nature of presidential systems. This suggests that parliamentarism, combined with proportional representation, should be the ideal end goal of reforms that seek to improve voter representation (cf. Santos, 2020, pp. 16-17).

14.6 Avoiding Pathocracy: A Top Priority

When it comes to governance, it may be more important to avoid the worst than to achieve the very best. In other words, rather than striving for anything like political perfection, perhaps the most pressing task is to steer clear of catastrophic failure modes that put humanity down a disastrous path that entails vast amounts of suffering. A specific such failure mode that is particularly worrying is "pathocracy" — rule by individuals with malevolent personality traits (Lobaczewski, 2006, ch. 5; Taylor, 2019; Althaus & Baumann, 2020).

14.6.1 The Peril of Malevolent Rulers

In their essay "Reducing long-term risks from malevolent actors", David Althaus and Tobias Baumann explore the risk of having people with malevolent traits in power, by which they mean people who score high on the Dark Tetrad traits of psychopathy, narcissism, Machiavellianism, or sadism. There is some evidence suggesting that people with such traits are disproportionately likely to gain power, and that there is a high risk that they will cause great harm if they do (Althaus & Baumann, 2020).

Two reasons suggest that malevolent individuals are more likely to gain power. First, their willingness to use whatever means required, particularly their willingness to cheat and be manipulative (Machiavellianism), may give them an advantage over other contenders for power, especially in the absence of institutions that can enforce norms and laws against such behavior. Second, psychological studies suggest that people who score high in psychopathy, narcissism, and Machiavellianism are also significantly more *motivated* to become dominant and powerful (Bennett, 1988; Jonason & Ferrell, 2016; Taylor, 2019).

Taken together, this suggests that people with malevolent traits may both be more able (at least under certain circumstances) *and* more motivated to gain power. And history lends further support to this picture, as outliers in terms of Dark Tetrad scores — such as Hitler, Stalin, and Mao — appear to be vastly overrepresented among the most powerful individuals in history (cf. Fallon, 2011; Hughes, 2018, ch. 2-3; Althaus & Baumann, 2020, Appendix B).

The elevated risk of harm posed by such individuals is likewise supported by various lines of evidence. For example, Hitler, Stalin, and Mao all played critical roles in some of history's greatest atrocities — e.g. World War II, the Holocaust, the Gulag, and the Cultural Revolution. And while these atrocities no doubt had many causes, it is plausible that the extreme malevolence of these individuals was a significant contributing factor (Althaus & Baumann, 2020, Appendix A).

In general, malevolent dictators seem to have influenced international cooperation in a markedly negative direction, which gives us reason to think that future malevolent leaders would increase the risk of great power wars and international conflict. There are also strong reasons to think that malevolent rulers increase the spread of political extremism, increase the risk of a global totalitarian regime, and increase domestic conflict (Althaus & Baumann, 2020). Additionally, such rulers seem likely to impede and reverse moral progress, which could have catastrophic consequences both in the short and the long term (cf. Section 11.12.2).

14.6.2 Beneficial Interventions

What can be done to reduce the risk of pathocracy? One suggestion is to increase the overall awareness and priority devoted to the problem. Such awareness-raising work should likely also inform people about the difficulty of *detecting* malevolent traits, at least in skillfully manipulative individuals, since people may greatly overestimate their own ability to detect them — especially when the malevolent individual in question belongs to one's own party or ideology (cf. Achen & Bartels, 2016, ch. 10). In other words, it might be necessary to explain why this problem is considerably more serious and more difficult to address than most people tend to assume.

A related measure is to advance research on the nature and detection of malevolent traits. This may include a better understanding of the causes of malevolent traits (e.g. in genetic and environmental terms), as well as neuroscientific developments that enable us to detect a lack of empathetic concern and the presence of extreme sadism in response to others' distress (Lobaczewski, 2006, ch. 4; Althaus & Baumann, 2020, "Advancing the science of malevolence").

If our technologies for detecting malevolent traits were to become sufficiently reliable, and if knowledge about the dangers of malevolent traits got sufficiently widespread, it could perhaps become the norm that aspiring leaders would go through screening procedures for malevolent traits. The result of such screenings could serve as an important source of information for voters, and not least be a positive signal for aspiring leaders who are eager to prove their non-malevolence (Althaus & Baumann, 2020, "Manipulation-proof measures of malevolence").

There are also many political measures that can be taken to prevent malevolent rulers from gaining and misusing power. Perhaps the single most important factor is whether a country has democratic institutions that entail the protection of free speech and constraints on power, since such institutions generally seem better able to maintain stability and avoid malevolent leaders (cf. Gibler & Randazzo, 2011; Althaus & Baumann, 2020, "Political interventions"). Hence, interventions that promote such institutions appear helpful, including interventions that strengthen existing democratic institutions against democratic backsliding. The promotion of (greater degrees of) parliamentarism might be particularly beneficial in this regard, since parliamentary systems tend to be more stable, less prone to coups, and better able to remove bad leaders compared to presidential systems (Santos, 2020, ch. 1). Indeed, Hitler's rise to power — perhaps the most famous case of democratic backsliding — may have been partly enabled by the semi-presidential nature of the Weimar Republic, including an emergency decree in the Weimar constitution that Hitler exploited to avoid checks on his power (Santos, 2020, pp. 81-82, p. 113; 2021a).

Another potential risk factor for a malevolent takeover is a high level of political polarization (Althaus & Baumann, 2020, "Political interventions").

In particular, if political polarization is high, and if people feel outright threatened by the "other side", it seems more likely that partisans will ignore signs of malevolence and rally behind a strong leader regardless. A highly polarized political environment could thus make the difference between whether a malevolent individual stays in power or not. For example, US president Richard Nixon resigned in part because people in his own party eventually opposed him, yet if he had been president in a more polarized age, perhaps more people from his own party would have supported him regardless, and in effect kept him in power (cf. Shenkman, 2016, pp. 118-120). To be clear, my point here is not that Nixon was a particularly malevolent individual (though some have argued that he was in fact highly narcissistic, Harden, 2021), but simply that political polarization plausibly could help a malevolent individual gain and stay in power.

Specific interventions that seem promising for reducing political polarization include some of those mentioned earlier, such as advocating parliamentarism and proportional representation, as well as pushing for a political culture that is more charitable and cooperative (see Chapter 4).

Lastly, since high levels of Dark Tetrad traits appear more common among men, it may also be beneficial to promote gender equality and thereby increase the proportion of female leaders (Althaus & Baumann, 2020, "Political interventions"). This could be helpful for other reasons as well, such as decreasing the propensity for violent aggression among leaders, which also tends to be significantly higher among men (Wrangham & Peterson, 1996; Tuschman, 2013, ch. 13).

14.7 Marginal Realist Implications

Having reviewed some suggestions for how democracy might be updated or improved, let us now turn to the question of which projects seem most worth prioritizing, on the margin, by those seeking to reduce suffering.

14.7.1 Promoting and Securing Liberal Democracy as the Main Priority?

It could well be that the difference between autocracy and modern liberal democracy is more significant, overall, than further improvements to liberal democracy in its most functional manifestations. For example, the best liberal democracies of today — while woefully imperfect in many ways — do seem to provide a near-perfect protection of civil liberties, including free speech in particular. Contemporary autocracies, in contrast, create just the opposite: an effective *suppression* of civil liberties.

There is thus almost a zero-to-one difference between oppressive autocracies and contemporary liberal democracies, at least in this crucial respect. And this is a crucial respect indeed: recall that civil liberties serve as the precondition for many important endeavors, such as moral progress, peaceful compromise, and keeping powerful actors — including malevolent ones — in check (see Chapter 11). Given this significant difference, as well as the other significant differences between liberal democracies and autocracies reviewed in Section 14.3, it is only natural to wonder whether the best interventions we can pursue are ones that promote liberal democracy, either by advancing liberal democracy in places that currently have little or none of it, or by securing existing liberal democracies against democratic backsliding.

The aim of promoting modern liberal democracy also has the advantage of not being particularly speculative (compared to the aim of promoting some novel form of governance). There really is a clear difference between liberal democracies and autocracies, supported by numerous lines of evidence. Liberal representative democracy has been realized with decent (comparative) success in many countries, it seems better at preventing malevolent rule compared to all other tried systems, and we have considerable evidence about which forms of representative democracy work better than others (e.g. parliamentary systems appear better than presidential ones). New forms of government, by contrast, have less of an evidentiary base and track record supporting them, meaning that we can be less sure of the value of promoting them, and about which forms of them, if any, work well.

However, the case for prioritizing the promotion of liberal democracy also requires that we can identify promising interventions that help advance this aim, *and* that these interventions are not already being pursued to such a degree that other, more neglected pursuits would be a better use of marginal resources. Fortunately, it seems that there are a number of promising interventions for securing and promoting democracy, as outlined in the next section. But it is also true that there already is a considerable level of funding devoted to this aim. For instance, various foreign policy institutions in the US collectively devote more than two billion dollars each year to the promotion of democracy. Yet much of this money seems tied to the promotion of US foreign policy interests in particular, and hence may not be spent optimally from an impartial perspective (Schonfeld, 2020). Moreover, the right marginal efforts could perhaps significantly increase this amount, considering both that the promotion of democracy is a widely endorsed aim and that two billion dollars is not *that* much to spend on such a key aim on the stage of global politics.

Finally, it is worth noting that there could be a bias against the cause of securing and promoting liberal democracy. After all, this is not a particularly novel, impressive, or exciting cause to advocate. Indeed, compared to many of the proposals outlined above, it seems rather mundane and conventional — perhaps even boring. Yet novelty, impressiveness, and excitement should ideally not determine our priorities, our psychological need for these things notwithstanding.

14.7.2 Interventions for Promoting and Securing Liberal Democracy

It is an open question which interventions are most effective at advancing and securing democracy, yet we can at least point to some plausible candidates. In terms of securing liberal democracy, we have already identified a couple of interventions that may be promising, namely to promote parliamentarism (in presidential democracies as well as in emerging democracies), and to push for voting systems that reduce winner-take-all dynamics, especially in countries without proportional representation. In more concrete terms, Tiago Santos recommends stronger advocacy efforts aimed at the promotion of parliamentarism, similar to ongoing efforts to promote democracy in general (Santos, 2020, ch. 6).

Promising and non-coercive interventions have also been identified when it comes to the advancement of democracy in countries with weak democratic institutions. One such intervention is foreign aid that is conditioned on the implementation of democratic reforms (Schonfeld, 2020). As one study noted, "over a decade of empirical research indicates that foreign aid specifically for democracy promotion is remarkably successful at improving the survival and institutional strength of fragile democracies" (Heinrich & Loftis, 2019, abstract; see also Ziaja, 2020).

Another intervention with considerable empirical support is to hire independent parties to inspect a country's electoral processes. Such election monitoring has been found effective in reducing election fraud and manipulation, which some scholars argue are among the greatest threats to democracy globally (Hyde, 2007; Cheeseman & Klaas, 2018; Schonfeld, 2020).

The interventions mentioned above only seem applicable in countries where some degree of democracy is already established. Unfortunately, it is more difficult to identify well-supported interventions when it comes to wholly autocratic states, where democratization is most needed. Yet some interventions that may be promising include:

- Setting up sanctions against the wealthy elites that surround and empower autocrats (cf. Bueno de Mesquita & Smith, 2012; Navalny, 2021).

- Facilitating a safer exchange of information among citizens in autocracies (e.g. through encrypted communication services, cf. Pavlova, 2020).

- Conducting and publicizing anonymous surveys of the unpopularity of the prevailing system (to create common knowledge about its widespread disapproval, cf. Section 10.9.4).

- Helping individual citizens escape from authoritarian regimes, which may also increase awareness of the ongoing oppression and human rights violations in those regimes (see e.g. libertyinnorth korea.org).

- Pursuing advocacy and capacity building in favor of anti-totalitarian aims (cf. Drescher, 2017).

It seems valuable to further explore the effectiveness of these strategies, including the risk of provoking a ruthless backlash. Also important to keep in mind, in this context, are the effects that decades of totalitarian rule will have had on the cultural psychology of its citizens, and how such a thoroughly manipulated psychology cannot be changed overnight (cf. Section 6.2; Henrich, 2020, p. 219).

14.7.3 Other Interventions: Exploring Novel Proposals in Weaker Forms?

The broad line of argument laid out above is by no means conclusive, and hence does not rule out that endeavors other than the promotion of liberal democracy could be similarly or even more promising on the margin. These other endeavors may include pushing for one or more of the many proposed alternatives and improvements to modern democracy explored in this chapter.

A general point worth making about these proposals, especially regarding the suggested alternatives to democracy — i.e. futarchy, epistocracy, sortition, and algorithmic governance — is that they might be more promising in a weaker form compared to their purest form. That is, rather than having these proposed systems wholly *replace* our current form of democracy, it may be better to adopt certain *elements* of these proposals, in effect implementing them to a greater degree than we currently do. This would probably also be among the best paths toward testing such proposals in any case, and toward eventually implementing them to even greater degrees, if they do prove desirable.

So rather than having prediction markets *determine* policies (along with votes on values), one could, more modestly, have prediction markets *inform* policy decisions to a greater extent. Rather than implementing epistocracy, one could work to create institutions that collate the views of confirmed experts in order to convey these views to voters and policy makers. (Prediction markets could be one example of such an institution, but it is by no means the only one; groups of forecasters with a track record of accurate predictions is another example, cf. Tetlock, 2015.) Rather than fully replacing representative democracy with lottocracy, one could have a randomly selected citizens' assembly that provides inputs on existing policy proposals and perhaps puts forward proposals of its own (cf. Fishkin, 2018). Rather than having a purely algorithmic government, one could use advanced software to a greater extent in governance decisions.

These proposals could also be combined in various ways. For instance, one could have a lottocracy in which policy-makers are able to draw on prediction markets, panels of confirmed experts, and advanced software in their decision-making. They could also, of course, draw on official opinion polls, to add a greater element of direct democracy.

14.7.4 Comparing Proposals

What follows is a brief and highly tentative (marginal realist) evaluation of some of the main proposals outlined in this chapter. Each proposal is followed by a number from –10 to 10 that is meant to convey my own rough estimate of how promising it would be to advance the given proposal at this point; though different efforts pertaining to these respective proposals will obviously vary in terms of how beneficial they are. Note also that there might well be proposals that deserve greater priority than the ones reviewed here.

Futarchy: As hinted above, the first step toward the implementation of futarchy would likely be to use prediction markets to a greater extent in various institutions. So the question, from a marginal realist perspective, is roughly whether it makes sense to push for such a greater use of prediction markets. A number of social scientists argue that prediction markets hold great promise for improving institutional decision-making, which surely speaks in favor of prediction markets (Arrow et al., 2008). Yet the general-purpose nature of prediction markets, and the consequent (relatively) wide interest in them, also suggest that pushing for a greater use of prediction markets is unlikely to be among the very best uses of marginal resources by those seeking to reduce suffering — not least considering that we currently have little reason to think that futarchy would ultimately work better than does modern liberal democracy. In sum, testing and implementing prediction markets to a greater extent may be beneficial, but we hardly have grounds for considering it a uniquely promising use of marginal resources. Estimate Score: 1.

Epistocracy: In its weaker forms, epistocracy would amount to some version of "giving greater influence to those with expertise". This seems to be something that many people are already pushing for in various ways (and which perhaps a similar number of people are pushing against). In its stronger forms, epistocracy appears to have various downsides. Perhaps most damning for its practical realization is that epistocracy seems likely to leave a large fraction of the population — those consistently unable to pass the relevant knowledge tests — with a feeling of being unfairly disempowered and excluded, which could in turn fuel political resentment and polarization. There is thus reason to doubt that pushing for epistocracy is a good use of marginal resources, and to perhaps even consider it harmful overall. Estimate Score: –3.

Sortition: This institution has already been used in weaker forms in countries such as Spain and Ireland — e.g. an Irish citizens' assembly made a policy proposal that resulted in a referendum that changed the Irish constitution (Hennig, 2018) — and there has recently been a surge in countries using randomly selected citizens' assemblies to provide policy inputs on specific issues (see e.g. Sortition Foundation, 2021). The implementation of "greater degrees" of sortition thus seems quite feasible. Yet whether a greater use of citizens' assemblies will have positive effects overall is unclear. Sortition does have some theoretical virtues to recommend it — for instance, there are reasons to think it could reduce our tendency to view politics through a zero-sum lens. But these virtues mostly apply to a condition in which sortition has replaced elected politicians, not necessarily to marginal increases in the use of citizens' assemblies. And whether a complete lottocracy is better than electoral liberal democracy as we know it is also unclear given its untested nature (in a modern context). So while sortition probably merits inclusion in a portfolio of governance options worth exploring further, its effects still seem too uncertain at this point for its promotion to be regarded as a high priority. Estimate Score: 3.

Algorithmic governance: Proposals for algorithmic governance are still very much at an early stage, and hence it is unclear what exactly one would push for here. It seems that the most promising next steps lie in further research, such as exploring design options and analyzing the potential risks and benefits. This may well be worth prioritizing by those able to do such work, perhaps especially with an eye to worst-case failure modes and how these can best be prevented. On the other hand, such research could also be premature at this point, when we still do not know which form, if any, algorithmic governance is likely to take; and there is a real risk that premature research could be harmful (e.g. by leading to massive resource investments into ill-conceived research programs). Estimate Score: 5 for work to explore its risks and benefits; –3 for work to push for its implementation at this point.

Sentiocracy: Among the proposals explored here, this is perhaps the most promising one from a marginal realist perspective concerned with the reduction of suffering. It is a proposal that can readily be pursued within the framework of contemporary liberal democracy (Cochrane, 2018, ch. 3), it can be pursued in gradual steps, and early such steps are already being pursued with some success. Moreover, the general public already expresses a fairly high level of support for taking the interests of non-human animals into account in our political decisions, which suggests that dedicated marginal pushes for such institutional change could gain support and be highly impactful (see Section 10.9.4; Rethink Priorities, 2021; Chaney et al., 2021). The promotion of sentiocracy is also highly neglected compared to many of the other proposals explored here, including the promotion of sortition, which various organizations are singularly devoted to. In terms of long-term effects, a greater realization of sentiocracy could be highly significant in that it may set a precedent for granting (greater) consideration to all sentient beings in our political decisions going forward. Estimate Score: 7.

Direct democracy: As mentioned earlier, the mixed literature and mixed considerations on direct democracy render it doubtful that its promotion should be a high priority. Estimate Score: 0.

Voting reform and (increasing) parliamentarism: These institutional changes have already been recommended above, both for reducing risks of malevolent actors and for securing liberal democracy. They have considerable evidence to recommend them, and they also seem fairly realistic to push for given their mainstream nature. Of course, these systemic changes are not applicable everywhere — among existing democracies, they are most pressing in presidential states without proportional voting systems. But seeing that the world's richest and most powerful country, i.e. the United States, is precisely such a country, it may still be a high priority to support reforms in this direction. Perhaps the main consideration that speaks against prioritizing voting reforms with marginal resources is that a relatively large number of people are already pursuing such reforms, especially compared to neglected proposals such as (increasing) sentiocracy. Likewise, a consideration that speaks against pushing for parliamentarism is that it appears difficult to create such constitutional change. Yet the importance and the seemingly robust evidence in favor of these institutional changes could well mean that their realization deserves to be among our highest priorities, despite their respective crowdedness and low tractability. Estimate Score: 6.

Advancing liberal democracy: As argued above, this is a plausible priority given the benefits of liberal democracy as well as the considerable evidence behind interventions such as democracy aid and election monitoring. Yet an argument against considering it a top priority, on the margin, is that it is not nearly as neglected as other promising causes, such as the promotion of sentiocracy or parliamentarism. Estimate Score: 6.

14.8 Plausible Proxies and Democracy

Once again, the proxies outlined in Chapter 9 serve to highlight and elaborate on some of the points made above.

14.8.1 Greater Levels of Cooperation

The greater peace within and between democracies compared to autocracies suggests that the promotion of democracy is helpful for the proxy aim of increasing cooperation and reducing risks of conflict. Likewise, the greater stability and domestic peace of parliamentary systems, as well as the lower war involvement of countries with proportional representation, suggest that this aim is best served by the promotion of proportional parliamentary systems in particular, at least over non-proportional presidential ones.

Given that the alternative systems reviewed here have not yet been implemented on a large scale, there is currently little evidence on whether they would tend to increase or reduce cooperation and peace. Hence, the promotion of liberal democracy seems safer and better supported than does the promotion of any alternative system (relative to the aim of increasing cooperation and peace).

This is not to say that alternative systems might not in fact be better. But given that much testing and massive investments would be required to gain good evidence on this question, there are reasons to doubt that investments into testing alternative systems are as promising for advancing cooperation as are investments into the promotion of liberal democracy. One reason is that it is unlikely that we will ever gain such evidence on a scale remotely similar to the scale of evidence we have in the case of contemporary democracy, with numerous countries that have implemented it for several decades.

Another reason relates to the magnitude of the difference between democracies and autocracies in terms of how conducive they are to cooperation and peace versus conflict and violence. This sizable difference suggests that it is urgent to push for well-supported improvements, whereas it seems comparatively less urgent to test uncertain alternatives to democracy — alternatives that might just be slightly better at securing cooperation (compared to the significant difference between liberal democracy and autocracy), and which may well be worse.

14.8.2 Better Values

The propensity of liberal democracy to reduce conflict and promote cooperation is also a reason to think that liberal democracy is more conducive to value improvements than are other tried systems, as peaceful and cooperative dialogue seems a precondition for such improvements. The same can be said about the greater liberty of liberal democracies: it, too, seems a prerequisite for improving our values and for avoiding value regression (see Section 11.12.2).

In terms of how we can advance systems of government that are conducive to good values, it again seems plausible that it is better to promote modern liberal democracy than to push for novel systems. One reason lies in the argument outlined in the previous section: we do not know whether alternative systems would be better than liberal democracy with respect to value improvements, and it is expensive and difficult to amass reliable evidence on this question on a large scale. In contrast, we have strong evidence that liberal democracy represents a clear improvement over other tried forms of government.

Perhaps the main reason to think that the promotion of liberal democracy is better than the advancement of alternative systems (with respect to improving values) is that the best liberal democracies already manage to provide close to a perfect protection of civil liberties. That is, given that strong civil liberties are a key factor — perhaps *the* key factor — for improving values, and given that the best liberal democracies are near-optimal at protecting civil liberties, it seems plausible that the promotion of liberal democracy is a better way to support value improvements than is the promotion of novel systems whose ability to protect civil liberties is unknown.

In terms of marginal efforts to improve liberal democracy, perhaps one of the best things we can do to entrench better values in our institutions and in society at large is to promote sentiocracy — working to gradually increase the concern for and representation of non-human beings in the political process, and thus to make sentiocracy the future of democracy (Cochrane, 2018, ch. 3).

14.8.3 Greater Capacity to Reduce Suffering

The proxy aim of increasing our overall ability to reduce suffering yields broadly similar conclusions. Liberal democracy seems the best form of government tried so far when it comes to fostering the capabilities and insights that are required for us to reduce suffering effectively — e.g. better insights into practical ethics and social science (cf. Tomasik, 2013d). This is in large part because liberal democracy has proved uniquely effective at providing people the freedom to pursue such progress and development (cf. Section 11.12.3). And for reasons similar to those reviewed in the previous two sections — reasons relating to the scale of evidence that supports liberal democracy, as well as the sizable difference between liberal democracy and other tried systems — it seems likely that liberal democracy is the system of government that is most rational to advance and secure in order to increase humanity's capacity to reduce suffering.

14.9 Conclusion

Modern liberal democracy seems significantly better than other tried systems of government, across a wide range of important measures. Indeed, the difference between liberal democracy and autocracy is so great that it may be more significant than the difference between modern liberal democracy and any (potentially) better alternative, in which case assisting the development of liberal democracy and preventing democratic backsliding may generally be more important than identifying and implementing even better alternatives.

We have reviewed a number of proposed alternatives to modern democracy in this chapter, and while some of them appear promising and worth exploring further — especially in their weaker forms — it does not currently seem warranted to consider the promotion of any of these alternatives a top priority. Promoting and securing liberal democracy over autocracy, on the other hand, does seem a justified and pressing priority. Yet these conclusions are still consistent with devoting some resources to further exploring alternatives to modern liberal democracy.

Beyond alternatives, we have examined some proposed improvements to modern democracy. The most promising of these seem to be (greater degrees of) parliamentarism and proportional voting systems (where these are absent), as well as greater political consideration and representation of non-human beings in the political process. The prevention of pathocracy should also be considered a top priority, which in turn lends further support to the priority of promoting and securing democracy in general, including parliamentarism and better voting systems in particular, as these appear protective against pathocracy.

In sum, while it would be strange if liberal democracy in its current form happened to be an ideal institution — as some of the possible improvements reviewed in this chapter indeed imply it is not — it nonetheless seems the best and safest institution to promote and further improve at this point, given the evidence we currently have.

PART V

SUMMARY

15

An Early Step in a Larger Project

Before summarizing the policy recommendations of the preceding chapters, it is worth emphasizing a few qualifications and limitations. These qualifications may feel redundant and repetitive, as I have already hinted at them in passing a couple of times, but I nonetheless consider it crucial to bring them out more clearly, so as to explain how the policy analyses of the previous chapters are to be viewed and contextualized. Namely, as an early step and an invitation for further work and discussion.

15.1 Limited Scope

A key qualification to re-emphasize is the limited scope of my analysis. While the last few chapters have covered many of the most prominent concepts and issues in political philosophy, there are obviously still many important issues that have not been covered here. A single book cannot cover every significant political issue, and this book certainly has no pretense to such exhaustiveness.

Ideally, we will pursue similar and more elaborate analyses of *all* major policy areas, seeking to provide insights and recommendations about policies conducive to suffering reduction in each respective area.

15.2 Tentative Conclusions

No less important to stress is the provisional and uncertain nature of the recommendations inferred in previous chapters. Indeed, this point holds true on a couple of levels. For one, there are many important questions that have yet to be thoroughly investigated, by anyone, and explorations of these questions could surely help update and refine many of the conclusions drawn here.

Beyond that, there are plenty of relevant insights that people have *already* gathered, yet which I have not included in my analysis due to my ignorance of these insights, or due to a failure on my part to realize the relevance of certain insights. Thus, if one thinks the preceding analysis neglects findings *a*, *b*, and *c*, and indeed ignores the entire fields of *X*, *Y*, and *Z*, my reply will likely be that this critique is correct. And I would — and *do* — encourage people with knowledge of such findings and fields to contribute their insights to this larger, open-ended project of reasoned politics, a project that should obviously not be tied to the limited perspective of any one person. After all, there is much evidence that our overall judgments on empirical questions tend to become better as we factor in more perspectives (Tetlock, 2015, ch. 3).

However, it is also important not to overstate the uncertainty of the foregoing analysis. For example, to say that there is significant uncertainty is not to say that all our conclusions are extremely vulnerable to change, such that a tiny bit of contradictory evidence should radically overturn our conclusions — least of all when it comes to those conclusions that have a wide range of convergent considerations and evidence behind them. And I do believe that a fair number of the recommendations inferred in previous chapters *are* reasonably certain and robust, including the core recommendations outlined in the previous five chapters. When we have fairly strong evidence in favor of certain conclusions, similarly strong evidence will be required to overturn these conclusions. But it is still true that we always need to be open to such counter-evidence.

15.3 Three Broad Goals

In sum, the aim of the preceding analysis (Part IV) has been three-fold. First, I have tried to infer some plausible policy recommendations for those seeking to reduce suffering. It is my hope that these recommendations can help inform the political decisions of compassionate political actors, and thereby aid us in creating positive real-world change for sentient beings.

Second, I have sought to encourage further exploration into how we can best reduce suffering at the political level, and indeed to urge an entire research program focused on this critical question so that we can gain more refined answers that enable still more effective real-world action.

Third, and most generally, I have tried to demonstrate and exemplify — however imperfectly — a rough method for how we can use empirical evidence and theoretical considerations to infer policy recommendations based on a given set of moral values. My example surely has many shortcomings, but I hope it nonetheless gives a better sense of how the general two-step ideal could be employed, and that it in turn can help motivate others to further pursue this ideal of reasoned politics.

16

Party Example: Alliance of Reason and Compassion

This final chapter is written as a political program of a hypothetical political party, the Alliance of Reason and Compassion (ARC). The point of this program is in part to provide a brief summary of some of the main policy recommendations inferred in the previous chapters, and in part to stir our political imagination with a more vivid sense of what it would be like to see these ideas implemented in political practice.

To clarify, I do not mean to suggest that it is necessarily ideal to form a new party of this kind. While starting such a party could be worthwhile in some cases, it may often be better to try to nudge existing parties in the directions outlined below. Nor do I mean to suggest that my framing of this program is optimal or politically salable — though perhaps it could be feasible to frame a political program in roughly this way in a few decades, if we manage to progress toward a more reasoned political equilibrium.

Lastly, it must be stressed that the following is not intended to be a *complete* political program. Again, there are many important political issues that I have not touched upon in this book, and since this chapter primarily seeks to summarize the conclusions drawn in previous chapters, the program presented below will be similarly limited in scope. That said,

I do think the following provides a decent sketch of the *core* of a political program animated by the ideas presented in this book.

Manifesto of the Alliance of Reason and Compassion

We think the prevailing approach to politics is deeply flawed. Too much energy is spent on political theater rather than sense and substance. The premise that politics must consist chiefly in zero-sum conflict has been bought all too uncritically, at the expense of the view that politics can consist mostly in cooperative decision-making, based on reasoned values and empirical evidence, with the aim of creating win-win solutions when possible. We believe the time has come to realize this ideal of value- and evidence-based politics.

Doing Politics Better

Two Pillars of Reasonable Politics: Moral Reflection and Empirical Investigation

We believe politics is to be based on carefully reflected ethical values. We affirm open discussion and transparency about these values, both when it comes to our own values and the values of society at large. While some value differences are unavoidable, we think it is a mistake to sidestep moral reflection altogether, and to simply resign to "differences of opinion" without exploring the best reasons for or against people's respective views. We believe values can be informed and often improved by reasoned arguments, and reflecting on values can likewise help each of us gain more clarity about what matters and what is worth prioritizing. We view the project of clarifying and improving our values as a collaborative project that everyone can benefit from engaging in, and which carries great potential for further advancement.

In addition to basing our policies on carefully reflected values, we believe it is paramount to be guided by the best available evidence. In particular, we believe political policies should ideally be supported with reference both to underlying values and empirical data. Given a certain set of values, it is essentially an empirical question how we can best satisfy these values, which renders it puzzling that empirical evidence does not play a larger role in political debates. We believe political discourse needs to focus more on empirical evidence and less on spin and rhetoric, and we strive to do our part to move politics more in this direction.

Reducing Political Biases

We aspire to be critical of our biased minds. Just as it can no longer be denied that the Earth revolves around the Sun, we can no longer deny the profusely biased nature of the human mind that has been documented by modern psychological research. But unlike the heliocentric picture, whose once insistent denial has now been widely overcome, this more recent knowledge concerning our political biases has yet to be spread and integrated fully into our culture. We strongly believe this needs to change.

Specifically, we think it is important to be aware of our tendency to engage in political loyalty signaling, and to be mindful of our "hot cognition" that reflexively paints an unduly favorable picture of our own political tribes and views, while unconsciously portraying other political groups and views in a profoundly unfavorable light. Both of these tendencies underscore the need to be charitable toward political opponents and their views, so as to correct for the distortions created by these tendencies. Other pitfalls to be aware of and mitigate include our susceptibility to extreme political overconfidence, our inclination to let our political views be dictated by our most immediate intuitions, and our tendency to view politics through a lens of zero-sum conflict rather than searching for win-win solutions.

While succumbing to such instinctive modes of thought and behavior may feel right and compelling in the moment, it is our conviction that they ultimately make politics worse for everyone, and hence that it is best to strive to limit their influence. Given that our minds are the seat of all our beliefs and attitudes about politics, it is only reasonable that we make it a priority to understand the common function and pitfalls of our political minds, and that we seek to transcend these pitfalls rather than blindly allowing them to dictate our views.

Our Values and Approach

Extreme Suffering Deserves Special Priority

Extreme suffering carries an unspeakable and overriding moral urgency that cries out for relief. We therefore believe that the reduction of extreme suffering deserves a foremost priority in our political decisions, and place this aim at the core of our fundamental values. This is not to say that the prevention of extreme suffering is the *only* aim guiding our decisions, which it decidedly is not (see, for example, our Three Robust Aims below). But we do believe extreme suffering warrants unique and extensive consideration in politics, and certainly far more consideration than it currently receives.

Excluding No One: Politics for All Sentient Beings

We likewise believe that suffering matters regardless of *who* is experiencing it. Our political decisions should not disregard suffering and individual interests on the basis of irrelevant criteria such as skin color, sexuality, or species membership. All suffering matters and warrants consideration in our political decisions, and hence compassion for all sentient beings is a core value guiding our politics.

A Realistic and Principled Approach to Politics

Grand ideals are of little value if we are not realistic in our efforts to actualize them. We are therefore dedicated to a strategic and pragmatic approach to politics, being willing to engage in compromises when necessary, while also being principled and unyielding when necessary.

In general, we seek to find win-win solutions to political problems, and we think such solutions are often more feasible than the adversarial format of modern politics suggests; different political objectives can often be reconciled in gainful ways, and diverse political groups are usually in greater agreement on core values than the media or these political groups themselves are inclined to project. Such widely shared core values include the importance of preventing intense suffering, which is something most political actors agree strongly on, even as they might differ on exactly how important this goal is compared to other things. We hope to see a future in which all political actors work together to create a future with less extreme suffering.

Good political outcomes also require consistent adherence to solid principles. We believe in honesty, integrity, and transparency, as we are convinced that these virtues and principles represent the best way to build a better, more cooperative future.

Three Robust Aims

The following are three broad aims that we believe are conducive to good political outcomes relative to a wide range of commonly endorsed values, including the reduction of suffering. We therefore try to steer toward these positive aims in our political decisions.

Securing Cooperation

We aim to reduce the risk of conflict between individuals, groups, and nations, and to promote peaceful cooperation. This aim is worth highlighting and pursuing since virtually all other aims we care about depend on cooperation and the avoidance of conflicts, and not least because major conflicts are among the main risk factors for truly catastrophic outcomes that everyone wants to avoid.

Improving Values

We seek to facilitate the improvement of society's values. It is clear that humanity's values have improved in various ways over the course of history, and there is no reason to think that this process of moral progress has reached its final stage today. In fact, it is clear that humanity's values have the potential to improve much further, not least when it comes to the moral consideration we extend to non-human animals, as well as the lack of concern for suffering we often display in our decisions.

We therefore seek to promote greater reflection and more open discussions on values, such as by putting discussion of ethical values on the political agenda, and by contributing to the public discussion on values ourselves. We believe that ethics should ideally be a key part of everyone's education and of our political discourse at large.

Advancing Society's Ability to Solve Important Problems

Improving society's values is not enough. We also need to develop the capacities and resources that enable us to *act* on our best values. This aim has extensive implications, as it entails sensible investments across a wide range of endeavors. Specifically, it requires us to invest in the many insights and technologies, including social technologies, that increase our ability to steer away from bad outcomes and toward better ones. Hence we do not, as a party, seek to advance just any set of capacities, but particularly those that support a wiser and more peaceful path forward.

Our Policies and Principles

A World Without Slaughterhouses

We believe the suffering of non-human beings is one of the most pressing political issues. Thankfully, the scope and importance of animal suffering is now being recognized ever more widely. Indeed, the vast majority of people already believe that many non-human animals feel pain and that this pain matters. But we have yet to bring our political practice and institutions into alignment with these convictions. This is the challenge of our time.

We strive to move politics in a direction where we consider the suffering of *all* the beings who will be affected by our decisions. This includes the suffering of wild animals, as well as the victims of human exploitation who are tormented and killed by the billions each year. In terms of policy, we will work to move society toward outlawing all industrial practices that impose suffering on non-human beings for trivial reasons, such as mere taste and fashion preferences. In short, we work for a civilization without slaughterhouses, the only kind worthy of the name. Additionally, we work to move society toward a state in which we pursue scientific research on, and eventually implement, large-scale interventions that help alleviate the suffering of non-human beings in nature.

We will seek to inform the broader public about the sentience of non-human animals, and about the moral arguments against disregarding the suffering of sentient beings based on their species membership, an unjustified form of discrimination known as "speciesism". Informing the public, and not least politicians, about the public's own stated views on the importance of animal suffering is likewise a priority for us. We believe that highlighting the contrast between these stated views and society's harmful practices is among the best ways to accelerate our path toward a society that helps rather than harms non-human animals.

Freedom

We strongly support personal freedom and civil liberties for people everywhere. We are aware that individual freedom can be associated with certain risks, and these are worth being honest and transparent about. But we nevertheless believe that basic liberties, such as freedom of speech and the freedom to act as one wants (within reasonable limits), represent a strong force for good, all things considered. These basic liberties serve, among other things, to protect against and undermine oppressive structures; they enable us to reflect on our values and to live our lives accordingly; and they are a precondition for moral progress.

We believe the best way to address the risks and harms associated with liberty is to advance norms and laws that target these harms directly, such as social norms that discourage deliberately hurtful speech, and laws against pollution and other negative byproducts of free action. This enables us to limit such downsides in efficient ways, while still preserving the basic individual freedom of everyone.

Finally, we believe that society's conception of liberty needs to be radically updated, in that it should not entail the freedom to impose suffering on non-human animals. Thus, when we as a society declare that people have the freedom to act as they want as long as it does not harm others, we must be clear that non-human animals also count as "others" who are to be respected and spared from harm when possible. And our laws should reflect this view.

Equality

We affirm the equal consideration of equal interests, and we believe that political policies should be guided by this principle as far as is practicable. This essentially amounts to not privileging any individual or group without good reason, and to extending undiminished consideration to the suffering of all sentient beings. We will work to move our society, laws, and politics in this more equal and impartial direction.

When it comes to economic inequality, we believe that lower levels of inequality would be a good thing for various reasons, not least because it can help increase social cohesion and trust. However, we acknowledge that it is difficult to identify the policies that best achieve this aim, especially considering that these policies also need to be consistent with other important political aims and principles. In terms of concrete proposals, we see a negative income tax as a potential way to reduce both poverty and inequality, and as a possible step toward a simpler and more efficient tax policy. This is not to say that we necessarily endorse this policy, but rather that we would like to see it discussed in greater depth, and to see small-scale experiments that can help us learn more about its effects.

In general, we would like to see a more balanced discussion of economic inequality. We will seek to contribute to such discussions ourselves by highlighting some of the many uncertainties and tradeoffs that are involved in the relevant policy decisions.

Justice

We believe that a just society is one that grants a towering priority to the prevention of suffering. The closer our society comes to the ideal of protecting individuals from severe, involuntary harm, the more just it will be. We will work to make society more just in this compassionate sense of the word.

Our stance on criminal justice derives largely from this same ideal. We therefore endorse a forward-looking criminal justice system whose core aim is harm prevention, seeking to protect *all* sentient beings from deliberate harm, with a strong focus on preventing crimes that cause extreme suffering.

In addition to preventing crime, we believe that the justice system should stop criminalizing victimless "crimes" that do not impose suffering on anyone. Consequently, we support the decriminalization of peaceful drug use and voluntary euthanasia, coupled with strong safeguards against their respective risks of abuse.

Consistent with the three robust aims listed above, we further believe that the criminal justice system should help secure high levels of cooperation, and help provide a condition in which we can work together to improve our values and advance our ability to solve important problems. These aims require stable and even-handed laws and institutions, and such stability and fairness represent another broad aim that we strive to promote.

Democracy

We believe liberal democracy is by far the best form of government tried to date. We therefore consider it important to aid and protect liberal democracy, both locally and globally. In particular, we think parliamentary liberal democracy with proportional voting has the most evidence to recommend it, and we support efforts to help move governance more in that direction when possible.

While we believe that contemporary politics is deeply flawed, we also acknowledge that it could be far worse, and that we need to actively prevent it from deteriorating. A specific pitfall we need to guard against in this respect is the risk of ending up with malevolent individuals in power, which history suggests is a serious danger. We will work to put the prevention of such malevolent rulers on the political agenda, and support ways to make democracy more robust against this risk.

That said, we also think our current society is too complacent about democracy in its modern form. To say that liberal democracy is better than the tried alternatives is not to say that we should stop innovating and improving democracy. Supporting liberal democracy is consistent with efforts to improve it further and to tentatively explore forms of governance that are different from the prevailing one. We thus endorse small-scale experiments to test whether institutions like prediction markets and randomly selected citizens' assemblies could be used to improve policy decisions and our political culture in general. We are in favor of using such experiments to update our political institutions in gradual and evidence-based ways.

A critical improvement that we support is to grant significant representation to non-human beings in the political process. Just as it cannot be justified to exclude non-human beings from moral consideration, neither, we maintain, can it be justified to exclude our fellow sentient beings from genuine political representation. Which exact form this representation should ideally take stands as an open question to be explored, but it is clear to us that we need to move in this direction. A true democracy is a sentientist democracy.

In short, our mission is to advance reasoned and compassionate politics for all sentient beings.

APPENDICES

Appendix A

Does Voting Make Sense?

An issue worth briefly addressing is whether voting in democratic elections is a sensible use of an individual voter's time and effort. After all, some economists, such as Mancur Olson, have argued that it is irrational to vote given that one's vote is exceedingly unlikely to influence the final outcome (Brennan, 2011, p. 28). But there are a number of reasons to think that a vote can in fact be quite influential in expectation, and that voting indeed should be considered important.

First, since the outcome of an election can itself be highly consequential, the expected influence of a single vote can still be significant despite a very low probability of swaying the outcome. As Rob Wiblin notes in relation to voting in the US:

> Over the next four years the US federal government will spend about $17.5 trillion. [...] That's $53,000 for each American, or $129,000 for each vote cast in 2016. If you multiply all that spending through a 1 in 10 million chance of changing the outcome, in a swing state like New Hampshire, it comes to $1.75 million. That's the fraction of the budget you might 'expect' to influence by voting in a swing state, in the statistical sense of expectation. (Wiblin, 2020)

And as Wiblin goes on to write, the budget need not be particularly flexible for a vote to matter, since even apparently small differences can be quite large in a national budget: "For example, if one party will spend 0.5% of GDP on foreign aid, and the other will spend 0.3%, a vote with a 1 in 10 million chance of changing the outcome would shift — in expectation — $17,800 into foreign aid" (Wiblin, 2020).

Yet how the national budget gets used is, of course, not the only thing that one's vote has a chance of influencing, as it can also (marginally) influence which values and beliefs that will come to power and get promulgated — e.g. whether one ends up with representatives who call for peace and cooperation rather than the opposite. And such differences may well be even more significant than differences in how the budget will be spent (Wiblin, 2020).

Furthermore, there is reason to think that a vote is not wasted even if one's preferred candidate loses, since more votes to a losing candidate can help signal support for that candidate and their message, which may then marginally influence the winning candidate(s) in their political work and messaging going forward (Yudkowsky, 2008).

Perhaps most important, there is the influence that one's individual voting behavior and affirmed voting norms have on the voting behavior and norms of others. We do not vote in a vacuum, but rather in a network in which we exert some influence on the propensity of family, friends, and political peers to vote (cf. Fowler & Christakis, 2009). And even small differences in the voting norms accepted by different political factions may change entire elections.

For instance, in the 2000 US presidential election, George W. Bush famously won Florida by 537 votes, corresponding to a 0.009 percent margin, which suggests that just a tiny difference in the respective voting norms of Democrats and Republicans could have changed the outcome of the entire election. This is an unusual example, of course, but it does serve to show that small differences in voting norms can be extremely consequential, and how it could be positively harmful to spread the sentiment that voting makes no difference, especially among informed voters concerned about reducing suffering.

However, merely arguing that our individual voting behavior can be influential in expectation is not sufficient to establish that voting makes sense on the margin. One could still end up voting for a suboptimal candidate or party (e.g. due to the difficulty of predicting outcomes), in which case it may have been better *not* to vote. This is indeed a real risk, and it does somewhat dampen the expected value of one's vote (cf. Baumann, 2017b).

Nonetheless, *if* one has a particular set of moral values and decent knowledge both of the most relevant issues and the positions of the main political candidates, and *if*, based on these values and this knowledge, one comes to the conclusion that one candidate seems clearly and robustly better than the others, then voting for that candidate probably *is* significantly better, despite the uncertainty. After all, the error bar extends in both directions, meaning that one's preferred candidate might also be markedly *better* than one's estimates suggest. Of course, if the difference between competing candidates seems unclear, then voting may be less consequential, yet one should still remember the signaling effects of not voting, and how these influence not only that single election but also future elections.

Appendix B

Hidden Challenges to the Two-Step Ideal

It is worth exploring some of the main obstacles to moving our politics toward greater conformity with the two-step ideal, especially in terms of challenges posed by our hidden motives (cf. Simler & Hanson, 2018). Some of the potential challenges raised below are admittedly quite speculative in nature — they are plausible hypotheses more than they are solidly corroborated claims. Yet it still seems worthwhile to flag these plausible challenges in order to get more of a clue about why so little of our politics comes close to conforming to the two-step ideal, and to get a better sense of how we should navigate so as to realize this ideal.

B.1 Why We Might Prefer Vagueness

As noted in Chapter 1, the two-step ideal can help bring greater clarity to our political discussions. However, there are various reasons why we might generally prefer vagueness over clarity. That is, while the two-step ideal would have us distinguish normative and empirical issues, and thus help us to clarify our views on these respective matters, the prevailing lack of distinction between these levels gives us more wiggle room and plausible deniability regarding our views and motives, and most of us might secretly want that.

To be sure, the main reasons that animate such a (putative) preference for vagueness will probably vary between different groups, such as politicians, political philosophers, and voters in general. But most of the reasons to favor vagueness outlined in this section nonetheless seem to apply, with some plausibility, to all such groups, even as the relative significance of these reasons probably differs across groups.

B.1.1 Sheltering Loyalty Signaling

If we have a relatively clear set of moral values, and if we express a strong commitment to basing our preferred policies on the best available evidence, wherever it may lead us, we will be relatively constrained in cases where the evidence strongly indicates that a certain policy satisfies our values better than do the alternatives. This constraint might be highly unwelcome if the policy in question is controversial, or if it is otherwise out of line with the policy views of the people we consider our political peers. Many of us likely prioritize the avoidance of such peer disagreements — which may feel like outright disloyalty — higher than we care to admit, especially on key political issues (cf. Achen & Bartels, 2016, ch. 8-9; Simler, 2016; Simler & Hanson, 2018, ch. 16).

By muddling our values and empirical beliefs into a homogeneous brown soup, we avoid this uncomfortable situation, and we can keep on signaling loyalty to our peers and support partisan policies without being worried about the empirical facts that might emerge. Granted, this story is quite conjectural, yet it is worth noting that we see a similar pattern with many religious beliefs. That is, religious doctrines are often vague and difficult to falsify, which helps them serve their social functions without being too vulnerable to challenges posed by facts (cf. Rue, 2005, Part I; Simler & Hanson, 2018, ch. 15).

B.1.2 Minimizing Attack Surface

Another reason we may prefer to be vague about our values is that such vagueness can protect us from attacks from political opponents — a reason that seems especially relevant to politicians and political parties. A clear set of values will tend to have significant weaknesses in the eyes of most people, and hence openly committing to such values will likely leave such weaknesses exposed for others to criticize. In contrast, if we are vague about our values, there will be fewer such vulnerabilities to attack, and any accusation about supposedly unpalatable implications of our core values can more readily be deflected and denied.

This would still, of course, leave us open to the accusation that our values are vague and muddled. But in an equilibrium where few political actors display clarity about their values, or seem aware of the potential benefits of such clarity — and hence where such accusations are unlikely to ever be raised — this may be considered an acceptable price.

B.1.3 We Do Not Stand By Our High-Minded Values

A related reason we might prefer vagueness is that we may not in fact stand by our idealized values in practice, not least because the true implications of our ideals can be quite costly. For example, many people would probably consider themselves fairly impartial and cosmopolitan in terms of their values. Yet such values are in strong tension with many of the most popular policies in existing countries, as these policies effectively devote vastly more resources to domestic citizens compared to citizens in foreign countries (not to mention the extreme disregard that the policies of all countries show toward non-human beings).

In other words, it is a matter of common sense within our current political paradigm that different nations should spend far more resources on their own citizens than they should spend on citizens elsewhere. This does not strike us as suspect in the least. But if we loudly declared our values to be impartial and cosmopolitan, then this strong ingroup favoritism would indeed seem suspect and in strong tension with our values. Committing to such value statements may be highly inconvenient if we secretly prefer to maintain the ingroup-favoring paradigm.

In general, the fully extrapolated implications of our high-minded values might be too demanding and other-favoring to our liking, and hence choosing to keep our values in the dark — or at least choosing to only clarify them when asked — may be a much cheaper and quietly preferred solution. Such muffled values can give us the discretion to pursue self-serving ends while minimizing the risk of being charged with hypocrisy relative to our (vaguely affirmed) high-minded values.

B.2 The Two-Step Ideal and Political Philosophy

Beyond the challenges mentioned above, there are likely additional challenges to the two-step ideal that apply to the academic field of political philosophy in particular.

B.2.1 Lack of Originality

One such challenge is that it is not particularly original or interesting to simply say "follow the empirical data", and to allow this to determine our politics so strongly (along with the normative step). Indeed, to say that we should follow the empirical data not only fails to signal one's political loyalties — something that academics are by no means above caring about — but it also fails to provide an impressive and distinctive position at the level of political theory. In fact, it is profoundly *un*impressive and *un*interesting to mostly refer the discussion onward to the empirical level. And as Daniel Dennett argues, many people, including philosophers, would rather come up with an interesting and original contribution that becomes famous than solve an important problem without being similarly recognized (Dennett, 1999).

Additionally, even if an individual in isolation were to transcend such motivations, the reality is that the academic world, and academic journals in particular, decidedly do not. That is, academia, including academic philosophy, tends to incentivize certain things that further people's careers and publication records, such as originality and impressiveness, not real-world importance per se (Jason Brennan: "Political philosophy still seems to reward people for working on very abstract topics that don't really matter" Brennan, 2021; see also Nesse, 2008; Simler & Hanson, 2018, ch. 9).

Consequently, an academic who pursues that which is important yet unimpressive and unoriginal will be facing a strong headwind in an uphill battle. This is bad news for the two-step ideal. After all, the most plausible moral values could in some sense be very uninteresting and unoriginal, as could the most plausible empirical views. Yet putting these things together might nonetheless be supremely important, a complete lack of impressiveness notwithstanding.

B.2.2 The Structure of Academia

What makes matters worse is that the move to empirical issues may be seen as a step beyond the turf of political philosophy. Thus, besides reasons pertaining to originality and impressiveness, such a move of letting policy recommendations rest strongly on empirical analyses might also be discouraged by academia's division into different fields that tend to train people — and encourage them to publish — strictly *within* their respective disciplines. People may then (rightly) feel like disapproved impostors when attempting to pursue such empirical analyses, and they might furthermore incur disapproval from certain turf-sensitive philosophers who think that this move cedes too much ground from political philosophy toward purely empirical fields, and hence to experts in these other fields.

In terms of more formal constraints, it may simply not be possible to get published if one tries to do highly empirical work within political philosophy, even if the work in question were both original and impressive. And if one then chooses to publish such empirical work in other fields — which would likely be difficult if the work seeks to derive policy implications relative to certain normative views — it may be next to impossible to get a job in political philosophy due to hiring practices that require publications that fall squarely within the traditional standards of the field.

So even if there were no informal disapproval and no turf-sensitivity, purely formal constraints might still prevent the kind of normatively guided empirical work that would be recommended by the two-step ideal. And publication norms that favor publications on fashionable topics may have a similarly restrictive effect. (Jason Brennan again: "At the end of the day, researchers try to publish in the best journals they can because that's where the money and prestige is. They will tend to work on whatever topics are sexy because that's what it takes to publish" Brennan, 2021.)

To be clear, the claim here is not that it is rare for work in political philosophy to be cross-disciplinary and informed by empirical analyses. The claim is merely that there appear to be certain forces that effectively push against *some* work of this kind, especially work that is not particularly impressive or distinctive by academic standards, as well as work that seeks to derive policy recommendations through empirical analyses in a genuinely open-ended way. Such work sadly does seem quite rare.

B.2.3 Inconvenient Frailty

Lastly, a significant impediment to the two-step ideal is that the true epistemic brokenness of the human mind, especially in the realm of politics, is hardly something welcome or flattering for anyone to hear about. That is, as hinted in Part II of this book, a reasoned approach to politics, and adherence to the two-step ideal in particular, seems to require a basic self-awareness about our primitive moral and political psychology — not least when it comes to the influence of our crude intuitions, "hot cognition", and loyalty signaling. Cultivating an awareness of these devious mechanics of our own minds should arguably be the very *first* step of political philosophy, yet it is often given no attention at all. And this is somewhat understandable given how inconvenient it is to establish a shared recognition of these crude tendencies.

For not only will a greater such awareness invite others to look for and see these primitive dynamics more clearly in ourselves, and thereby expose our own embarrassing primitivities, but it is also likely to be received poorly when we tell others, including esteemed political philosophers, that *their* political cognition is in many ways deeply primitive and tribal, at least by nature — i.e. unless they make a serious effort to do better.

In particular, it may be difficult for us to recognize that much of our epistemic brokenness is a direct product of our social and coalitional nature itself (cf. Simler, 2016; Tooby, 2017). After all, we tend to prize our social peers and coalitions, so it might be especially inconvenient to admit that they are often the greatest source of our epistemic brokenness — e.g. due to the seductive drive to signal our loyalties to them and to use beliefs as mediators of bonding, which often comes at a high cost to our epistemic integrity (Simler, 2016).

Being the messenger who brings such disrespectful news is hardly the best thing one can do for one's social life, or for one's academic career, which in effect represents another possible force against dispassionate adherence to the two-step ideal. In other words, these prohibitive social dynamics may serve to suppress the truth about our own epistemic shortcomings to an extent that markedly reduces our ability to mitigate these shortcomings, thereby hampering our adherence to the ideals of reasoned politics, even in the realm of academic political philosophy.

The challenges outlined above, though somewhat speculative, do represent reasons to think that greater adherence to the two-step ideal will be even more difficult to achieve than one might naively expect. But this is again not to say that it is unrealistic or fruitless to work toward a greater such adherence, which seems both achievable and worthwhile despite the challenges reviewed above (the points made in Sections 1.5 and 4.6 about the feasibility of change stand just the same). My main recommendations for overcoming these challenges are still those outlined in Section 1.7 and Chapter 4.

Acknowledgments

Deep thanks go to my colleagues at the Center for Reducing Suffering (CRS), who have provided extensive comments and feedback on the book during the writing process. The book has to a large extent been a group effort, which has helped shape it for the better. I feel very lucky to be part of such a strong and supportive team. In particular, I wish to thank Teo Ajantaival, Tobias Baumann, and Winston Oswald-Drummond for their encouraging feedback and support.

Sincere thanks also go to Dan Hageman, Skyler Lehto, Simon Möller, Alexandr "Nil" Shchelov, Chiara, and others for providing generous funding that has made this book possible.

For their feedback on the book, I thank Riikka Ajantaival, David Althaus, Kaare Andersen, Sabine Brels, Dario Citrini, Laurence Currie-Clark, Michael Dello-Iacovo, David Enoch, James Faville, Daniel Görtz, Robin Hanson, Oscar Horta, Phoenix Huber, Sille Juul Kjærbo, Andrew Knight, Simon Knutsson, Jonathan Leighton, David Mannheim, Jamie Mayerfeld, Rupert McCallum, David Moss, David Pearce, Joachim Robert, Tiago Santos, Sebastian Sudergaard Schmidt, Jeff Sebo, Karthik Sekar, Alexandr "Nil" Shchelov, Pablo Stafforini, Cynthia Stewart, and Brian Tomasik.

I owe special gratitude to Jamie Mayerfeld and Richard Ryder, who both nudged me toward focusing on politics when commenting on my previous book. *Reasoned Politics* has been heavily inspired by Richard's book *Putting Morality Back Into Politics* and by Jamie's *Suffering and Moral Responsibility*.

David Pearce also deserves heartfelt thanks, as always, for his help with the book and for all the inspiration and support that his work and friendship have provided me over the years. I am likewise grateful to Ailin, Magnus, Joachim, Sille, Sebastian, Joe, and Jess for their support and friendship over the years.

Special thanks to Mikkel for his role in shaping the earliest seeds of the book, and to Kirsten and Lars for their extensive help and support.

Finally, I thank Chiara for her immensely helpful feedback and encouragement, and not least for being my dea dell'amore. Mi ispiri a creare un mondo migliore con te. ♥

Bibliography

Aarøe, L. & Petersen, M. (2013). Hunger games: Fluctuations in blood glucose levels influence social welfare support. *Psychological Science*, 24(12), pp. 2550-2556.

Achen, C. & Bartels, L. (2012). Blind Retrospection: Why Shark Attacks Are Bad For Democracy. https://www.vanderbilt.edu/csdi/research/CSDI_WP_05-2013.pdf

Achen, C. & Bartels, L. (2016). *Democracy for Realists: Why Elections Do Not Produce Responsive Government.* Princeton University Press.

Agren, D. (2020). Mexico's drug war leaves 39,000 unidentified bodies in its morgues. https://www.theguardian.com/world/2020/sep/22/mexicos-drug-war-leaves-39000-unidentified-bodies-in-its-morgues

Ajantaival, T. (2021a). Positive roles of life and experience in suffering-focused ethics. https://forum.effectivealtruism.org/posts/t3St6Fz4DmHtKfgqm/positive-roles-of-life-and-experience-in-suffering-focused

Ajantaival, T. (2021b). Minimalist axiologies and positive lives. https://forum.effectivealtruism.org/posts/5gPubzt79QsmRJZnL/minimalist-axiologies-and-positive-lives

Akbari, M. et al. (2020). An experimental study of kin and ethnic favoritism. *Economic Inquiry*, 58(4), pp. 1795-1812.

Alexander, S. (2018). Conflict vs. Mistake. https://slatestarcodex.com/2018/01/24/conflict-vs-mistake/

Alford, J. et al. (2005). Are Political Orientations Genetically Transmitted? *American Political Science Review*, 99(2), pp. 153-167.

Althaus, D. & Baumann, T. (2020). Reducing long-term risks from malevolent actors. https://forum.effectivealtruism.org/posts/LpkXtFXdsRd4rG8Kb/reducing-long-term-risks-from-malevolent-actors

Althaus, D. & Gloor, L. (2016). Reducing Risks of Astronomical Suffering: A Neglected Priority. https://longtermrisk.org/reducing-risks-of-astronomical-suffering-a-neglected-priority/

American Veterinary Medical Association. (2013). Literature Review on the Welfare Implications of Swine Castration. https://www.avma.org/KB/Resources/LiteratureReviews/Documents/swine_castration_bgnd.pdf

Amodio, D. et al. (2007). Neurocognitive correlates of liberalism and conservatism. *Nature Neuroscience*, 10, pp. 1246-1247.

Amy, D. (2011). *Government Is Good: An Unapologetic Defense of a Vital Institution*. Dog Ear Publishing.

Anderson, C. et al. (2015). Is the desire for status a fundamental human motive? A review of the empirical literature. *Psychological Bulletin*, 141(3), pp. 574-601.

Anderson, J. & Tyler, L. (2018). Attitudes Toward Farmed Animals in the BRIC Countries. https://faunalytics.org/wp-content/uploads/2018/09/BRIC-Full-Report.pdf

Andorno, R. & Baffone, C. (2014). Human Rights and the Moral Obligation to Alleviate Suffering. In Green, R. & Palpant, N. (eds.), *Suffering and Bioethics*. Oxford University Press.

André, L. (2019). The relevance of sentience: Shaping nonanthropocentric politics (master's thesis). University of Minho. https://repositorium.sdum.uminho.pt/bitstream/1822/64187/2/Lara%20de%20Mendon%C3%A7a%20Andr%C3%A9.pdf

Animal Ethics. (2012/2019). Speciesism. https://www.animal-ethics.org/ethics-animals-section/speciesism/

Animal Ethics. (2013/2016). Working for a future with fewer harms to wild animals. https://www.animal-ethics.org/working-for-a-future-with-fewer-harms-to-wild-animals/

Animal Ethics. (2014). Why we should give moral consideration to sentient beings rather than ecosystems. https://www.animal-ethics.org/sentience-section/relevance-of-sentience/why-we-should-consider-sentient-beings-rather-than-ecosystems/

Animal Ethics. (2016a). Why wild animal suffering matters. https://www.animal-ethics.org/wild-animal-suffering-section/wild-animal-suffering-matters/

Animal Ethics. (2016b). Rescuing trapped animals. https://www.animal-ethics.org/wild-animal-suffering-section/helping-animals-in-the-wild/rescuing-trapped-animals/

Animal Ethics. (2017). Animals and politics. https://www.animal-ethics.org/animals-and-politics/

Animal Ethics. (2018). The importance of the future. https://www.animal-ethics.org/importance-of-the-future/

Animal Ethics. (2020a). *Introduction to wild animal suffering: A guide to the issues*. Animal Ethics. https://www.animal-ethics.org/wp-content/uploads/Introduction_to_Wild_Animal_Suffering.pdf

Animal Ethics. (2020b). Rescuing animals. https://www.animal-ethics.org/wild-animal-suffering-video-course-unit-8/

Animal Ethics. (2020c). Various ways to help wild animals in need. https://www.animal-ethics.org/wild-animal-suffering-video-course-unit-9/

Animal Ethics. (2020d). Vaccinating animals in the wild. https://www.animal-ethics.org/wild-animal-suffering-video-course-unit-10/

Animal Ethics. (2020e). Ethical theories and nonhuman animals. https://www.animal-ethics.org/wild-animal-suffering-video-course-unit-15/

Animal Ethics. (2020f). Reasons for promoting welfare biology as an academic field. https://www.animal-ethics.org/wild-animal-suffering-video-course-unit-21/

Animal Ethics. (2021). Suffering-focused ethics. https://www.animal-ethics.org/ethics-animals-section/ethical-theories-nonhuman-animals/suffering-focused-ethics/

Animal Ethics. (2022). Strategic considerations for effective wild animal suffering work. https://www.animal-ethics.org/strategic-considerations-for-effective-wild-animal-suffering-work/

APPC. (2016). Americans' knowledge of the branches of government is declining. http://cdn.annenbergpublicpolicycenter.org/wp-content/uploads/Civic_knowledge_survey_Sept_2016.pdf

Arrow, K. et al. (2008). The Promise of Prediction Markets. *Science*, 320(5878), pp. 877-878.

Aveek. (2012). Can Global Egalitarians Defend the Welfare State? https://socialproblemsarelikemaths.blogspot.com/2012/06/can-global-egalitarians-defend-welfare.html

Bailenson, J. et al. (2008). Facial Similarity between Voters and Candidates Causes Influence. *Public Opinion Quarterly*, 72(5), pp. 935-961.

Bailey, J. (1997). *Utilitarianism, Institutions, and Justice.* Oxford University Press.

Bakunin, M. (1873/1990). *Statism and Anarchy.* Cambridge University Press.

Balcombe, J. (2016). *What a Fish Knows: The Inner Lives of Our Underwater Cousins.* Scientific American/Farrar, Straus, and Giroux.

Balcombe, J. (2021). *Super Fly: The Unexpected Lives of the World's Most Successful Insects.* Penguin Books.

Bar-On, Y. et al. (2018). The biomass distribution on Earth. *PNAS*, 115(25), pp. 6506-6511.

Baron, J. & Jost, J. (2019). False Equivalence: Are Liberals and Conservatives in the United States Equally Biased? *Perspectives on Psychological Science*, 14(2), pp. 292-303.

Barone, G. & Mocetti, S. (2016). Inequality and Trust: New Evidence From Panel Data. *Economic Inquiry*, 54(2), pp. 794-809.

Bartels, L. (1996). Uninformed Votes: Information Effects in Presidential Elections. *American Journal of Political Science*, 40(1), pp. 194-230.

Baumann, T. (2017a). S-risks: An introduction. http://centerforreducingsuffering.org/intro/

Baumann, T. (2017b). Uncertainty smooths out differences in impact. https://prioritizationresearch.com/uncertainty-smoothes-out-differences-in-impact/

Baumann, T. (2018). A typology of s-risks. https://centerforreducingsuffering.org/a-typology-of-s-risks/

Baumann, T. (2019). Risk factors for s-risks. https://centerforreducingsuffering.org/risk-factors-for-s-risks/

Baumann, T. (2020a). Is most expected suffering due to worst-case outcomes? https://s-risks.org/wp-content/uploads/2020/01/Is_most_expected_suffering_due_to_worst_case_scenarios_.pdf

Baumann, T. (2020b). Thoughts on electoral reform. https://forum.effectivealtruism.org/posts/8Rn2gw7escCc2Rmb7/thoughts-on-electoral-reform

Baumann, T. (2020c). Improving our political system: An overview. https://centerforreducingsuffering.org/improving-our-political-system-an-overview/

Baumann, T. (2020d). Representing future generations in the political process. https://centerforreducingsuffering.org/representing-future-generations-in-the-political-process/

Baumann, T. (2020e). Arguments for and against a focus on s-risks. https://centerforreducingsuffering.org/arguments-for-and-against-a-focus-on-s-risks/

Baumann, T. (2020f). Longtermism and animal advocacy. https://centerforreducingsuffering.org/longtermism-and-animal-advocacy/

Baumann, T. (2021). How can we reduce s-risks? https://centerforreducingsuffering.org/research/how-can-we-reduce-s-risks/

Baumann, T. (2022). Career advice for reducing suffering. https://centerforreducingsuffering.org/research/career-advice-for-reducing-suffering/

Beggs, T. & Anderson, J. (2020). Beliefs About Fish and Chickens & Their Relation to Animal-Positive Behaviors. https://osf.io/862k9/

Bellafiore, R. (2020). An Update on Charitable Giving. https://www.jec.senate.gov/public/index.cfm/republicans/2020/9/an-update-on-charitable-giving

Benjamin, D. et al. (2012). The genetic architecture of economic and political preferences. *PNAS*, 109(21), pp. 8026-8031.

Bennett, J. (1988). Power and influence as distinct personality traits: Development and validation of a psychometric measure. *Journal of Research in Personality*, 22(3), pp. 361-394.

Bentham, J. (1789/2007). *An Introduction to the Principles of Morals and Legislation.* Dover Publications.

Berger, P. (1974). *Pyramids of Sacrifice: Political Ethics and Social Change.* Basic Books.

Berlin, I. (1969/2002). Two Concepts of Liberty. In Berlin, I., *Four Essays on Liberty*, Oxford University Press.

Beshkar, M. (2008). The presence of consciousness in the absence of the cerebral cortex. *Synapse*, 62(7), pp. 553-556.

Birch, J. (2017). Animal sentience and the precautionary principle. *Animal Sentience*, 16(1).

Blanken, P. et al. (2010). Outcome of long-term heroin-assisted treatment offered to chronic, treatment-resistant heroin addicts in the Netherlands. *Addiction*, 105(2), pp. 300-308.

Boehm, C. (1999/2001). *Hierarchy in the Forest: The Evolution of Egalitarian Behavior.* Harvard University Press.

Bogenschneider, K. & Corbett, T. (2010). *Evidence-Based Policymaking: Insights from Policy-Minded Researchers and Research-Minded Policymakers.* Routledge.

Bollard, L. (2018). Ending factory farming. https://www.youtube.com/watch?v=WcAaWL0geRU

Bonnardel, Y. (2020). Should we attack speciesism or humanism? https://veganoptioncanada.org/en/opinion-en/should-we-attack-speciesism-or-humanism/

Bostrom, N. (2011). Information Hazards: A Typology of Potential Harms from Knowledge. *Review of Contemporary Philosophy*, 10, pp. 44-79.

Bostrom, N. (2014). *Superintelligence: Paths, Dangers, Strategies.* Oxford University Press.

Bostrom, N. & Ord, T. (2006). The Reversal Test: Eliminating Status Quo Bias in Applied Ethics. *Ethics*, 116(4), pp. 656-679.

Bouchard T. et al. (1990). Sources of human psychological differences: The Minnesota Study of Twins Reared Apart. *Science*, 250(4978), pp. 223-228.

Boyce, C. et al. (2010). Money and happiness: Rank of income, not income, affects life satisfaction. *Psychol Sci*, 21(4), pp. 471-475.

Boyer, P. & Petersen, M. (2012). The naturalness of (many) social institutions: Evolved cognition as their foundation. *Journal of Institutional Economics*, 8, pp. 1-25.

Bradley, B. (2018). Contemporary Consequentialist Theories of Virtue. In Snow, N. (ed.), *The Oxford Handbook of Virtue.* Oxford University Press.

Braithwaite, V. (2010). *Do Fish Feel Pain?* Oxford University Press.

Brandt, R. (1984). Utilitarianism and Moral Rights. *Canadian Journal of Philosophy*, 14(1), pp. 1-19.

Brehm, S. & Brehm, J. (1981). *Psychological Reactance: A Theory of Freedom and Control.* Academic Press.

Brels, S. (2017). A Global Approach to Animal Protection. *Journal of International Wildlife Law & Policy*, 20(1), pp. 105-123.

Brennan, J. (2011). *The Ethics of Voting.* Princeton University Press.

Brennan, J. (2016). *Against Democracy.* Princeton University Press.

Brennan, J. (2021). AMA: Jason Brennan, author of "Against Democracy" and creator of a Georgetown course on EA. https://forum.effectivealtruism.org/posts/z3S3ZejbwGe6BFjcz/ama-jason-brennan-author-of-against-democracy-and-creator-of

Breyer, D. (2015). The Cessation of Suffering and Buddhist Axiology. *Journal of Buddhist Ethics*, 22, pp. 533-560.

Brockway, J. (2021). Speciesism And Diet. https://faunalytics.org/speciesism-and-diet/

Brown, C. (2015). Fish intelligence, sentience and ethics. *Anim Cogn*, 18(1), pp. 1-17.

Brown, D. (1991). *Human Universals.* McGraw-Hill.

Bryant, C. (2019). We Can't Keep Meating Like This: Attitudes towards Vegetarian and Vegan Diets in the United Kingdom. *Sustainability*, 11(23): 6844.

Bueno de Mesquita, B. & Smith, A. (2012). *The Dictator's Handbook: Why Bad Behavior Is Almost Always Good Politics*. PublicAffairs.

Burger, J. (2009). Replicating Milgram: Would people still obey today? *American Psychologist*, 64(1), pp. 1-11.

Burnheim, J. (1985/2014). *Is Democracy Possible? The Alternative to Electoral Politics*. JUP.

Bushman, B. (1988). The Effects of Apparel on Compliance: A Field Experiment with a Female Authority Figure. *Personality and Social Psychology Bulletin*, 14, pp. 459-467.

Buttrick, N. et al. (2017). Inequality and well-being. *Current Opinion in Psychology*, 18, pp. 15-20.

Buttrick, N. & Oishi, S. (2017). The psychological consequences of income inequality. *Social and Personality Psychology Compass*, 11(3): e12304.

Bøggild, T. & Petersen M. (2016). The Evolved Functions of Procedural Fairness: An Adaptation for Politics. In Shackelford, T. & Hansen, R. (eds.), *The Evolution of Morality*. Springer.

Caplan, B. (2007). *The Myth of the Rational Voter: Why Democracies Choose Bad Policies*. Princeton University Press.

Caplan, B. (2008). The Totalitarian Threat. In Bostrom, N. et al. (eds.), *Global Catastrophic Risks*. Oxford University Press.

Capps, A. (2013a). Debeaking Video Shows Standard Practice on Free Range Egg Farms. https://freefromharm.org/animal-cruelty-investigation/debeaking-video-shows-standard-practice-on-free-range-egg-farms/

Capps, A. (2013b). From Bacon to Holiday Ham. https://freefromharm.org/animal-cruelty-investigation/day-in-the-life-christmas-ham-pig/

Caprioli, M. & Trumbore, P. (2006). First Use of Violent Force in Militarized Interstate Disputes, 1980-2001. *Journal of Peace Research*, 43(6), pp. 741-749.

Carlier, A. & Treich, N. (2020). Directly Valuing Animal Welfare in (Environmental) Economics. *International Review of Environmental and Resource Economics*, 2020, 14(1), pp. 113-152.

Carlin, R. & Love, G. (2013). The Politics of Interpersonal Trust and Reciprocity: An Experimental Approach. *Political Behavior*, 35, pp. 43-63.

Carr, J. (2015). What Have We Learned About the Performance of Council-Manager Government? A Review and Synthesis of the Research. *Public Administration Review*, 75(5), pp. 673-689.

Carter, S. & Huston, J. (2018). Universal Basic Income Research. https://www.effectivealtruism.org/articles/ea-global-2018-ubi/

Casal Bértoa, F. & Rama, J. (2021). Polarization: What Do We Know and What Can We Do About It? *Frontiers in Political Science*, 3: 687695.

Cassino, D. (2015). Ignorance, Partisanship Drive False Beliefs about Obama, Iraq. http://publicmind.fdu.edu/2015/false/

Cavalieri, P. (1991). Principle of Liberty or Harm Principle? *Between the Species*, 7(3), pp. 161-164.

Caviola, L. (2017). Against naive effective altruism. https://www.youtube.com/watch?v=-2oRgxxafXk

Caviola, L. et al. (2019). The moral standing of animals: Towards a psychology of speciesism. *J Pers Soc Psychol*, 116(6), pp. 1011-1029.

Caviola, L. et al. (2022). Population ethical intuitions. *Cognition*, 218: 104941.

Center for Responsive Politics. (2020). Net Worth of 2020 Presidential Candidates. https://www.opensecrets.org/2020-presidential-race/financial-disclosures-and-net-worth

Chaney, P. et al. (2021). Exploring the Substantive Representation of Non-Humans in UK Parliamentary Business: A Legislative Functions Perspective of Animal Welfare Petitions, 2010–2019. *Parliamentary Affairs*, gsab036, https://doi.org/10.1093/pa/gsab036

Cheeseman, N. & Klaas, B. (2018). *How to Rig an Election*. Yale University Press.

Chenoweth, E. & Stephan, M. (2011). *Why Civil Resistance Works: The Strategic Logic of Nonviolent Conflict*. Columbia University Press.

Cheon, B. et al. (2011). Cultural influences on neural basis of intergroup empathy. *Neuroimage*, 57(2), pp. 642-650.

Chester, D. & DeWall, C. (2018). Personality correlates of revenge-seeking: Multidimensional links to physical aggression, impulsivity, and aggressive pleasure. *Aggress Behav*, 44(3), pp. 235-245.

Chesterton, G. (1929). *The Thing*. Sheed & Ward.

Chiavacci, D. (2005). Changing egalitarianism? Attitudes regarding income and gender equality in contemporary Japan. *Japan Forum*, 17(1), pp. 107-131.

Choe, J. (2008). Income inequality and crime in the United States. *Economics Letters*, 101(1), pp. 31-33.

Christakis, N. (2019). *Blueprint: The Evolutionary Origins of a Good Society*. Little, Brown Spark.

Christiano, T. (2011). An Instrumental Argument for a Human Right to Democracy. *Philosophy & Public Affairs*, 39(2), pp. 142-176.

Christiano, T. & Sameer, B. (2006/2021). Democracy. https://plato.stanford.edu/entries/democracy/

Cochrane, A. (2010). *An Introduction to Animals and Political Theory*. Palgrave Macmillan.

Cochrane, A. (2012). *Animal Rights Without Liberation: Applied Ethics and Human Obligations*. Columbia University Press.

Cochrane, A. (2013). From human rights to sentient rights. *Critical Review of International Social and Political Philosophy*, 16(5), pp. 655-675.

Cochrane, A. (2018). *Sentientist Politics: A Theory of Global Inter-Species Justice*. Oxford University Press.

Cochrane, A. (2020). *Should Animals Have Political Rights?* Polity Press.

Cohen, S. (2001). *States of Denial: Knowing About Atrocities and Suffering.* Polity Blackwell Publishers.

Conard, E. (2016). *The Upside Of Inequality: How Good Intentions Undermine the Middle Class.* Portfolio.

Conner, T. et al. (2017). Let them eat fruit! The effect of fruit and vegetable consumption on psychological well-being in young adults: A randomized controlled trial. *PLoS One,* 12(2): e0171206.

Conway, L. et al. (2017). Donald Trump as a Cultural Revolt Against Perceived Communication Restriction: Priming Political Correctness Norms Causes More Trump Support. *Journal of Social and Political Psychology,* 5(1), pp. 244-259.

Cosmides, L. & Tooby, J. (1992). Cognitive adaptations for social exchange. In Barkow, J. et al. (eds.), *The Adapted Mind.* Oxford University Press.

Cosmides, L. & Tooby, J. (1997). Evolutionary Psychology: A Primer. https://www.cep.ucsb.edu/primer.html

Cowen, T. (2003). Policing nature. *Environmental Ethics,* 25(2), pp. 169-182.

Cowles, C. (2019). *War on Us: How the War on Drugs and Myths About Addiction Have Created a War on All of Us.* Fidalgo Press.

Crisp, R. (1992). Utilitarianism and the Life of Virtue. *The Philosophical Quarterly,* 42(167), pp. 139-160.

Curry, O. (2019). What's Wrong with Moral Foundations Theory, and How to get Moral Psychology Right. https://behavioralscientist.org/whats-wrong-with-moral-foundations-theory-and-how-to-get-moral-psychology-right/

Dahl, R. (2006). *On Political Equality.* Yale University Press.

Daly, M. et al. (2014). A social rank explanation of how money influences health. *Health Psychol,* 34(3), pp. 222-230.

Damasio, A. (1994/2006). *Descartes' Error: Emotion, Reason, and the Human Brain.* Vintage Books.

Danaher, J. et al. (2017). Algorithmic governance: Developing a research agenda through the power of collective intelligence. *Big Data & Society,* 4(2), pp. 1-21.

Davidow, B. (2013). Why Most People Don't Care About Wild-Animal Suffering. https://reducing-suffering.org/why-most-people-dont-care-about-wild-animal-suffering/

DeBruine, L. (2002). Facial resemblance enhances trust. *Proc R Soc Lond B,* 269, pp. 1307-1312.

DeCelles, K. & Norton, M. (2016). Physical and situational inequality on airplanes predicts air rage. *PNAS,* 113(20), pp. 5588-5591.

De Freitas, J. et al. (2019). Common knowledge, coordination, and strategic mentalizing in human social life. *PNAS,* 116(28), pp. 13751-13758.

Delannoi, G. & Dowlen, O. (eds.) (2010). *Sortition: Theory and Practice.* Imprint Academic.

Dennett, D. (1999). Dennett's Deal. https://www.edge.org/conversation/daniel_c_dennett-dennetts-deal

DeScioli, P. (2016). The side-taking hypothesis for moral judgment. *Current Opinion in Psychology*, 7, pp. 23-27.

Deseret News. (1996). Online Document: How the Public Views Animal Rights. https://www.deseret.com/1996/8/20/19261207/online-document-how-the-public-views-animal-rights

Dierickx, S. et al. (2016). Euthanasia in Belgium: Trends in reported cases between 2003 and 2013. *CMAJ*, 188(16): E407-E414.

DiGiovanni, A. (2021). A longtermist critique of "The expected value of extinction risk reduction is positive". https://forum.effectivealtruism.org/posts/RkPK8rWigSAybgGPe/a-longtermist-critique-of-the-expected-value-of-extinction-2

Ditto, P. et al. (2019a). At Least Bias Is Bipartisan: A Meta-Analytic Comparison of Partisan Bias in Liberals and Conservatives. *Perspectives on Psychological Science*, 14(2), pp. 1-19.

Ditto, P. et al. (2019b). Partisan Bias and Its Discontents. *Perspectives on Psychological Science*, 14(2), pp. 304-316.

Doğruyol, B. et al. (2019). The five-factor model of the moral foundations theory is stable across WEIRD and non-WEIRD cultures. *Personality and Individual Differences*, 151: 109547.

Dohmen, T. et al. (2015). Patience and the Wealth of Nations. Working paper. http://humcap.uchicago.edu/RePEc/hka/wpaper/Dohmen_Enke_etal_2016_patience-wealth-nations.pdf

Dolinski, D. et al. (2017). Would You Deliver an Electric Shock in 2015? Obedience in the Experimental Paradigm Developed by Stanley Milgram in the 50 Years Following the Original Studies. *Social Psychological and Personality Science*, 8(8), pp. 927-933.

Dorjsuren, B. (2020). Norway's Prison System Benefits Its Economy. https://borgenproject.org/norways-prison-system/

Dowlen, O. (2008). *The Political Potential of Sortition: A Study of the Random Selection of Citizens for Public Office*. Imprint Academic.

Drescher, D. (2017). Cause Area: Human Rights in North Korea. https://forum.effectivealtruism.org/posts/werW78GfeAgBRbvF3/cause-area-human-rights-in-north-korea

Drutman, L. (2020). *Breaking the Two-Party Doom Loop: The Case for Multiparty Democracy in America*. Oxford University Press.

Drutman, L. (2021). Why The Two-Party System Is Effing Up U.S. Democracy. https://fivethirtyeight.com/features/why-the-two-party-system-is-wrecking-american-democracy/

Drutman, L. & Strano, M. (2021). What We Know About Ranked-Choice Voting. https://www.newamerica.org/political-reform/reports/what-we-know-about-ranked-choice-voting/

Dullaghan, N. et al. (2021). Rethink Priorities poll: US attitudes towards insects. https://drive.google.com/file/d/1g3t2BNANVHGC4rsII9Lx5hzqNRi5yNy4/view

Duverger, M. (1954/1976). *Political Parties: Their Organization and Activity in the Modern State.* Cambridge University Press.

Dyson, L. (2016). A forgotten Space Age technology could change how we grow food. https://www.youtube.com/watch?v=c8WMM_PUOj0

Earp, B. et al. (2021). Racial Justice Requires Ending the War on Drugs. *The American Journal of Bioethics*, 21(4), pp. 4-19.

Economist Intelligence Unit (2021). Democracy Index 2020 In sickness and in health? https://www.dnevnik.bg/file/4170840.pdf

Eisnitz, G. (2009). *Slaughterhouse: The Shocking Story of Greed, Neglect, And Inhumane Treatment Inside the U.S. Meat Industry.* Prometheus.

Enoch, D. (2021). Politics and Suffering (draft paper). https://davidenoch.huji.ac.il/sites/default/files/david.enoch/files/politics_and_suffering.pdf

Everett, J. et al. (2016). Inference of trustworthiness from intuitive moral judgments. *J Exp Psychol Gen*, 145(6), pp. 772-787.

Everett, J. et al. (2018). The costs of being consequentialist: Social inference from instrumental harm and impartial beneficence. *Journal of Experimental Social Psychology*, 79, pp. 200-216.

Fajnzylber, P. et al. (2002). Inequality and Violent Crime. *Journal of Law and Economics*, 45(1), pp. 1-39.

Fallon, J. (2011). The Mind of a Dictator. https://www.youtube.com/watch?v=bs1Re2-NAD4

Farb, N. et al. (2012). The Mindful Brain and Emotion Regulation in Mood Disorders. *Canadian Journal of Psychiatry*, 57(2), pp. 70-77.

Faria, C. (2014). Equality, priority and nonhuman animals. *Dilemata: International Journal of Applied Ethics*, 14, pp. 225-236.

Faria, C. & Horta, O. (2019). Welfare Biology. In Fischer, B. (ed.), *The Routledge Handbook of Animal Ethics*. Routledge

Faria, C. & Paez, E. (2019). It's splitsville: Why animal ethics and environmental ethics are incompatible. *American Behavioral Scientist*, 63(8), pp. 1047-1060.

Fatke, M. (2017). Personality Traits and Political Ideology: A First Global Assessment. *Political Psychology*, 38(5), pp. 881-899.

Feinberg, M. et al. (2012). Liberating reason from the passions: Overriding intuitionist moral judgments through emotion reappraisal. *Psychol Sci*, 23(7), pp. 788-795.

Felice, W. (1996). *Taking Suffering Seriously: The Importance of Collective Human Rights.* State University of New York Press.

Fernbach, P. et al. (2013). Political Extremism Is Supported by an Illusion of Understanding. *Psychological Science*, 24(6), pp. 939-946.

Ferreira, S. (2017). Portugal's radical drugs policy is working. Why hasn't the world copied it? https://www.theguardian.com/news/2017/dec/05/portugals-radical-drugs-policy-is-working-why-hasnt-the-world-copied-it

Fischhoff, B. et al. (1977). Knowing with Certainty: The Appropriateness of Extreme Confidence. *Journal of Experimental Psychology: Human Perception and Performance,* 3(4), pp. 552-564.

Fishcount. (2014). Humane slaughter. http://fishcount.org.uk/ fish-welfare-in-commercial-fishing/humane-slaughter

Fishcount. (2019). Numbers of fish caught from the wild each year. http://fishcount.org. uk/fish-count-estimates-2/numbers-of-fish-caught-from-the-wild-each-year

Fishkin, J. (2018). *Democracy When the People Are Thinking: Revitalizing Our Politics Through Public Deliberation.* Oxford University Press.

Fishkin, J. et al. (2000). Deliberative polling and public consultation. *Parliamentary Affairs,* 53(4), pp. 657-666.

Fleischman, D. (in press). Animal Ethics and Evolutionary Psychology. In Shackelford, T. (ed.), *The SAGE Handbook of Evolutionary Psychology.* SAGE Publications.

Forbes. (2020). Forbes Billionaires 2020. https://www.forbes.com/billionaires/

Foulkes, I. (2001). Democracy at its most direct in Appenzell. https://www.swissinfo.ch/ eng/democracy-at-its-most-direct-in-appenzell/245320

Fowler, J. & Christakis, N. (2009). *Connected: The Surprising Power of Our Social Networks.* Little, Brown and Company.

Frank, J. (2008). Is there an "animal welfare Kuznets curve"? *Ecological Economics,* 66(2-3), pp. 478-491.

Frankfurt, H. (2015). *On Inequality.* Princeton University Press.

Freedom House. (2017). Freedom of the Press 2017. https://freedomhouse.org/sites/ default/files/2020-02/FOTP_2017_booklet_FINAL_April28_1.pdf

Freinacht, H. (2017). *The Listening Society: A Metamodern Guide to Politics, Book One.* Metamoderna.

Freinacht, H. (2019). *Nordic Ideology: A Metamodern Guide to Politics, Book Two.* Metamoderna.

Frey, B. & Stutzer, A. (2000). Happiness, Economy and Institutions. *The Economic Journal,* 110, pp. 918-938.

Friedman, B. (2005/2006). *The Moral Consequences of Economic Growth.* Vintage Books.

Friedman, B. (2006a). The Moral Consequences of Economic Growth. *Society,* 43(2), pp. 15-22.

Friedman, D. (1973/2014). *The Machinery of Freedom: Guide to a Radical Capitalism.*

Friedman, D. (1981). Problems with Libertarianism. https://www.youtube.com/ watch?v=197mWvLs04c

Friedman, J. (2006b). Democratic competence in normative and positive theory: Neglected implications of "the nature of belief systems in mass publics". *Critical Review,* 18(1-3), pp. 1-43.

Friedman, J. (2019). *Power without Knowledge: A Critique of Technocracy.* Oxford University Press.

Friedman, M. (1962/2002). *Capitalism and Freedom.* University of Chicago Press.

Fukuyama, F. (1992). *The End of History and the Last Man.* Free Press.

Future of Life Institute. (2017). The Future of AI — What Do You Think? https://futureoflife.org/superintelligence-survey/

Gajic, M. & Gamser, D. (2018). Freedom Barometer Human Rights Index. http://freedombarometer.org/files/download/Human_Rights_Index_2018_final.pdf

Galef, J. (2021). *The Scout Mindset: Why Some People See Things Clearly and Others Don't.* Portfolio.

Garfield, Z. et al. (2019). The evolutionary anthropology of political leadership. *The Leadership Quarterly*, 30(1), pp. 59-80.

Garner, R. (2005). *The Political Theory of Animal Rights.* Manchester University Press.

Garner, R. (2017). Animals and democratic theory: Beyond an anthropocentric account. *Contemporary Political Theory*, 16(4), pp. 459-477.

Garrido J. et al. (2011). Protection against Tuberculosis in Eurasian Wild Boar Vaccinated with Heat-Inactivated *Mycobacterium bovis. PLoS One*, 6(9): e24905.

Gellers, J. (2020). *Rights for Robots: Artificial Intelligence, Animal and Environmental Law.* Routledge.

Gelpi, C. & Griesdorf, M. (2001). Winners or Losers? Democracies in International Crisis, 1918–94. *American Political Science Review*, 95(3), pp. 633-647.

Gerring, J. et al. (2009). Are Parliamentary Systems Better? *Comparative Political Studies*, 42(3), pp. 327-359.

Gesley, J. (2021). On This Day in 1984: Women's Suffrage in Liechtenstein. https://blogs.loc.gov/law/2021/07/on-this-day-in-1984-womens-suffrage-in-liechtenstein/

Gibler, D. & Randazzo, K. (2011). Testing the Effects of Independent Judiciaries on the Likelihood of Democratic Backsliding. *American Journal of Political Science*, 55(3), pp. 696-709.

Gilens, M. (2005). Inequality and Democratic Responsiveness. *The Public Opinion Quarterly*, 69(5), pp. 778-796.

GiveWell. (2014). Your Dollar Goes Further Overseas. https://www.givewell.org/giving101/Your-dollar-goes-further-overseas

Gloor, L. (2016/2019). The Case for Suffering-Focused Ethics. https://longtermrisk.org/the-case-for-suffering-focused-ethics/

Gloor, L. (2017). Tranquilism. https://longtermrisk.org/tranquilism/

Gloor, L. (2018). Cause prioritization for downside-focused value systems. https://longtermrisk.org/cause-prioritization-downside-focused-value-systems/

Goldberg, S. et al. (2020). The experimental effects of psilocybin on symptoms of anxiety and depression: A meta-analysis. *Psychiatry Research*, 284: 112749.

Goldsmith, F. (2021). Animal Welfare (Sentience) Bill. https://bills.parliament.uk/publications/41515/documents/260

Goodin, R. (1995). *Utilitarianism as a public philosophy.* Cambridge University Press.

Goodman, C. (2009). *Consequences of Compassion: An Interpretation and Defense of Buddhist Ethics.* Oxford University Press.

Graham, J. et al. (2013). Moral Foundations Theory: The pragmatic validity of moral pluralism. *Advances in Experimental Social Psychology*, 47, pp. 55-130.

Greene, J. (2013). *Moral Tribes: Emotion, Reason and the Gap Between Us and Them*. Penguin Group.

Greenwald, G. (2009). Drug Decriminalization in Portugal: Lessons for Creating Fair and Successful Drug Policies. https://www.cato.org/sites/cato.org/files/pubs/pdf/greenwald_whitepaper.pdf

Greger, M. (2015). *How Not to Die: Discover the Foods Scientifically Proven to Prevent and Reverse Disease*. Flatiron Books.

Greger, M. (2020a). Pandemics: History & Prevention. https://www.youtube.com/watch?v=7_ppXSABYLY

Greger, M. (2020b). *How to Survive a Pandemic*. Flatiron Books.

Guerrero, A. (2014). Against Elections: The Lottocratic Alternative. *Philosophy and Public Affairs*, 42(2), pp. 135-178.

Gwartney, J. et al. (2019). Economic Freedom of the World: 2019 Annual Report. https://www.fraserinstitute.org/sites/default/files/economic-freedom-of-the-world-2019.pdf

Hacker, J. & Pierson, P. (2016). *American Amnesia: How the War on Government Led Us to Forget What Made America Prosper*. Simon & Schuster.

Hafenbrack, A. et al. (2014). Debiasing the mind through meditation: Mindfulness and the sunk-cost bias. *Psychol Sci*, 25(2), pp. 369-376.

Haidt, J. (2001). The emotional dog and its rational tail: A social intuitionist approach to moral judgment. *Psychol Rev*, 108(4), pp. 814-834.

Haidt, J. (2012). *The Righteous Mind: Why Good People Are Divided by Politics and Religion*. Pantheon Books.

Haidt, J. (2013). 2013 Boyarsky Lecture. https://www.youtube.com/watch?v=b86dzTFJbkc

Haidt, J. et al. (2000). Moral Dumbfounding: When Intuition Finds No Reason. http://theskepticalzone.com/wp/wp-content/uploads/2018/03/haidt.bjorklund.working-paper.when-intuition-finds-no-reason.pub603.pdf

Hajjar, L. (2013). *Torture: A Sociology of Violence and Human Rights*. Routledge.

Halpern, C. (2002). *Suffering, Politics, Power: A Genealogy in Modern Political Theory*. State University of New York Press.

Hannon, M. (2021). Disagreement or Badmouthing? The Role of Expressive Discourse in Politics. In Edenberg, E. & Hannon, M. (eds.), *Political Epistemology*. Oxford University Press.

Hanson, R. (2007). Policy Tug-O-War. https://www.overcomingbias.com/2007/05/policy_tugowar.html

Hanson, R. (2013). Shall We Vote on Values, But Bet on Beliefs? *Journal of Political Philosophy*, 21(2), pp. 151-178.

Hanson, R. (2018). The Model to Beat: Status Rank. https://www.overcomingbias.com/2018/03/the-model-to-beat-status-rank.html

Hanson, R. (2019a). Best Cause: New Institution Field Trials. https://www.overcomingbias.com/2019/03/best-cause-new-mechanism-field-trials.html

Hanson, R. (2019b). Expand vs Fight in Social Justice, Fertility, Bioconservatism, & AI Risk. https://www.overcomingbias.com/2019/05/expand-vs-fight-social-justice-fertility-bioconservatism-and-ai-risk.html

Hanson, R. et al. (2006). Information aggregation and manipulation in an experimental market. *Journal of Economic Behavior & Organization*, 60(4), pp. 449-459.

Hanson, R. & Yudkowsky, E. (2013). The Hanson-Yudkowsky AI-Foom Debate. https://intelligence.org/files/AIFoomDebate.pdf

Harden, J. (2021). All the World's a Stage: US Presidential Narcissism and International Conflict. *International Studies Quarterly*, 65(3), pp. 825-837.

Harris, J. (2021). Key Lessons From Social Movement History. https://www.sentienceinstitute.org/blog/key-lessons-from-social-movement-history

Harris, J. & Reese, J. (2021). The Moral Consideration of Artificial Entities: A Literature Review. https://arxiv.org/abs/2102.04215

Harris, S. (2010/2011). *The Moral Landscape: How Science Can Determine Human Values.* Free Press.

Hatemi, P. et al. (2011). A Genome-Wide Analysis of Liberal and Conservative Political Attitudes. *The Journal of Politics*, 73(1), pp. 271-285.

Hatemi, P. et al. (2014). Genetic Influences on Political Ideologies: Twin Analyses of 19 Measures of Political Ideologies from Five Democracies and Genome-Wide Findings from Three Populations. *Behav Genet*, 44(3), pp. 282-294.

Hatemi, P. & McDermott, R. (2012). The Genetics of Politics: Discovery, Challenges, and Progress. *Trends in Genetics*, 28(10), pp. 525-533.

Haukkala, H. (2018). Policy Makers Love Their Children Too. https://www.effectivealtruism.org/articles/ea-global-2018-policy-makers-love-their-children-too/

Healy, A. et al. (2010). Irrelevant events affect voters' evaluations of government performance. *PNAS*, 107(29), pp. 12804-12809.

Heath, C. & Heath, D. (2007). *Made to Stick: Why Some Ideas Survive and Others Die.* Random House.

Heinrich, T. & Loftis, M. (2019). Democracy aid and electoral accountability. *Journal of Conflict Resolution*, 63(1), pp. 139-166.

Hemel, D. & Fleischer, M. (2017). Atlas Nods: The Libertarian Case for a Basic Income. *Wisconsin Law Review.* https://chicagounbound.uchicago.edu/cgi/viewcontent.cgi?article=13519&context=journal_articles

Hennig, B. (2017). *The End of Politicians: Time for a Real Democracy.* Unbound.

Hennig, B. (2018). The Irish Citizens' Assembly chooses representatives by lottery, not election. https://www.buildinganewreality.com/the-irish-citizens-assembly-chooses-representatives-by-lottery-not-election/

Henrich, J. (2015). *The Secret of Our Success: How Culture Is Driving Human Evolution, Domesticating Our Species, and Making Us Smarter.* Princeton University Press.

Henrich, J. (2020). *The WEIRDest People in the World: How the West Became Psychologically Peculiar and Particularly Prosperous.* Farrar, Straus and Giroux.

Henrich, J. et al. (2010). The weirdest people in the world? *Behav Brain Sci*, 33(2-3), pp. 61-83.

Henrich, J. et al. (2012). The puzzle of monogamous marriage. *Phil Trans R Soc B*, 367, pp. 657-669.

Henrich, N. & Henrich, J. (2007). *Why Humans Cooperate: A Cultural and Evolutionary Explanation*. Oxford University Press.

Herrán, M. (2017). The big lie. https://manuherran.com/the-big-lie/

Hibbing, J. et al. (2013). *Predisposed: Liberals, Conservatives, and the Biology of Political Differences*. Routledge.

Hidalgo, C. (2019a). A bold idea to replace politicians. https://www.youtube.com/watch?v=CyGWML6cI_k

Hidalgo, C. (2019b). Augmented Democracy FAQ. https://www.peopledemocracy.com/

History. (2017/2019). War on Drugs. https://www.history.com/topics/crime/the-war-on-drugs

Hobbes, T. (1651/2017). *Leviathan*. Early Modern Texts.

Holmes, S. & Sunstein, C. (1999/2000). *The Cost of Rights: Why Liberty Depends on Taxes*. W. W. Norton & Company.

Holness-Tofts, A. (2020). Poor meat eater problem. https://forum.effectivealtruism.org/posts/mGLYpBXvN3F2KCAP5/poor-meat-eater-problem

Hölzel, B. et al. (2011). How does mindfulness meditation work? Proposing mechanisms of action from a conceptual and neural perspective. *Perspectives on Psychological Science*, 6, pp. 6537-6559.

Hooker, B. (2002). *Ideal Code, Real World: A Rule-Consequentialist Theory of Morality*. Oxford University Press.

Hooley, D. (2018). The Political Status of Nonhuman Animals (PhD thesis). https://tspace.library.utoronto.ca/bitstream/1807/89821/3/Hooley_Daniel_201806_PhD_thesis.pdf

Horta, O. (2010a). Debunking the Idyllic View of Natural Processes: Population Dynamics and Suffering in the Wild. *Télos*, 17, pp. 73-88.

Horta, O. (2010b). What Is Speciesism? *Journal of Agricultural and Environmental Ethics*, 23, pp. 243-266.

Horta, O. (2013a). Zoopolis, interventions and the State of Nature. *Law, Ethics and Philosophy*, 1, pp. 113-125.

Horta, O. (2013b). Expanding Global Justice: The Case for the International Protection of Animals. *Global Policy*, 4(4), pp. 371-380.

Horta, O. (2014). The Scope of the Argument from Species Overlap. *Journal of Applied Philosophy*, 31(2), pp. 142-154.

Horta, O. (2015). The Problem of Evil in Nature: Evolutionary Bases of the Prevalence of Disvalue. *Relations: Beyond Anthropocentrism*, 3(1), pp. 17-32.

Horta, O. (2016). Egalitarianism and Animals. *Between the Species*, 19(1), pp. 109-143.

Horta, O. (2017a). Population Dynamics Meets Animal Ethics: The Case for Aiding Animals in Nature. In Woodhall, A. & Garmendia da Trindade, G. (eds.), *Ethical and Political Approaches to Nonhuman Animal Issues*. Palgrave Macmillan.

Horta, O. (2017b). Animal Suffering in Nature: The Case for Intervention. *Environmental Ethics*, 39(3), pp. 261-279.

Horta, O. (2018). Concern for wild animal suffering and environmental ethics: What are the limits of the disagreement? *Les ateliers de l'éthique*, 13(1), pp. 85-100.

Horta, O. (2019). Promoting Welfare Biology as the Study of Wild Animal Suffering. https://www.youtube.com/watch?v=GOuQ7gPIU7Q&

Horta, O. (2020). Oscar Horta of the University of Santiago de Compostela on How We Can Best Help Wild Animals. https://www.sentienceinstitute.org/podcast/episode-13.html

Huang, K. et al. (2019). Veil-of-ignorance reasoning favors the greater good. *Proc Natl Acad Sci*, 116(48), pp. 23989-23995.

Huemer, M. (2013). *The Problem of Political Authority: An Examination of the Right to Coerce and the Duty to Obey*. Palgrave Macmillan.

Huemer, M. (2019). *Dialogues on Ethical Vegetarianism*. Routledge.

Hughes, C. & Stevens, A. (2010). What Can We Learn from the Portuguese Decriminalization of Illicit Drugs? *The British Journal of Criminology*, 50(6), pp. 999-1022.

Hughes, I. (2018). *Disordered Minds: How Dangerous Personalities Are Destroying Democracy*. Zero Books.

Hughes, J. (2017). Algorithms and Posthuman Governance. *Journal of Posthuman Studies*, 1(2), pp. 166-184.

Hyde, S. (2007). The Observer Effect in International Politics: Evidence from a Natural Experiment. *World Politics*, 60, pp. 37-63.

Illescas, S. & Genovés, V. (2008). Efficacy of a psychological treatment for sex offenders. *Psicothema*, 20(1), pp. 4-9.

Illing, S. (2018). Epistocracy: A political theorist's case for letting only the informed vote. https://www.vox.com/2018/7/23/17581394/against-democracy-book-epistocracy-jason-brennan

Imai, K. & Lo, J. (2021). Robustness of Empirical Evidence for the Democratic Peace: A Nonparametric Sensitivity Analysis. *International Organization*, 75(3), pp. 901-919.

Institute for Economics & Peace. (2021). Global Peace Index 2021. https://www.economicsandpeace.org/wp-content/uploads/2021/06/GPI-2021-web.pdf

Ipsos MORI. (2014). Perceptions are not reality: Things the world gets wrong. https://www.ipsos.com/ipsos-mori/en-uk/perceptions-are-not-reality-things-world-gets-wrong

Iyer, R. et al. (2012). Understanding Libertarian Morality: The Psychological Dispositions of Self-Identified Libertarians. *PLoS One*, 7(8): e42366.

Jabr, F. (2018). It's Official: Fish Feel Pain. https://www.smithsonianmag.com/science-nature/fish-feel-pain-180967764/

Jain, P. (2019). *An Introduction to Jain Philosophy*. DK Printworld.

Jansa, J. (2019). Inequality is higher in some states like New York and Louisiana because of corporate welfare. https://theconversation.com/inequality-is-higher-in-some-states-like-new-york-and-louisiana-because-of-corporate-welfare-126406

Jensen, H. (2001). John Stuart Mill's Theories of Wealth and Income Distribution. *Review of Social Economy*, 59(4), pp. 491-507.

Johannsen, K. (2017). Animal Rights and the Problem of r-Strategists. *Ethical Theory and Moral Practice*, 20, pp. 333-345.

Johannsen, K. (2020). *Wild Animal Ethics: The Moral and Political Problem of Wild Animal Suffering*. Routledge.

Jonason, P. & Ferrell, J. (2016). Looking under the hood: The psychogenic motivational foundations of the Dark Triad. *Personality and Individual Differences*, 94, pp. 324-331.

Jones, G. (2020). *10% Less Democracy: Why You Should Trust Elites a Little More and the Masses a Little Less*. Stanford University Press.

Jönsson, K. et al. (2008). Tardigrades survive exposure to space in low Earth orbit. *Current Biology*, 18(17), pp. 729-731.

Jordahl, H. (2007). Inequality and Trust. https://www.ifn.se/Wfiles/wp/wp715.pdf

Käfer, A. (2018). How Authoritarian Regimes Create a Climate of Fear. https://www.bosch-stiftung.de/en/news/how-authoritarian-regimes-create-climate-fear

Kahan, D. et al. (2013). Motivated Numeracy and Enlightened Self-Government. *Behavioural Public Policy*, 1, pp. 54-86.

Kahneman, D. (2011). *Thinking, Fast and Slow*. Farrar, Straus and Giroux

Kanai, R. et al. (2011). Political Orientations Are Correlated with Brain Structure in Young Adults. *Current Biology*, 21(8), pp. 677-680.

Kang, Y. et al. (2014). The nondiscriminating heart: Lovingkindness meditation training decreases implicit intergroup bias. *Journal of Experimental Psychology: General*, 143(3), pp. 1306-1313.

Keown, D. (1992/2001). *The Nature of Buddhist Ethics*. Palgrave Macmillan.

King-Nobles, H. (2019). Fish Welfare Initiative. https://www.youtube.com/watch?v=bePnsETp89c

Klein, J. (2010). How Can a Democracy Solve Tough Problems? http://content.time.com/time/magazine/article/0,9171,2015790,00.html

Klein, N. (2014/2015). *This Changes Everything: Capitalism vs. The Climate*. Simon & Schuster.

Klemmensen, R. et al. (2012). Heritability in Political Interest and Efficacy across Cultures: Denmark and the United States. *Twin Research and Human Genetics*, 15(1), pp. 15-20.

Knopf, T. (2019). Switzerland couldn't stop drug users. So it started supporting them. https://www.northcarolinahealthnews.org/2019/01/21/switzerland-couldnt-stop-drug-users-so-it-started-supporting-them/

Knutsson, S. (2021). The World Destruction Argument. *Inquiry*, 64(10), pp. 1004-1023.

Knutsson, S. & Munthe, C. (2017). A Virtue of Precaution Regarding the Moral Status of Animals with Uncertain Sentience. *Journal of Agricultural and Environmental Ethics*, 30(2), pp. 213-224.

Koenig, P. et al. (2007). CP7_E2alf: A safe and efficient marker vaccine strain for oral immunisation of wild boar against Classical swine fever virus (CSFV). *Vaccine*, 25(17), pp. 3391-3399.

Konczal, M. (2021). *Freedom From the Market: America's Fight to Liberate Itself from the Grip of the Invisible Hand*. The New Press.

Korsgaard, C. (2018). *Fellow Creatures: Our Obligations to the Other Animals*. Oxford University Press.

Krediet, E. et al. (2020). Reviewing the Potential of Psychedelics for the Treatment of PTSD. *Int J Neuropsychopharmacol*, 23(6), pp. 385-400.

Kriminalomsorgen. (2021). About the Norwegian Correctional Service. https://www.kriminalomsorgen.no/information-in-english.265199.no.html

Kropotkin, P. (1892/2006). *The Conquest of Bread*. AK Press.

Kunda, Z. (1990). The case for motivated reasoning. *Psychological bulletin*, 108(3), pp. 480-498.

Kurzban, R. (2011a). *Why Everyone (Else) Is a Hypocrite: Evolution and the Modular Mind*. Princeton University Press.

Kurzban, R. (2011b). Two problems with "self-deception": No "self" and no "deception". *Behavioral and Brain Sciences*, 34, pp. 32-33.

Kymlicka, W. (2018). Human rights without human supremacism. *Canadian Journal of Philosophy*, 48, pp. 763-792.

Lacalle, D. (2020). *Freedom or Equality: The Key to Prosperity Through Social Capitalism*. Post Hill Press.

Lancee, B. & van de Werfhorst, H. (2012). Income inequality and participation: A comparison of 24 European countries. *Social Science Research*, 41, pp. 1166-1178.

Landemore, H. (2020). *Open Democracy: Reinventing Popular Rule for the Twenty-First Century*. Princeton University Press.

Lane, R. et al. (1998). Neural correlates of levels of emotional awareness. Evidence of an interaction between emotion and attention in the anterior cingulate cortex. *J Cogn Neurosci*, 10(4), pp. 525-535.

Lanteaume, L. et al. (2007). Emotion Induction After Direct Intracerebral Stimulations of Human Amygdala. *Cerebral Cortex*, 17(6), pp. 1307-1313.

Laslier, J.-F. (2011). And the loser is... Plurality Voting. https://hal.archives-ouvertes.fr/hal-00609810/document

Latimer, J. et al. (2005). The Effectiveness of Restorative Justice Practices: A Meta-Analysis. *The Prison Journal*, 85(2), pp. 127-144.

Layne, C. (1994). Kant or Cant: The Myth of the Democratic Peace. *International Security*, 19(2), pp. 5-49.

Leblang, D. & Chan, S. (2003). Explaining Wars Fought by Established Democracies: Do Institutional Constraints Matter? *Political Research Quarterly*, 56(4), pp. 385-400.

Leighton, J. (2011). *The Battle for Compassion: Ethics in an Apathetic Universe*. Algora.

Leighton, J. (2015). The Battle for Compassion - a short film by Jonathan Leighton. https://www.youtube.com/watch?v=DBiKl_v5Mls

Leighton, J. (2017). Thriving in the Age of Factory Farming. https://medium.com/@jonleighton1/thriving-in-the-age-of-factory-farming-fbcca7121d67

Leighton, J. (2018). Ending the Agony: Access to Morphine as an Ethical and Human Rights Imperative. https://www.preventsuffering.org/wp-content/uploads/2018/03/Guide-to-morphine-access.pdf

Leighton, J. (2019). OPIS, a think-and-do tank for an ethic based on the prevention of suffering. https://medium.com/@jonleighton1/opis-a-think-and-do-tank-for-an-ethic-based-on-the-prevention-of-suffering-eb2baa3d5619

Leighton, J. (2020). Legalising Access to Psilocybin to End the Agony of Cluster Headaches. https://www.preventsuffering.org/wp-content/uploads/2020/11/Legalising-Access-to-Psilocybin-for-Cluster-Headaches-Policy-Paper.pdf

Leighton, J. (forthcoming). *The Tango of Ethics*.

Lerner, J. & Tetlock, P. (2003). Bridging individual, interpersonal, and institutional approaches to judgment and decision making: The impact of accountability on cognitive bias. In Schneider, S. & Shanteau, J. (eds.), *Cambridge series on judgment and decision making. Emerging perspectives on judgment and decision research*. Cambridge University Press.

Levine, S. et al. (2020). The logic of universalization guides moral judgment. *PNAS*, 117(42), pp. 26158-26169.

Lewis, G. (2016). Beware surprising and suspicious convergence. https://forum.effectivealtruism.org/posts/omoZDu8ScNbot6kXS/beware-surprising-and-suspicious-convergence

Lindauer, M. et al. (2020). Comparing the effect of rational and emotional appeals on donation behavior. *Judgment and Decision Making*, 15(3), pp. 413-420.

Linz, J. (1990). The Perils of Presidentialism. *Journal of Democracy*, 1(1), pp. 51-69.

Linz, J. & Valenzuela, A. (eds.) (1994). *The Failure of Presidential Democracy: Comparative Perspectives, Vol. 1-2*. Johns Hopkins University Press.

Linzey, A. (2009). *Why Animal Suffering Matters: Philosophy, Theology, and Practical Ethics*. Oxford University Press.

Lipsey, M. et al. (2001). Cognitive-Behavioral Programs for Offenders. *The Annals of the American Academy of Political and Social Science*, 578, 1, pp. 144-157.

Lobaczewski, A. (2006). *Political Ponerology*. Red Pill Press.

Lodge, M. & Taber, C. (2005). The Automaticity of Affect for Political Leaders, Groups, and Issues: An Experimental Test of the Hot Cognition Hypothesis. *Political Psychology*, 26(3), pp. 455-482.

Low, P. et al. (2012). The Cambridge Declaration on Consciousness. https://fcmconference.org/img/CambridgeDeclarationOnConsciousness.pdf

Lueke, A. & Gibson, B. (2015). Mindfulness meditation reduces implicit age and race bias: The role of reduced automaticity of responding. *Social Psychological and Personality Science*, 6(3), pp. 284-291.

Lueke, A. & Gibson, B. (2016). Brief mindfulness meditation reduces discrimination. *Psychology of Consciousness: Theory, Research, and Practice*, 3(1), pp. 34-44.

Madigan, M. & Karhu, E. (2018). The role of plant-based nutrition in cancer prevention. *J Unexplored Med Data*, 3: 9.

Maki, J. et al. (2017). Oral vaccination of wildlife using a vaccinia–rabies-glycoprotein recombinant virus vaccine (RABORAL V-RG*): A global review. *Vet Res*, 48(1): 57.

Mandel, A. (2018). Why Nobel Prize Winner Daniel Kahneman Gave Up on Happiness. https://www.haaretz.com/israel-news/.premium.MAGAZINE-why-nobel-prize-winnerdaniel-kahneman-gave-up-on-happiness-1.6528513

Mannetti, L. et al. (2016). All we need is the candidate's face: The irrelevance of information about political coalition affiliation and campaign promises. *Cogent Psychology*, 3(1), pp. 120-148.

Mannino, A. (2015). Humanitarian Intervention in Nature: Crucial Questions and Probable Answers. *Relations: Beyond Anthropocentrism*, 3(1), pp. 107-118.

Margalit, Y. (2013). Explaining Social Policy Preferences: Evidence from the Great Recession. *American Political Science Review*, 107(1), pp. 80-103.

Martin, C. et al. (2017). The nervous and visual systems of onychophorans and tardigrades: Learning about arthropod evolution from their closest relatives. *Journal of comparative physiology*, 203(8), pp. 565-590.

Mathison, E. (2018). Asymmetries and Ill-Being (PhD thesis). University of Toronto. https://tspace.library.utoronto.ca/bitstream/1807/92027/3/Mathison_Eric_201811_PhD_thesis.pdf

Matsusaka, J. (2005). Direct Democracy Works. *Journal of Economic Perspectives*, 19(2), pp. 185-206.

Matthews, D. (2019). Factory farms abuse workers, animals, and the environment. Cory Booker has a plan to stop them. https://www.vox.com/future-perfect/2019/12/20/21028200/factory-farms-abuse-workers-animals-and-the-environment-cory-booker-has-a-plan-to-stop-them

Mayerfeld, J. (1996). The Moral Asymmetry of Happiness and Suffering. *Southern Journal of Philosophy*, 34, pp. 317-338.

Mayerfeld, J. (1999). *Suffering and Moral Responsibility*. Oxford University Press.

Mayerfeld, J. (2008). In Defense of the Absolute Prohibition of Torture. *Public Affairs Quarterly*, 22(2), pp. 109-128.

Mayerfeld, J. (2016). *The Promise of Human Rights: Constitutional Government, Democratic Legitimacy, and International Law*. University of Pennsylvania Press.

McClendon, G. (2018). *Envy in Politics*. Princeton University Press.

McManus, R. & Ozkan, F. (2018). Who Does Better for the Economy? Presidents Versus Parliamentary Democracies. *Public Choice*, 176(3-4), pp. 361-387.

McNeill, B. (2017). Sadism Leads Certain People to Seek Vengeance, Study Finds. https://neurosciencenews.com/vengence-sadism-8077/

Mellers, B. & McGraw, A. (1999). How to improve Bayesian reasoning: Comment on Gigerenzer and Hoffrage (1995). *Psychological Review*, 106(2), pp. 417-424.

Mendez, M. (2017). A Neurology of the Conservative-Liberal Dimension of Political Ideology. *J Neuropsychiatry Clin Neurosci*, 29, pp. 86-94.

Mercier, H. (2020). *Not Born Yesterday: The Science of Who We Trust and What We Believe*. Princeton University Press.

Mercier, H. & Sperber, D. (2017). *The Enigma of Reason*. Harvard University Press.

Merkel, M. (2015). Using the legal system to fight factory farms. https://www.youtube.com/watch?v=za1aWllWfWs

Metzinger, T. (2003). *Being No One: The Self-Model Theory of Subjectivity*. MIT Press.

Metzinger, T. (2009). *The Ego Tunnel: The Science of the Mind and the Myth of the Self*. Basic Books.

Metzinger, T. (2017). Suffering. In Almqvist, K. & Haag, A. (eds.), *The Return of Consciousness*. Axel and Margaret Ax:son Johnson Foundation.

Metzinger, T. (2018). Towards a Global Artificial Intelligence Charter. https://www.blogs.uni-mainz.de/fb05philosophieengl/files/2018/10/Metzinger_2018_Global_Artificial_Intelligence_Charter_PE_614.547.pdf

Metzinger, T. (2021). Artificial Suffering: An Argument for a Global Moratorium on Synthetic Phenomenology. *Journal of Artificial Intelligence and Consciousness*, 8(1), pp. 1-24.

Milanovic, B. (2016). *Global Inequality: A New Approach for the Age of Globalization*. Harvard University Press.

Milgram, A. (2014). Why smart statistics are the key to fighting crime. https://www.youtube.com/watch?v=ZJNESMhIxQ0

Milgram, S. (1963). Behavioral study of obedience. *Journal of Abnormal and Social Psychology*, 67, pp. 371-378.

Milgram, S. (1974/2009). *Obedience to Authority: An Experimental View*. Harper & Row.

Mill, J. S. (1859/2002). *On Liberty*. Dover Publications.

Mill, J. S. (1861). *Considerations on Representative Government*. Parker, Son, and Bourn.

Mill, J. S. (1863/2007). *Utilitarianism*. Dover Publications.

Miller, D. (2017). Justice. https://plato.stanford.edu/entries/justice/

Miller, G. (1996). Political peacocks. *Demos Quarterly*, 10, pp. 9-11.

Miller, T. et al. (2021). 2021 Index of Economic Freedom. https://www.heritage.org/index/pdf/2021/book/2021_IndexOfEconomicFreedom_FINAL.pdf

Milligan, T. (2015). The political turn in animal rights. *Politics and Animals*, 1(1), pp. 6-15.

Minson, J. & Monin, B. (2011). Do-Gooder Derogation: Disparaging Morally Motivated Minorities to Defuse Anticipated Reproach. *Social Psychological and Personality Science*, 3(2), pp. 200-207.

Molloy, M. (2021). Are Insects the Next Victims of Massive Scale Factory Farming? https://idausa.org/news/insect-eating-europe/

Mood, A. & Brooke, P. (2010). Estimating the Number of Fish Caught in Global Fishing Each Year. http://fishcount.org.uk/published/std/fishcountstudy.pdf

Mood, A. & Brooke, P. (2012). Estimating the Number of Farmed Fish Killed in Global Aquaculture Each Year. http://fishcount.org.uk/published/std/fishcountstudy2.pdf

Mousseau, M. & Shi, Y. (1999). A Test for Reverse Causality in the Democratic Peace Relationship. *Journal of Peace Research*, 36(6), pp. 639-663.

Muehlhauser, L. & Salamon, A. (2012). Intelligence Explosion: Evidence and Import. http://intelligence.org/files/IE-EI.pdf

Murray, C. (2006). *In Our Hands: A Plan To Replace The Welfare State*. AEI Press.

Muthukrishna, M. (2020). Beyond Western, Educated, Industrial, Rich, and Democratic (WEIRD) Psychology: Measuring and Mapping Scales of Cultural and Psychological Distance. *Psychological Science*, 31(6), pp. 678-701.

Mutz, D. & Kim, E. (2017). The Impact of In-group Favoritism on Trade Preferences. *International Organization*, 71(4), pp. 827-850.

Nakamura, H. et al. (2014). Cold-hearted or cool-headed: physical coldness promotes utilitarian moral judgment. *Front Psychol*, 5: 1086.

Narvaez, D. (2008). The social intuitionist model: Some counter-intuitions. In Sinnott-Armstrong, W. (ed.), *Moral psychology, Vol. 2. The cognitive science of morality: Intuition and diversity*. MIT Press.

Navalny, A. (2021). Only action against corruption can solve the world's biggest problems. https://www.theguardian.com/commentisfree/2021/aug/19/action-against-corruption-russian-sanctions-oligarchs-alexei-navalny

Nelson, K. & Afonso, W. (2019). Ethics By Design: The Impact of Form of Government on Municipal Corruption. *Public Administration Review*, 79(4), pp. 591-600.

Nesse, R. (2008). Truth does not reside with smart university experts. https://www.edge.org/response-detail/10101

Neves, P. et al. (2016). A Meta-Analytic Reassessment of the Effects of Inequality on Growth. *World Development*, 78, pp. 386-400.

Neville, L. (2012). Do Economic Equality and Generalized Trust Inhibit Academic Dishonesty? Evidence From State-Level Search-Engine Queries. *Psychological Science*, 23(4), pp. 339-345.

Newman, M. (2004/2006). Power laws, Pareto distributions and Zipf's law. https://arxiv.org/pdf/cond-mat/0412004.pdf

Ng, Y-K. (1995). Towards welfare biology: Evolutionary economics of animal consciousness and suffering. *Biology and Philosophy*, 10, pp. 255-285.

Norris, J. (2016). Booklet Comparison Study – Pay Per Read #2 Jul 2016. https://veganoutreach.org/ppr-2016/

Norton, M. & Ariely, D. (2011). Building a Better America—One Wealth Quintile at a Time. *Perspectives on Psychological Science*, 6(1), pp. 9-12.

Norwood B. & Murray, S. (2018). FooDS Food Demand Survey. https://web.archive. org/web/20190806000018/http://agecon.okstate.edu/files/january%202018.pdf

Nozick, R. (1974/2013). *Anarchy, State, and Utopia*. Basic Books.

Nussbaum, M. (2011). *Creating Capabilities: The Human Development Approach*. Harvard University Press.

Nussbaum, M. (2022). *Justice for Animals: Our Collective Responsibility*. Simon & Schuster.

Oberhaus, D. (2019). A Crashed Israeli Lunar Lander Spilled Tardigrades on the Moon. https://www.wired.com/story/a-crashed-israeli-lunar-lander-spilled-tardigrades-on-the-moon/

OECD. (2022). Meat consumption. https://www.oecd-ilibrary.org/agriculture-and-food/meat-consumption/indicator/english_fa290fd0-en

Oishi, S. & Kesebir, S. (2015). Income Inequality Explains Why Economic Growth Does Not Always Translate to an Increase in Happiness. *Psychological Science*, 26(10), pp. 1630-1638.

O'Leary, K. (2006). *Saving Democracy: A Plan for Real Representation in America*. Stanford University Press.

Oleck, J. (2020). With 40,000 Americans Incarcerated For Marijuana Offenses, The Cannabis Industry Needs To Step Up, Activists Said This Week. https://www.forbes.com/sites/joanoleck/2020/06/26/with-40000-americans-incarcerated-for-marijuana-offenses-the-cannabis-industry-needs-to-step-up-activists-said-this-week/

Olson, M. (1965). *The Logic of Collective Action*. Harvard University Press.

Ord, T. (2005). Consequentialism and Decision Procedures (bachelor thesis). https://www.academia.edu/2781612/Consequentialism_and_Decision_Procedures

Ortiz-Ospina, E. & Roser, M. (2013/2017). Happiness and Life Satisfaction. https://ourworldindata.org/happiness-and-life-satisfaction

Ortoleva, P. & Snowberg, E. (2015). Overconfidence in Political Behavior. *The American Economic Review*, 105(2), pp. 504-535.

Page, B. et al. (2013). Democracy and the Policy Preferences of Wealthy Americans. *Perspectives on Politics*, 11, pp. 51-73.

Pániker, A. (2010). *Jainism: History, Society, Philosophy and Practice*. Motilal Banarsidass.

Parfit, D. (1995). *Equality or Priority*. University of Kansas.

Park, J. & Van Leeuwen, F. (2015). Evolutionary Perspectives on Social Identity. In Zeigler-Hill, V. et al. (eds.), *Evolutionary Perspectives on Social Psychology*. Springer.

Party for the Animals. (2020). Party for the Animals. https://www.partyfortheanimals.com/en/who-we-are

Pavlova, P. (2020). Did they crack the code? The importance of encryption for protest movements. https://www.openglobalrights.org/did-they-crack-the-code-the-importance-of-encryption-for-protest-movements/

Paxton, J. & Greene, J. (2010). Moral reasoning: Hints and allegations. *Top Cogn Sci*, 2(3), pp. 511-527.

Payne, K. (2017). *The Broken Ladder: How Inequality Affects the Way We Think, Live, and Die*. Viking.

Payne, K. et al. (2017). Economic inequality increases risk taking. *PNAS*, 114(18), pp. 4643-4648.

Pearce, D. (1995/2007). *The Hedonistic Imperative*. http://www.hedweb.com/hedab.htm

Pearce, D. (2007). The Abolitionist Project. https://www.abolitionist.com/

Pearce, D. (2012). The Antispeciesist Revolution. https://www.hedweb.com/transhumanism/antispeciesist.html

Pearce, D. (2015). A Welfare State for Elephants? A Case Study of Compassionate Stewardship. *Relations: Beyond Anthropocentrism*, 3(2), pp. 153-164.

Pearce, D. (2016). Compassionate Biology: How CRISPR-based "gene drives" could cheaply, rapidly and sustainably reduce suffering throughout the living world. https://www.gene-drives.com/

Pearce, D. (2017). *Can Biotechnology Abolish Suffering?* The Neuroethics Foundation.

Pearce, D. (2020). What does David Pearce think is the best strategy for reducing animal suffering? https://www.hedweb.com/quora/2015.html#slaughterhouses

Perreault, C. & Mathew, S. (2012). Dating the Origin of Language Using Phonemic Diversity. *PLoS One*, 7(4): e35289.

Perry, G. (2012). *Behind the Shock Machine: The Untold Story of the Notorious Milgram Psychology Experiments*. Scribe Publications.

Peters, A. (2016). Global Animal Law: What It Is and Why We Need It. *Transnational Environmental Law*, 5(1), pp. 9-23.

Petersen, M. (2015). Evolutionary Political Psychology: On the Origin and Structure of Heuristics and Biases in Politics. *Political Psychology*, 36, pp. 45-78.

Petersen, M. et al. (2013). Motivated Reasoning and Political Parties: Evidence for Increased Processing in the Face of Party Cues. *Polit Behav*, 35, pp. 831-854.

Petersen, M. & Laustsen, L. (2019). Upper-Body Strength and Political Egalitarianism: Twelve Conceptual Replications. *International Society of Political Psychology*, 40(2), pp. 375-394.

Peterson, E. (2017). Is Economic Inequality Really a Problem? A Review of the Arguments. *Social Sciences*, 6(4): 147.

Peterson, J. et al. (2020). Do people really become more conservative as they age? *Journal of Politics*, 82(2), pp. 600-611.

Peterson, R. & Palmer, C. (2017). Effects of physical attractiveness on political beliefs. *Politics and the Life Sciences*, 36(2), pp. 3-16.

Pettit, P. (1988). The Consequentialist Can Recognise Rights. *The Philosophical Quarterly*, 38(150), pp. 42-55.

Pew Research Center. (2014). Political Polarization in the American Public. https://www.pewresearch.org/politics/2014/06/12/political-polarization-in-the-american-public/

Pew Research Center. (2015). The Politics of Financial Insecurity.
https://www.pewresearch.org/politics/2015/01/08/
the-politics-of-financial-insecurity-a-democratic-tilt-undercut-by-low-participation/

Piketty, T. (2013/2017). *Capital in the Twenty-First Century*. Harvard University Press.

Pinker, S. (2002/2003). *The Blank Slate: The Modern Denial of Human Nature*. Penguin Books.

Pinker, S. (2011). *The Better Angels of Our Nature: Why Violence Has Declined*. Viking.

Pinker, S. (2012). Emotion, Reason and Moral Progress. https://www.youtube.com/watch?v=hgGEKBSOeEY

Pinker, S. (2016). The Elephant, the Emperor, and the Matzo Ball. https://www.youtube.com/watch?v=eay1-m7RpoU

Pinker, S. (2018). *Enlightenment Now: The Case for Reason, Science, Humanism, and Progress*. Viking.

Pizarro, D. & Bloom, P. (2003). The intelligence of the moral intuitions: Comment on Haidt (2001). *Psychol Rev*, 110(1), pp. 193-196.

Plant, M. & Singer, P. (2021). Why drugs should be not only decriminalised, but fully legalised. https://www.newstatesman.com/international/2021/05/why-drugs-should-be-not-only-decriminalised-fully-legalised

Plous, S. (1993). *The Psychology of Judgment and Decision Making*. McGraw-Hill.

Popper, K. (1945/2011). *The Open Society and Its Enemies*. Routledge.

Popper, K. (1963/2002). *Conjectures and Refutations: The Growth of Scientific Knowledge*. Routledge & Kegan Paul.

Pratto, F. et al. (1994). Social dominance orientation: A personality variable predicting social and political attitudes. *Journal of Personality and Social Psychology*, 67(4), pp. 741-763.

Price, M. et al. (2002). Punitive sentiment as an anti-free rider psychological device. *Evolution and Human Behavior*, 23, pp. 203-231.

Price, M. & Launay, J. (2018). Increased Wellbeing from Social Interaction in a Secular Congregation. *Secularism and Nonreligion*, 7(6), pp. 1-9.

Pronin, E. et al. (2002). The Bias Blind Spot: Perceptions of Bias in Self Versus Others. *Personality and Social Psychology Bulletin*, 28(3), pp. 369-381.

Putnam, H. (2002). *The Collapse of the Fact/Value Dichotomy and Other Essays*. Harvard University Press

Quispe-Torreblanca, E. et al. (2021). Inequality and Social Rank: Income Increases Buy More Life Satisfaction in More Equal Countries. *Personality and Social Psychology Bulletin*, 47(4), pp. 519-539.

Rasmussen, D. (2013). *The Pragmatic Enlightenment: Recovering the Liberalism of Hume, Smith, Montesquieu, and Voltaire*. Cambridge University Press.

Rawls, J. (1971/2005). *A Theory of Justice*. Harvard University Press.

Rawls, J. (1993). *Political Liberalism*. Columbia University Press.

Rawls, J. (2001). *Justice as Fairness: A Restatement*. Harvard University Press.

Reese, J. (2016). The Animal-Free Food Movement Should Move Towards An Institutional Message. https://medium.com/@jacyreese/the-animal-free-food-movement-should-move-towards-aninstitutional-message-534d7cd0298e

Reese, J. (2018). *The End of Animal Farming: How Scientists, Entrepreneurs, and Activists Are Building an Animal-Free Food System*. Beacon Press.

Reese, J. (2020). Institutional change and the limitations of consumer activism. *Palgrave Communications*, 6: 26.

Reporters Without Borders. (2020). 2020 World Press Freedom Index. https://rsf.org/en/ranking/2020

Rethink Priorities. (2021). Submission of Evidence to Animal Welfare (Sentience) Bill. https://committees.parliament.uk/writtenevidence/37632/html/

Riffkin, R. (2015). In U.S., More Say Animals Should Have Same Rights as People. https://news.gallup.com/poll/183275/say-animals-rights-people.aspx

Riggs, F. (1997). Presidentialism versus Parliamentarism: Implications for Representativeness and Legitimacy. *International Political Science Review*, 18(3), pp. 253-278.

Ritchie, H. & Roser, M. (2017/2019). Meat and Dairy Production. https://ourworldindata.org/meat-production

Ritchie, H. & Roser, M. (2018/2019). Causes of Death. https://ourworldindata.org/causes-of-death

Ritchie, H. & Roser, M. (2021). Seafood Production. https://ourworldindata.org/fish-and-overfishing

Roemer, J. (1998). *Equality of Opportunity*. Harvard University Press.

Rogoff, K. (2021). Tackling cross-country inequality is the key to global stability. https://www.theguardian.com/business/2021/may/04/tackling-cross-country-inequality-is-the-key-to-global-stability

Rorheim, A. & Roll Spinnangr, I. (2016/2019). Effective Drug Policy: An Evidence-based Approach. https://ea-foundation.org/files/effective-drug-policy.pdf

Rosato, S. (2003). The Flawed Logic of Democratic Peace Theory. *The American Political Science Review*, 97(4), pp. 585-602.

Rosenfeld, D. (2019). Ethical Motivation and Vegetarian Dieting: The Underlying Role of Anti-speciesist Attitudes. *Anthrozoös*, 32(6), pp. 785-796.

Roser, M. (2016/2019). Human Rights. https://ourworldindata.org/human-rights

Roser, M. & Herre, B. (2013/2019). Democracy. https://ourworldindata.org/democracy

Roser, M. & Ortiz-Ospina, E. (2013a/2016). Income Inequality. https://ourworldindata.org/income-inequality

Roser, M. & Ortiz-Ospina, E. (2013b/2019). Global Extreme Poverty. https://ourworldindata.org/extreme-poverty

Ross, W. D. (1930/2002). *The Right and the Good*. Oxford University Press.

Ross, W. D. (1939). *Foundations of Ethics*. Oxford University Press.

Rothbard, M. (1973/2020). *For a New Liberty: The Libertarian Manifesto*. Ludwig von Mises Institute.

Rothbard, M. (1982/2002). *The Ethics of Liberty*. New York University Press.

Rowe, A. (2020). The scale of direct human impact on invertebrates. https://osf.io/psvk2/

Rozenblit, L. & Keil, F. (2002). The misunderstood limits of folk science: An illusion of explanatory depth. *Cogn Sci*, 26(5), pp. 521-562.

Rue, L. (2005). *Religion Is Not about God: How Spiritual Traditions Nurture our Biological Nature and What to Expect When They Fail*. Rutgers University Press.

Ryder, R. (2001). *Painism: A Modern Morality*. Centaur Press.

Ryder, R. (2006). *Putting Morality Back Into Politics*. Imprint Academic.

Ryder, R. (2011). *Speciesism, Painism and Happiness: A Morality for the Twenty-First Century*. Imprint Academic.

Ryder, R. (2018). Interview with Richard Ryder. https://www.youtube.com/watch?v=nZWcY7Xt0VM

Saghafian, F. et al. (2018). Fruit and vegetable consumption and risk of depression: Accumulative evidence from an updated systematic review and meta-analysis of epidemiological studies. *British Journal of Nutrition*, 119(10), pp. 1087-1101.

Sandel, M. (2009). *Justice: What's the Right Thing to Do?* Farrar, Straus and Giroux.

Santos, T. (2020). *Why Not Parliamentarism?* Wordzworth.

Santos, T. (2021a). We learned some wrong lessons about the rise of Nazis. https://whynotparliamentarism.com/f/we-learned-some-wrong-lessons-about-the-rise-of-nazis

Santos, T. (2021b). Glorious algorithm. https://whynotparliamentarism.com/f/glorious-algorithm

Sapolsky, R. (2017). *Behave: The Biology of Humans at Our Best and Worst*. Penguin Press.

Scala, D. & Johnson, K. (2017). Political Polarization along the Rural-Urban Continuum? The Geography of the Presidential Vote, 2000–2016. *The ANNALS of the American Academy of Political and Social Science*, 672(1), pp. 162-184.

Scanlon, T. (2018). *Why Does Inequality Matter?* Oxford University Press.

Schedler, A. (2006). *Electoral Authoritarianism: The Dynamics of Unfree Competition*. Lynne Rienner Publishers.

Schein, C. & Gray, K. (2017). The Theory of Dyadic Morality: Reinventing Moral Judgment by Redefining Harm. *Personality and Social Psychology Review*. 22(1), pp. 32-70.

Schonfeld, B. (2020). Democracy Promotion as an EA Cause Area. https://forum.effectivealtruism.org/posts/dTconqCtsmHQsNwo9/democracy-promotion-as-an-ea-cause-area-1

Schreiber, D. et al. (2013). Red brain, blue brain: Evaluative processes differ in democrats and republicans. *PLoS One*, 8: e52970.

Schubert, S. (2016). What if politics was rational? https://www.youtube.com/watch?v=aghkRPTE2B8

Schubert, S. et al. (2017). Considering Considerateness: Why communities of do-gooders should be exceptionally considerate. https://www.

centreforeffectivealtruism.org/blog/considering-considerateness-why-communities-of-do-
gooders-should-be/

Schukraft, J. (2020). Intervention Profile: Ballot Initiatives. https://
forum.effectivealtruism.org/posts/2LdswNsEZAgDfJDzo/
intervention-profile-ballot-initiatives

Schulz, J. et al. (2019). The Church, intensive kinship, and global psychological
variation. *Science*, 366(6466): eaau5141.

Schulz, W. & Raman, S. (2020). *The Coming Good Society: Why New Realities Demand
New Rights*. Harvard University Press.

Schwardmann, P. & van der Weele, J. (2019). Deception and self-deception. *Nat Hum
Behav*, 3(10), pp. 1055-1061.

Scully, M. (2002). *Dominion: The Power of Man, the Suffering of Animals, and the Call to
Mercy*. St. Martin's Press.

Sebo, J. (2019). A utilitarian case for animal rights. https://www.youtube.com/
watch?v=vELWCTgA9oA

Sebo, J. (2022). *Saving Animals, Saving Ourselves: Why animals matter for pandemics,
climate change, and other catastrophes*. Oxford University Press.

Selinger, W. (2019). *Parliamentarism: From Burke to Weber*. Cambridge University Press.

Sen, A. (1999). *Development as Freedom*. Anchor Books.

Sentience Institute. (2017). Survey of US Attitudes Towards Animal Farming
and AnimalFree Food October 2017. https://www.sentienceinstitute.org/
animal-farming-attitudes-survey-2017

Shapiro, I. (2003). *The Moral Foundations of Politics*. Yale University Press.

Shenkman, R. (2016). *Political Animals: How Our Stone-Age Brain Gets in the Way of
Smart Politics*. Basic Books.

Shklar, J. (1982). Putting Cruelty First. *Daedalus*, 111(3), pp. 17-27.

Shklar, J. (1989). The Liberalism of Fear. In Rosenblum, N. (ed.), *Liberalism and the
Moral Life*. Harvard University Press.

Shklar, J. (1992). *The Faces of Injustice*. Yale University Press.

Shklar, J. (2019). *On Political Obligation*. Yale University Press.

Shooster, J. (2018). Factory Farming is Illegal. https://jayforjustice.wordpress.
com/2018/08/06/factory-farming-is-illegal/

Shriver, A. (2014). The Asymmetrical Contributions of Pleasure and Pain to Animal
Welfare. *Cambridge Quarterly of Healthcare Ethics*, 23(2), pp. 152-162.

Sidgwick, H. (1874/1981). *The Methods of Ethics*. Hackett Pub. Co.

Sidgwick, H. (1891/2012). *The Elements of Politics*. Cambridge University Press.

Silver, J. & Silver, E. (2017). Why are conservatives more punitive than liberals? A moral
foundations approach. *Law and Human Behavior*, 41(3), pp. 258-272.

Simler, K. (2016). Crony Beliefs. https://meltingasphalt.com/crony-beliefs/

Simler, K. & Hanson, R. (2018). *The Elephant in the Brian: Hidden Motives in Everyday
Life*. Oxford University Press.

Singer, J. (2020a). Tulsi Gabbard on veganism, climate change, and what gives her hope. https://vegnews.com/2020/2/tulsi-gabbard-on-veganism-climate-change-and-what-gives-her-hope

Singer, P. (1975/2009). *Animal Liberation*. HarperCollins Publishers.

Singer, P. (1979/2011). *Practical Ethics*. Cambridge University Press.

Singer, P. (1999). *A Darwinian Left: Politics, Evolution, and Cooperation*. Weidenfeld & Nicolson.

Singer, P. (2018). Using Technology to Reduce Suffering. https://www.youtube.com/watch?v=teGzSp5mybc&

Singer, P. (2020b). *Why Vegan?* Penguin Books.

SIPRI. (2021). World military spending rises to almost $2 trillion in 2020. https://www.sipri.org/media/press-release/2021/world-military-spending-rises-almost-2-trillion-2020

Smart, R. (2018). Evidence on the Effectiveness of Heroin-Assisted Treatment. https://www.rand.org/content/dam/rand/pubs/working_papers/WR1200/WR1263/RAND_WR1263.pdf

Smets, T. et al. (2011). Attitudes and Experiences of Belgian Physicians Regarding Euthanasia Practice and the Euthanasia Law. *Journal of Pain and Symptom Management*, 41(3), pp. 580-593.

Smith, K. (2011). Why Not Plutocracy: Apathy Runs Deep Edition. https://modeledbehavior.wordpress.com/2011/12/21/why-not-plutocracy-apathy-runs-deep-edition/

Sortition Foundation. (2021). Sortition goes wild. https://www.sortitionfoundation.org/sortition_goes_wild

Soryl, A. et al. (2021). The Case for Welfare Biology. *Journal of Agricultural and Environmental Ethics*, 34: 7.

Souva, M. & Prins, B. (2006). The Liberal Peace Revisited: The Role of Democracy, Dependence, and Development in Militarized Interstate Dispute Initiation, 1950–1999. *International Interactions*, 32, pp. 183-200.

Sowell, T. (1980/1996). *Knowledge and Decisions*. Basic Books.

Sowell, T. (2009). *Intellectuals and Society*. Basic Books.

St Clair, T. (2002). Farming without subsidies – a better way. Why New Zealand agriculture is a world leader. https://www.politico.eu/article/viewpoint-farming-without-subsidies-a-better-way-why-new-zealand-agriculture-is-a-world-leader/

Strossen, N. (2018/2020). *Hate: Why We Should Resist It with Free Speech, Not Censorship*. Oxford University Press.

Sumaila, U. et al. (2019). Updated estimates and analysis of global fisheries subsidies. *Marine Policy*, 109: 103695.

Sumner, L. (1987). *The Moral Foundation of Rights*. Clarendon Press.

Sumner, L. (1996). *Welfare, Happiness, and Ethics*. Oxford University Press.

Sumner, L. (2011). *Assisted Death: A Study in Ethics and Law*. Oxford University Press.

Sunstein, C. (2009). The Rights of Animals: A Very Short Primer. https://www.all-creatures.org/articles/ar-therights.html

Sunstein, C. (2019). *How Change Happens.* MIT Press.

Sussman, A. et al. (2013). Competence ratings in US predict presidential election outcomes in Bulgaria. *Journal of Experimental Social Psychology*, 49(4), pp. 771-775.

SWI. (2019). Swiss to vote on banning factory farming. https://www.swissinfo.ch/eng/animal-rights_swiss-to-vote-on-banning-factory-farming/45233958

Sychev, O. & Protasova, I. (2020). The Relationships between Moral Foundations, Social Beliefs and Attitudes towards Economic Inequality among Russian Youth: A Case Study of Altai Krai. *Journal of Psychology and Pedagogics*, 17(4), pp. 705-718.

Sætra, H. (2020). A shallow defence of a technocracy of artificial intelligence: Examining the political harms of algorithmic governance in the domain of government. *Technol Soc*, 62: 101283.

Sønderskov, K. & Dinesen, P. (2014). Danish Exceptionalism: Explaining the Unique Increase in Social Trust over the Past 30 Years. *European Sociological Review*, 30(6), pp. 782-795.

Taber, C. & Lodge, M. (2006). Motivated Skepticism in the Evaluation of Political Beliefs. *American Journal of Political Science*, 50(3), pp. 755-769.

Taft, C. (2016). *Motivational Methods for Vegan Advocacy: A Clinical Psychology Perspective.* Vegan Publishers.

Talbott, W. (2005). *Which Rights Should Be Universal?* Oxford University Press.

Talbott, W. (2010). *Human Rights and Human Well-Being.* Oxford University Press.

Talhelm, T. et al. (2015). Liberals Think More Analytically (More "WEIRD") Than Conservatives. *Personality and Social Psychology Bulletin*, 41(2), pp. 250-267.

Taylor, J. (2015). How to Change Public Opinion. https://www.niskanencenter.org/how-to-change-public-opinion/

Taylor, S. (2019). Pathocracy. https://www.psychologytoday.com/us/blog/out-the-darkness/201907/pathocracy

Teffer, P. (2019). Study: EU spends 18-20% of budget on livestock farming. https://euobserver.com/economic/144137

Temkin, L. (1993). *Inequality.* Oxford University Press.

Tetlock, P. (2005). *Expert Political Judgment.* Princeton University Press.

Tetlock, P. (2015). *Superforecasting: The Art and Science of Prediction.* Crown.

Tetrick, J. (2013). The Future of Food: Josh Tetrick at TEDxEdmonton. https://www.youtube.com/watch?v=QVTkdpfeb8A

Thornton, M. (1991). Alcohol Prohibition Was a Failure. https://www.cato.org/policy-analysis/alcohol-prohibition-was-failure

Toft, F. (2013). Dyreambulancerne kørte 24 gange om dagen sidste år. https://www.beredskabsinfo.dk/brandvaesen/dyreambulancerne/

Tomasello, M. (1999/2009). *The Cultural Origins of Human Cognition.* Harvard University Press.

Tomasik, B. (2006). On the Seriousness of Suffering. https://reducing-suffering.org/on-the-seriousness-of-suffering/

Tomasik, B. (2007). How Much Direct Suffering Is Caused by Various Animal Foods? https://reducing-suffering.org/how-much-direct-suffering-is-caused-by-various-animal-foods/

Tomasik, B. (2008/2018). Climate Change and Wild Animals. https://reducing-suffering.org/climate-change-and-wild-animals/

Tomasik, B. (2009/2019). How Many Wild Animals Are There? https://reducing-suffering.org/how-many-wild-animals-are-there/

Tomasik, B. (2011/2019). Risks of Astronomical Future Suffering. https://longtermrisk.org/risks-of-astronomical-future-suffering/

Tomasik, B. (2013a/2018). Gains from Trade through Compromise. https://longtermrisk.org/gains-from-trade-through-compromise/

Tomasik, B. (2013b/2017). Intention-Based Moral Reactions Distort Intuitions about Wild Animals. https://reducing-suffering.org/intention-based-moral-reactions-distort-intuitions-about-wild-animals/

Tomasik, B. (2013c/2018). Why Honesty Is a Good Policy. https://reducing-suffering.org/why-honesty-is-a-good-policy/

Tomasik, B. (2013d/2015). Differential Intellectual Progress as a Positive-Sum Project. https://longtermrisk.org/differential-intellectual-progress-as-a-positive-sum-project/

Tomasik, B. (2013e/2015). Charity Cost-Effectiveness in an Uncertain World. https://longtermrisk.org/charity-cost-effectiveness-in-an-uncertain-world/

Tomasik, B. (2013f/2016). Possible Ways to Promote Compromise. https://longtermrisk.org/possible-ways-to-promote-compromise/

Tomasik, B. (2014a/2016). A Lower Bound on the Importance of Promoting Cooperation. https://longtermrisk.org/a-lower-bound-on-the-importance-of-promoting-cooperation/

Tomasik, B. (2014b/2017). Reasons to Be Nice to Other Value Systems. https://longtermrisk.org/reasons-to-be-nice-to-other-value-systems/

Tomasik, B. (2014c/2019). Why I Don't Support Eating Insects. https://reducing-suffering.org/why-i-dont-support-eating-insects/

Tomasik, B. (2014d/2018). Will Space Colonization Multiply Wild-Animal Suffering? https://reducing-suffering.org/will-space-colonization-multiply-wild-animal-suffering/

Tomasik, B. (2015a). The Importance of Wild-Animal Suffering. *Relations: Beyond Anthropocentrism*, 3(2), pp. 133-152.

Tomasik, B. (2015b). A Small Mechanical Turk Survey on Ethics and Animal Welfare. https://reducing-suffering.org/a-small-mechanical-turk-survey-on-ethics-and-animal-welfare/

Tomasik, B. (2016). Preventing Extreme Suffering Has Moral Priority. https://www.youtube.com/watch?v=RyA_eF7W02s

Tondani, D. (2009). Universal Basic Income and Negative Income Tax: Two different ways of thinking redistribution. *The Journal of Socio-Economics*, 38(2), pp. 246-255.

Tooby, J. (2017). Coalitional Instincts. https://www.edge.org/response-detail/27168

Tooby J. & Cosmides, L. (2010). Groups in Mind: The Coalitional Roots of War and Morality. In Høgh-Olesen, H. (ed.), *Human Morality and Sociality: Evolutionary and Comparative Perspectives*. Palgrave Macmillan.

Trammell, P. (2021). Dynamic Public Good Provision under Time Preference Heterogeneity: Theory and Applications to Philanthropy. https://philiptrammell.com/static/PatienceAndPhilanthropy.pdf

Trivers, R. (2011). *The Folly of Fools: The Logic of Deceit and Self-Deception in Human Life*. Basic Books.

Trujillo, C. et al. (2019). Complex Oscillatory Waves Emerging from Cortical Organoids Model Early Human Brain Network Development. *Cell*, 25(4), pp. 558-569.

Tuckness, A. & Wolf, C. (2016). *This Is Political Philosophy: An Introduction*. John Wiley & Sons, Blackwell.

Turchin, P. (2013a). Return of the oppressed. https://aeon.co/essays/history-tells-us-where-the-wealth-gap-leads

Turchin, P. (2013b). The Double Helix of Inequality and Well-Being. https://peterturchin.com/cliodynamica/the-double-helix-of-inequality-and-well-being/

Turchin, P. (2016). *Ages of Discord: A Structural-demographic Analysis of American History*. Beresta Books.

Tuschman, A. (2013). *Our Political Nature: The Evolutionary Origins of What Divides Us*. Prometheus Books.

Tyson, L. (2013). Taking the law into our own hands. https://www.youtube.com/watch?v=rsTu9X9QnNM

Uchiyama, R. et al. (2021). Cultural Evolution of Genetic Heritability. *Behavioral and Brain Sciences*, published online: https://doi.org/10.1017/S0140525X21000893

Uslaner, E. & Brown, M. (2005). Inequality, Trust, and Civic Engagement. *American Politics Research*, 33(6), pp. 868-894.

Vaintrob, L. (2021). Issues with futarchy. https://forum.effectivealtruism.org/posts/E4QnGsXLEEcNysADT/issues-with-futarchy

Valdesolo, P. & DeSteno, D. (2006). Manipulations of Emotional Context Shape Moral Judgment. *Psychological Science*, 17(6), pp. 476-477.

van de Haar, E. (2015a). *Degrees of Freedom: Liberal Political Philosophy and Ideology*. Routledge.

van de Haar, E. (2015b). The Meaning of "Liberalism". https://www.libertarianism.org/publications/essays/lets-clear-liberal-mess

van der Plas, E. et al. (2010). Amygdala volume correlates positively with fearfulness in normal healthy girls. *Soc Cogn Affect Neurosci*, 5, pp. 424-431.

Van Reybrouck, D. (2016/2018). *Against Elections*. Seven Stories Press.

Vargas, A. et al. (2020). Psilocybin as a New Approach to Treat Depression and Anxiety in the Context of Life-Threatening Diseases—A Systematic Review and Meta-Analysis of Clinical Trials. *Biomedicines*, 8(9): 331.

Vásquez, I. & McMahon, F. (2020). The Human Freedom Index 2020: A Global Measurement of Personal, Civil, and Economic Freedom. https://www.fraserinstitute.org/sites/default/files/human-freedom-index-2020.pdf

Vicario, C. et al. (2018). The effect of hunger and satiety in the judgment of ethical violations. *Brain Cogn*, 125, pp. 32-36.

Villamor Iglesias, A. (2018). The overwhelming prevalence of suffering in Nature. *Revista de Bioética y Derecho*, 42, pp. 181-195.

Vinding, M. (2014). *Why We Should Go Vegan*. https://www.smashwords.com/books/view/409738

Vinding, M. (2015). *Speciesism: Why It Is Wrong and the Implications of Rejecting It*. https://www.smashwords.com/books/view/539674

Vinding, M. (2016a/2020). *Reflections on Intelligence*. https://www.smashwords.com/books/view/655938

Vinding, M. (2016b). Animal Advocates Should Focus On Antispeciesism, Not Veganism. https://magnusvinding.com/2020/05/04/animal-advocates-should-focus-on-antispeciesism-not-veganism/

Vinding, M. (2017). Notes on the Utility of Anti-Speciesist Advocacy. https://magnusvinding.com/2017/10/24/notes-on-the-utility-of-anti-speciesist-advocacy/

Vinding, M. (2018). In Defense of Nuance. https://magnusvinding.com/2018/08/29/in-defense-of-nuance/

Vinding, M. (2020a). *Suffering-Focused Ethics: Defense and Implications*. Ratio Ethica. https://magnusvinding.files.wordpress.com/2020/05/suffering-focused-ethics.pdf

Vinding, M. (2020b). Ten Biases Against Prioritizing Wild-Animal Suffering. https://magnusvinding.com/2020/07/02/ten-biases-against-prioritizing-wild-animal-suffering/

Vinding, M. (2020c). Compassionate Free Speech. https://magnusvinding.com/2020/07/28/compassionate-free-speech/

Vinding, M. (2020d). Why altruists should be cooperative. https://centerforreducingsuffering.org/why-altruists-should-be-cooperative/

Vinding, M. (2020e). Suffering and happiness: Morally symmetric or orthogonal? https://centerforreducingsuffering.org/suffering-and-happiness-morally-symmetric-or-orthogonal/

Vinding, M. (2020f). Underappreciated consequentialist reasons to avoid consuming animal products. https://magnusvinding.com/2020/10/03/underappreciated-consequentialist-reasons/

Vinding, M. (2020g). On fat-tailed distributions and s-risks. https://centerforreducingsuffering.org/on-fat-tailed-distributions-and-s-risks/

Vinding, M. (2021). Suffering-focused ethics and the importance of happiness. https://magnusvinding.com/2021/01/12/the-importance-of-happiness/

Vinding, M. (forthcoming). *Essays on Suffering-Focused Ethics*. Ratio Ethica.

Vrselja, Z. et al. (2019). Restoration of brain circulation and cellular functions hours postmortem. *Nature*, 568, pp. 336-343.

Wang, X. et al. (2014). Fruit and vegetable consumption and mortality from all causes, cardiovascular disease, and cancer: Systematic review and dose-response meta-analysis of prospective cohort studies. *BMJ*, 349: g4490.

Weale, A. (2020). *Modern Social Contract Theory*. Oxford University Press.

Weeden, J. & Kurzban, R. (2014). *The Hidden Agenda of the Political Mind: How Self-Interest Shapes Our Opinions and Why We Won't Admit It*. Princeton University Press.

Westfall, R. et al. (2019). The Influence of Physical Attractiveness on Belief in a Just World. *Psychological Reports*, 122(2), pp. 536-549.

White, M. (2011/2013). *Atrocities: The 100 Deadliest Episodes in Human History*. W. W. Norton & Company.

Wiblin, R. (2020). If you care about social impact, why is voting important? https://80000hours.org/articles/is-voting-important/

Wilson, T. (2014). Slaughterhouse 'sadism': Campaign calls for CCTV in abattoirs to end cruelty. https://www.mancunianmatters.co.uk/life/15122014-slaughterhouse-sadism-campaign-calls-for-cctv-in-abattoirs-to-end-cruelty/

Wiltermuth, S. & Heath, C. (2009). Synchrony and Cooperation. *Psychological Science*, 20(1), pp. 1-5.

Wolf, C. (1995). Contemporary Property Rights, Lockean Provisos, and the Interests of Future Generations. *Ethics*, 105(4), pp. 791-818.

Wolf, C. (1996). Social Choice and Normative Population Theory: A Person Affecting Solution to Parfit's Mere Addition Paradox. *Philosophical Studies*, 81, pp. 263-282.

Wolf, C. (1997). Person-Affecting Utilitarianism and Population Policy. In Heller, J. & Fotion, N. (eds.), *Contingent Future Persons*. Kluwer Academic Publishers. https://web.archive.org/web/20190410204154/https://jwcwolf.public.iastate.edu/Papers/JUPE.HTM

Wolf, C. (2004). O Repugnance, Where Is Thy Sting? In Tännsjö, T. & Ryberg, J. (eds.), *The Repugnant Conclusion*. Kluwer Academic Publishers.

Wolfers, J. & Zitzewitz, E. (2004). Prediction markets. *Journal of Economic Perspectives*, 18(2), pp. 107-126.

Wolff, J. (1996). *An Introduction to Political Philosophy*. Oxford University Press.

Wood, A. et al. (2012). An evolutionary based social rank explanation of why low income predicts mental distress: A 17 year cohort study of 30,000 people. *Journal of Affective Disorders*, 136(3), pp. 882-888.

World Animal Protection. (2020). Animal Protection Index. https://api.worldanimalprotection.org/indicators

World Health Organization. (2010). Violence prevention: The evidence. https://apps.who.int/iris/handle/10665/77936

World Inequality Database. (2020). World Inequality Database. https://wid.world/world/

World Population Review. (2021a). Incarceration Rates By Country 2021. https://worldpopulationreview.com/country-rankings/incarceration-rates-by-country

World Population Review. (2021b). Recidivism Rates By Country 2021. https://worldpopulationreview.com/country-rankings/recidivism-rates-by-country

WPO. (2010). American Public Vastly Overestimates Amount of U.S. Foreign Aid. https://worldpublicopinion.net/american-public-vastly-overestimates-amount-of-u-s-foreign-aid/

Wrangham, R. & Peterson, D. (1996/1997). *Demonic Males: Apes and the Origins of Human Violence.* Houghton Mifflin Harcourt.

Yamagishi, K. (2003). Facilitating normative judgments of conditional probability: Frequency or nested sets? *Exp Psychol*, 50(2), pp. 97-106.

Yeomans, M. (2021). The straw man effect: Partisan misrepresentation in natural language. *Group Processes & Intergroup Relations*, published online: https://doi.org/10.1177/13684302211014582

Yudkowsky, E. (2008). Today's Inspirational Tale. https://www.lesswrong.com/posts/4SysgzYYJmErwHrWw/today-s-inspirational-tale

Zakaria, F. (2003). *The Future of Freedom: Illiberal Democracy at Home and Abroad.* W. W. Norton & Company.

Zaller, J. (1992). *The Nature and Origins of Mass Opinion.* Cambridge University Press.

Ziaja, S. (2020). More Donors, More Democracy. *The Journal of Politics*, 82(2), pp. 433-447.

Ziesche, S. & Yampolskiy, R. (2019). Do No Harm Policy for Minds in Other Substrates. *Journal of Evolution and Technology*, 29(2), pp. 1-11.

Zorzut, A. (2021). El Chapo's cartel torture and kill rivals before hanging naked bodies from bridge in brutal turf war. https://www.the-sun.com/news/3134510/el-chapos-cartel-torture-kill-and-hang-rivals/

Zwolinski, M. (2014). The Pragmatic Libertarian Case for a Basic Income Guarantee. https://web.archive.org/web/20211017094806/https://www.cato-unbound.org/2014/08/04/matt-zwolinski/pragmatic-libertarian-case-basic-income-guarantee

Printed in Poland
by Amazon Fulfillment
Poland Sp. z o.o., Wrocław